The Last Crusades

The Last Crusades
The Final Attempts by Christendom to Conquer
Jerusalem and the Holy Land, 1202-1272

The Fall of Constantinople
Edwin Pears

The Final Crusades
T. A. Archer

The Fourth Crusade
and
Letters of the Crusaders
Dana Carlton Monro

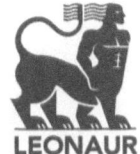

The Last Crusades
The Final Attempts by Christendom to Conquer Jerusalem and the Holy Land, 1202-1272
The Fall of Constantinople
by Edwin Pears
The Final Crusades
by T. A. Archer
The Fourth Crusade
and
Letters of the Crusaders
by Dana Carlton Monro

FIRST EDITION

Leonaur is an imprint of Oakpast Ltd
Copyright in this form © 2022 Oakpast Ltd

ISBN: 978-1-915234-46-9 (hardcover)
ISBN: 978-1-915234-47-6 (softcover)

http://www.leonaur.com

Publisher's Notes

The views expressed in this book are not necessarily those of the publisher.

Contents

The Preparations for a Crusade	7
Arrival in Venice	24
Departure to, Conquest of, and Stay in Zara	34
The Plot	40
From Zara to Corfu	64
From Corfu to Constantinople	70
Flight of the Emperor Alexis and Restoration of Isaac—Revolution in the City	81
The Assault, Capture, and Plunder of the City	107
The Fourth Crusade *Dana Carleton Munro*	129
The Final Crusades *T. A. Archer*	149
Letters of the Crusaders *Dana Carleton Munro*	183

CHAPTER 1

The Preparations for a Crusade

The fourth crusade began to be preached in 1197. The earlier successes of the third crusade, notwithstanding the quarrels of its leaders, had led the Christians of the West to believe that the progress of Mahometanism might yet be checked. In 1187 Saladin had captured Jerusalem. Guy of Lusignan had been taken prisoner. Many brave Templars and Hospitallers, with many a nameless soldier of the West, had suffered martyrdom rather than renounce the faith. The fall of Jerusalem had been the immediate cause of the third crusade. Our own Richard the Lion-hearted, whose sole claim to be remembered is his skill as a captain of Crusaders, Philip of France, one of the ablest of French kings, and Frederic Barbarossa, the Swabian Emperor of Western Rome, had, as we have seen, united to reconquer Christian territory in Syria.

Acre had been besieged, and after a two years' resistance, which had cost the Crusaders 300,000 men, had surrendered to Richard and Philip. Saladin had been defeated at Ascalon. Other places had been captured. But the victories and the results of the expedition fell far short of what might reasonably have been hoped for from the preparations which had been made by the three great sovereigns of the West. Jaffa had been taken by storm, but had been recaptured, and its Christian garrison massacred. Frederic was drowned in 1190. The quarrel between Philip and Richard had been espoused by their followers. In 1192 the English king quitted Syria, was shipwrecked, imprisoned, and went through some, at least, of the adventures which have associated the name of that sovereign with poetry and romance. Philip had returned home the same year.

The victories which the Crusaders had gained would be altogether barren if help were not shortly sent to the Christians in Palestine. The supplementary expedition had been a failure. The Crusaders who had remained behind, aided by the Armenian, Greek, and Syrian Christians, were doing their best to hold the territory which had been conquered, but every year saw that territory decreasing. Every traveller returning from Syria brought a prayer for immediate help from the survivors of the third crusade. It was necessary to act at once if any portion even of the wreck of the kingdom of Jerusalem were to be saved. Innocent the Third and some, at least, of the statesmen of the West were fully alive to the progress which Islam had made since the departure of the Western kings.

In 1197, however, after five years of weary waiting, the time seemed opportune for striking a new blow for Christendom. Saladin, the great *Sultan*, had died in 1193, and his two sons were already quarrelling about the partition of his empire. The contending divisions of the Arab Moslems were at this moment each bidding for the support of the Christians of Syria. The other great race of Mahometans which had threatened Europe, the Seljukian Turks, had made a halt in their progress through Asia Minor. We have seen that their empire was also divided against itself. Moreover, the great Asiatic horde which was shortly under Genghis Khan—perhaps the Prester John of the Middle Ages—to threaten the empire which the Seljukians had carved out of the eastern dominions of the New Rome, was already approaching, and the Seljukians were compelled to turn their attention to the formidable enemy of their own race which was threatening their rear.

Other special circumstances which rendered the moment favourable for a new crusade, combined with the profound conviction of the statesmen of the West of the danger to Christendom from the progress of Islam, urged Western Europe to take part in the new enterprise.

The reigning Pope, Innocent the Third, was the great moving spirit of the fourth crusade. He came to the pontificate in 1198, when he was thirty-seven years old. Innocent was a man versed in the learning of his age, and of unceasing and untiring energy. His restless activity forced him to take interest in every question of the day. To be interested in a question meant for him to be actively engaged in its solution. There was not a country in Europe in whose affairs he did not take a prominent part. Quarrels between kings, between barons; disputes, as in the case of our own John, between kings and their subjects; differences between abbeys and monasteries in the most remote countries, were examined personally and decided upon finally by him. The decision once taken, he took care to have it obeyed.

Nothing escaped his vigilance. No question was too large or too small to engage his attention. His vast correspondence is one of the marvels of the Middle Ages. His negotiations, not only with European sovereigns and their subjects, but with Leo the Great, King of Armenia, with the Bulgarians and with the Wallachs, were unceasing. His *legates* and cardinals were in every country, laying down the law of the sovereign Pontiff, scattering interdicts, issuing anathemas. He, perhaps, more than any other Pope, secured that the occupant of the pontifical chair should be listened to throughout Europe as one speaking with authority, that the Pope should be an independent sovereign, that the Church should owe obedience to the Pope alone among earthly sovereigns, and that the ruler of Rome should own no superior but God.

It is probably right to call the determination to carry out these designs ambition; but to understand the energy with which they were executed, one is forced to give Innocent credit for having believed that they were objects which it was desirable in the interests of mankind to attain. In his opinion he was called upon by divine right to govern Europe, to repress disorder, to put down civil war, to divert the fierce energy of Northern warriors away from anarchy into useful channels.

The world was turned upside down. The Holy Roman Empire was divided against itself. What is now Germany was the scene of constant and bloody wars. Italy was divided. Everywhere there was anarchy and confusion. Our fathers were right, no doubt, in opposing Innocent's designs in England, in seeing principally in his policy towards King John an attempt to advance the claims of the Papal See against the rights of Englishmen. Matthew Paris says that John knew the Pope as the most ambitious and proudest of men, a man insatiable after money and capable of every crime to obtain it, but history does not bear out his judgment.

Two schools of historians have discussed the character of Innocent. He stands before one as a clever Italian, an intriguing, ambitious priest, meddling in every business to advance the interests of the Church; and before the other party—that, namely, which believes in the Roman Catholic Church as the divine institution of the world—as the priest full of supernatural energy, of ability, and of success, the model Pontiff, the type pre-eminently of the Vicar of God.

Judging the man by the circumstances of his time, and putting aside his trivial weaknesses, one sees a clear-headed statesman who knew his own purpose and was tenacious of its realisation: one of the men who stamp their character upon the world's history in unmistakable outlines. It is in considering the amount of useful work done and the beneficial influence exerted by such Popes as Innocent, that we who are outside the Church of Rome come to understand how the belief in the inspired character of the Pope's official conduct has grown up. The character given of Innocent by a contemporary is borne out by his conduct during the fourth crusade:—

> A man of much discretion and kindliness, young indeed in years (he was thirty-seven when made Pope), but old in prudence, ripe in judgment, adorned by the uprightness of his character, of a noble race and commanding presence, a lover of what was right and good, a hater of iniquity and vice, so that he was called Innocent rather from his merit than from chance. (Gunther.)

But for us the important point is that during the eighteen years of his reign the most absorbing thought of Innocent, the purpose to which he most constantly adhered, was the deliverance of the Holy Land, (Hurter's *Hist. de Inno.* III.) His first act after he had ascended the pontifical throne was to announce to Monaco, the *Patriarch* of Jerusalem, his intention of proclaiming a crusade. Six months later he ordered the crusade to be preached, first in Italy and then throughout the rest of Europe. He sent letters to all princes, announcing to them his firm resolution to consecrate all his energy to this object. He said:—

> Who is there who would wish to shrink from the danger of the Cross when he remembers Him who bound Himself to the Cross to deliver us from the enemy? Arise, therefore, ye faithful; arise, gird on the sword and the buckler. Arise, and hasten to the help of Jesus Christ He Himself will lead your banner to victory. (*Epist.* i.)

As an inducement to those who were ready to join in the holy war, he promised pardon for past sins. He placed the lands of the princes and the goods of the Crusaders under the protection of the Holy See during their absence; he declared that those who borrowed money for the expedition should be exempted from the payment of interest. Princes were invited to compel the Jews, who were the principal money-lenders, to remit the payment of interest to intending Crusaders. Rulers were urged to forbid the Jews to engage in any business in case of their refusal.

Those who could not themselves take up the Cross were asked to provide substitutes, or at least to contribute to the expense. All who refused to give were warned that they incurred a grave responsibility. He ordered the clergy peremptorily to contribute a fixed portion of their revenue. He forbade the Venetians to furnish the Saracens with iron, ropes, wood, arms, galleys, ships, or any munitions of war whatever. Richard of England had made war on Philip of France. Innocent sent a cardinal to France to conclude a treaty for five years between the two sovereigns, and wrote himself to his *legate* in France:—

> If men perish, if the churches are weakened, if the poor are oppressed, if the French and the English incur danger on account of their kings—all this is of less consequence than the loss of Palestine, than the extermination of the Christian name; and yet this is what will happen if these kings prevent their warriors from going to reconquer what has been lost, from protecting those who have been threatened.

If the treaty were not accepted by the two kings, his firm resolution and that of his cardinals was to place the kingdom of the offender under an interdict, and to forbid, with the utmost rigour and severity, without regard to privileges and indulgences, the celebration of divine worship. Innocent pointed out that the time was opportune.

> By the dissensions which divide the Saracens, the Lord gives to Christian people the signal for the crusade. (*Inno. III.*)

Innocent, in his determination to leave no stone unturned for the accomplishment of his purpose, wrote also to Alexis, the Emperor in the New Rome, asking for his aid.

> Who can do more than you, seeing your nearness to the field where the battle must be fought, your riches and your power? Will Your Majesty put all other considerations on one side, and come to the help of Jesus Christ and of the country which He has won by His blood? The Pagans will flee before you, before your army, and you—you will share with the others in the pontifical favours.

The assumption of an authority was not likely to be welcome at Constantinople, but the letter shows at least how strong was the determination of the Pope to make the expedition a success. *Legates* were sent to the New Rome to negotiate with the emperor and the *patriarch* on the subject of the expedition and of the union of the two churches. The letter and the *legates* were treated with the utmost respect. The haughty tone of the Pope's letter and the experience which the Greeks had had of the last crusade were not likely, however, to produce a favourable reply.

The Emperor Alexis, in his answer, recalled that when Frederic, a few years earlier, had promised upon oath to pass through the empire peaceably, he had violated his promise. He had done great injury; he had fought Christians as well as Pagans, and yet, in spite of this, Alexis claimed that the Greeks, out of veneration for the object of the expedition, had furnished him with all that was necessary. Notwithstanding this just cause of complaint, Alexis concluded this part of his letter by promising that if the empire were able to preserve its tranquillity, he would favour the efforts which should be made for the delivery of the Holy Sepulchre.

As to the old question of the union of the two churches, the reply was that the best union would be brought about by each giving up its own will and submitting to the divine will. If the Pope wished to submit the doctrines in controversy to the examination of a Council, the Orthodox Church would take part in it. While admitting the zeal of the Pope for the glory of God, Alexis could not conceal his astonishment at hearing the Pope call the Roman Church the Universal Church, and the common mother of all the churches. That title belonged to the Church of Jerusalem. The old jealousy between the two Romes was not to be overcome, and, as usual, found vent in the religious questions which divided the two churches. Little aid was to be hoped for Constantinople, but only little had been expected.

Meanwhile in Western Europe the efforts of Innocent had met with more success. In every church a box had been placed to receive the gifts of those who had the holy cause at heart, and a Mass was ordered to be said weekly for the givers. Innocent again addressed himself to Philip of France. Christ Himself, he repeated, had given the signal for the crusade. Philip ought not only to permit his subjects to leave, but to force them to quit their homes on so important a mission. Innocent did all that he could in every European country, in order that the effort about to be made might prove successful.

The preacher of the new crusade, the Peter the Hermit who made known the Pope's wishes to the people of France and of Flanders, was a priest named Fulk, of Neuilly. If we can imagine a Wesley or a Whitefield with middle-age surroundings, we may obtain a glimpse of his character and of the secret of his influence. If, as Gibbon alleges, he was illiterate, his ignorance was not observed by his contemporaries.

It is true that after his ordination he had been reproached with ignorance; but in consequence of this reproach, or of his desire for knowledge, he went to the University of Paris, and returned to his parish to become a distinguished preacher. He was full of zeal and enthusiasm. Like many of the great preachers of the churches, he regarded his own time as especially given over to wickedness.

Contemporaries of his, monks and priests, had persuaded themselves that the world was shortly to come to an end, and that the mad confusion and anarchy of the time was one of the signs of the end. Fulk found in this belief the greater reason for putting right that which was wrong. He denounced iniquity in high places with the utmost fearlessness. Clergy and prelates felt the bitterness of his speech. In spite of ignominious treatment, threats, and imprisonment, he warned nobles and kings alike that they were travelling rapidly on the broad way to hell.

He denounced the new custom of lending money, which the Lombards had introduced into France, and spoke fiercely against avarice and sensuality. No danger could terrify him, no threat make him keep silence. His fervour made him popular with the people. At times his audience became so excited that men threw off their garments and offered their belts to the preacher, publicly confessing their sins and asking for public punishment. The people, rich and poor, came at last to hear him gladly. His fame had already reached Rome. Here, then, was the man whom Innocent had need of. His enthusiasm, his energy, his fearlessness, his apparent disinterestedness were to be made use of, as the Church of Rome has so often utilised the undisciplined enthusiasm which other churches have driven into opposition. The Pope commissioned him to preach the Cross in France, 'to use the gift of eloquence which God had given him for the good of the Holy Land.'

Fulk executed his commission in Normandy, Flanders, and Burgundy. His reputation as a preacher, a healer of the sick, and a worker of miracles had preceded him, and crowds everywhere went out to hear him and to be influenced by his preaching. According to the popular belief, virtue went out of him, and his clothes were sometimes torn to rags from the struggles of the masses to touch them in order that sickness might be healed. It is easy to say that Fulk lent himself to the imposture, but it is more probable that he, like other middle-age revivalists, believed himself to be a divine instrument, and the marvels attributed to him to be proofs of his mission. It must be said in favour of Fulk that he was willing to turn the popular enthusiasm into a useful channel.

'My garments,' said he, when the crowd pressed upon him, 'are not blessed, and have no charm about them; but look, I am going to bless and give virtue to this man's cloak.' At the same time, seizing upon one belonging to a bystander, he made the sign of the Cross upon it, in token that the wearer would join the crusade, and each one hastened to snatch a portion as a relic. His influence was marvellous and at times strangely exercised. If the crowd were too noisy, he obtained silence by solemnly cursing the noisiest. Sometimes he would lay about him lustily with his stick, while those who were wounded would kiss their wounds or the blood as sanctified by the man of God. Wherever he preached great numbers took the Cross, or contributed to the expenses of the crusade.

His greatest success was in the conversion of Theobald of Champagne. This nobleman, a nephew of Richard of England and of Philip of France, a young man of twenty-two, was already renowned in arms and in song. Eighteen hundred knights did homage as his vassals. During the truce between the Kings of England and France, he had called together a brilliant assemblage to engage in or witness a tournament. Fulk invited the knights to gain a more lasting glory by joining in the crusade. Theobald, Count Louis of Blois, and Simon de Montfort, father of our English hero of the same name, with a host of others, accepted the Cross.

Theobald, Earl of Champagne, was selected from his rank and ability to be the leader of the expedition. In his train were Geoffrey of Villehardouin, with many others of high rank. Under Theobald, the leaders were Baldwin of Flanders, whose wife was the sister of Theobald, Baldwin's brother Henry, Louis Earl of Blois, Simon de Montfort, and Count Hughes de St. Paul.

It may be mentioned here that the intention of the Crusaders, and probably also of Innocent, was that Richard of England should be the leader of the expedition. His death, however, in April 1199, put an end to this design. In one respect, however, his death contributed an element of success. Many of the French barons had joined him against Philip of France, and there can hardly be a doubt that but for his untimely death he would have defeated Philip. The hostility between the two sovereigns had been bitter.

'The devil is loose; take care of yourself,' had been Philip's warning to John when Richard had been released. The French barons who had fought on the side of Richard were glad on his death to escape the vengeance of Philip by joining the crusade. Among those who had been detached from the side of Philip by Richard, and had joined the revolt of the Bretons against him, was Theobald of Champagne himself, the appointed leader of the crusade. Baldwin of Flanders had in like manner declared for Richard, and probably joined the crusade the more readily on account of his death.

At the opening of the year 1200 a considerable number of nobles and others had undertaken to join the crusade. France and Flanders contributed the largest share, but Germany also furnished a considerable contingent. During the year many meetings or parliaments of the leaders of the expedition had been held, but they had been adjourned because the number of Crusaders was not judged to be sufficiently large to justify the leaders in making arrangements for the transport of the army beyond sea. Towards the end of the year, however, a parliament was held at Soissons, in which it was agreed that the time had come when preliminary arrangements might be undertaken for the chartering of a fleet. The decision arrived at was that six messengers should be sent to treat with Venice, with full powers to make such agreements for the transport of the army as they deemed necessary. Shortly after, the messengers set out on their journey.

Venice was chosen as being the city which was likeliest to furnish, if not the only city which could furnish, the large port of fleet of transports and convoys necessary. But the choice was in many respects an unfortunate one, and ultimately led to the failure of the fourth crusade. We have seen that Venice had occupied a neutral position between the East and the West. On many occasions she had owned allegiance to the New instead of the Old Rome, and although at the end of the twelfth century she had her special reasons for hostility towards her former protector, she was as little inclined as ever to render obedience either to the Pope in spiritual things, or to either of the rival claimants for the empire in the West in temporal things. The thunders of Innocent, which shook every other Western state, fell harmlessly upon Venice.

The struggles between Guelfs and Ghibelins, whether in Germany or Italy, aroused comparatively slight attention among her people. Innocent early in 1201 had declared for Otho, a nephew of Richard of England, the Guelphic claimant for the empire of the West, and had declared against Philip of Swabia, whom he had threatened with the penalties of the Church. But Venice cared little for such threats, and was ready to ally herself with Philip. Her great interest was to have a monopoly of the carrying trade by sea, and in order to preserve this she was ready with equal indifference to supply Crusaders and *Infidels* with contraband of war, or to transport the one or the other and their property whither they would.

Venice was now in the first springtime of her splendour.

The islands, which had themselves been constructed on the marshes, were already covered with stately buildings. The city had increased in wealth as Constantinople had declined.

The monopoly over the seas once possessed by Constantinople had long since been shared by the Republic, which recognised in the annual ceremony of the Bucentaur that her wealth was derived from commerce. She had been, as we have seen, specially favoured in the New Rome. The tone of her civilisation was that of Constantinople rather than that of any Western city. Her wealth, her distinction as a city whose civilisation was more advanced than that of any Western rival, were derived from her intercourse with the New Rome. The very aspect of her streets were a reproduction of what had been seen on the Golden Horn. Her famous church, dedicated to St. Mark, was but a reproduction on a smaller scale of the still more famous church of the Divine Wisdom of the Incarnate Word which existed in Constantinople.

The Crusaders of this and of former expeditions were profoundly impressed with the prosperity and magnificence of Venice. The New Rome was still the royal or imperial city but both cities evidently opened to the Crusaders new worlds of wealth, luxury, and civilisation. They marvelled much, says Robert de Clari, at the great riches they found in Venice, and numbers of contemporary writers bear testimony to the astonishment which her civilisation excited.

Of late years the Venetians had had difficulties with the New Rome. We have seen that these difficulties arose, in great measure, from the fact that the influence of Venice in Constantinople was no longer sufficient to exclude that of the other Italian republics. Isaac Angelos had, in 1187, and again in 1189, as we have also seen, concluded a new alliance, assuring to Venice her old privileges, together with the payment of a considerable indemnity. The consideration for the valuable concessions offered by the emperor was that the Venetians should place their fleet at the disposition of the empire, even in the case of a war against the Emperor in the West. This treaty was confirmed in 1199 by Alexis the Third.

In the spring of 1200, a quarrel took place at Constantinople between the Venetians and their great rivals the Pisans. The Venetians complained that their treaties had been violated; that the subsidies promised by the emperor had not been paid; above all, that the Pisans had been favoured at their expense, (Nicetas.) The *doge*, during the summer of the same year, sent an embassy to Alexis to demand the payment of arrears and the renewal of commercial privileges. Another embassy was sent six months later, and, indeed, the whole year was occupied with negotiations, which served only to show that it was improbable that the Republic should regain her supreme influence on the Bosphorus.

But the hostility to Constantinople reached its height when the Venetians learned that Alexis had, in May 1201, received an embassy from Genoa, and was negotiating with Ottobono della Croce, its leader, for the concession of privileges for trade in Romania which Venice had hitherto regarded as exclusively her own. From this time the *doge* appears to have determined to avenge the wrongs of his state on the ruler who had ventured to favour his rivals.

The Doge of Venice at this time was the famous Henry Dandolo. He was already a very old man, but full of energy, greedy of glory, exasperated against the empire, and devoted to the interests of the Republic. (Du Cange makes Dandolo ninety-two in 1200; but neither Villehardouin nor Andrea Dandolo use terms which would imply so great an age.) He was able to command with equal success an army or a fleet. Though he was nearly, if not quite, blind, he devoted an amount of attention and ability to the cares of government which places him in the first rank of Venetian administrators. The New Rome was the special object of his hatred.

The general belief after his death was that his eyes had been put out by order of the Emperor Alexis during his visit in 1172 or 1173 to Constantinople. (Daru, *Hist. of Venice*, i. Authorities are divided as to whether he was blind or only of weak sight.) What is certain is that he bore against the empire an inextinguishable hatred, which made him willing to embrace any project directed against its capital city. He possessed the entire confidence of his fellow-citizens. His influence in Venice was so great that when he subsequently embarked with the Crusaders his son was appointed Regent during the absence of his father.

The six messengers chosen by the Crusaders at Soissons arrived at Venice in February 1201. Four days after their arrival they were introduced to the Council and the *doge*, in a palace which was *bien riche et beau.* Their spokesman said:—

> Sire, we are come to thee on behalf of the noble barons of France, who have taken the sign of the Cross to avenge the shame of Jesus Christ, and to reconquer Jerusalem if God wills it. And because they know that no men can help them so well as you and your men, they pray that for God's sake you will have pity on the Land of Outremer, and on the shame of Jesus Christ, and that you will labour that they may have ships of war and transports.'

The Council took a week to consider what should be their reply. At the end of that time, the delegates of the Crusaders were informed that the Venetians were willing to provide ships to carry 4,500 horses, 9,000 esquires, 4,500 knights, and 20,000 infantry, together with provisions for nine months, in consideration of a payment of four *marks* per horse and two per man. The total sum therefore to be paid, reckoning the Venetian *mark* at a little over two pounds sterling, was about 180,000*l*. (M. de Wailly estimates the *mark* at fifty-two *francs*. So also does Sismondi. See also Heid.) This contract was to hold good for a year.

Besides this the Venetians promised to add for the love of God fifty armed galleys, in consideration that half of the money captured should belong to them. The terms were accepted by the delegates, were again submitted by Dandolo to the Council, and were approved. A solemn service was held in St. Mark's, and much enthusiasm displayed at the conclusion of what each believed a good bargain. Villehardouin, whose narrative of the crusade has long been the chief authority on the subject, was himself the spokesman of the delegates, and thanked the Venetians, on behalf of his brethren, that they had taken pity on Jerusalem, which was in slavery to the Turks, and that they were ready to aid in avenging the shame of Jesus Christ. The contract was signed early in April 1201, was referred to the barons, and was ratified at Corbie in the middle of May.

It had been decided from the first that the expedition should be directed towards Egypt as the best base of operations against the Mahometans in the Holy Land, though the plans and contract signed by the Venetians and the delegates contained the statement simply that the destination should be 'for the deliverance of the Holy Land.' The decision taken in the Council was kept secret from the army, to whom it was simply announced that the Crusaders would go beyond the sea (Villehardouin, c. iv.) Charts of the route were prepared and sealed, and it was agreed that the Crusaders should be in Venice by St. John's Day, 1202.

The *doge* and his Council on the one side and the delegates on the other swore solemnly to observe the terms of the arrangements entered into. The contract was then sent to the Pope, who approved it conditionally.

Innocent could not see without distrust the contract made with those who had shown their readiness to serve either Christians or Moslems, provided they paid. He would have preferred that the Pisans or the Genoese had been selected, and it was only on finding that no such arrangement could be made that he consented to accept the Venetians, (Inno. *Epist. ix.*) The conditions upon which he insisted showed the distrust which he entertained. He stipulated that there should be no attack made against a Christian state, and that a *legate* should accompany the army and watch over the expedition, in order to see that this article was complied with.

The leaders of the crusade had decided, as we have seen, that their operations should be directed against Egypt. Many considerations induced them to arrive at this conclusion. The passage through Romania had been found during previous crusades to be long and costly. Even when the Dardanelles had been passed, there remained the terrible march through Asia Minor, where the Turks hindered the progress of the Christians at every step, and where fever had rapidly thinned their ranks. The terrible experience of the last crusade had been that the great German Army, after winning every battle it had fought, had, by the time it reached the Holy Land, melted away.

The leaders wished to avoid this long and fatal route, and desired to be landed at some place where they could strike at the enemy before the army had been weakened by repeated contests, and wearied and demoralised by long marches through an unhealthy country. No place offered so many advantages from this point of view as Egypt A short sail over a pleasant sea and the Crusaders could be landed fresh and vigorous and prepared for battle. The cost of transporting an army to Alexandria would be far less than that of taking it to any other part of *paynimrie*.

The sea was the safest and most easily guarded road to keep open between the invading army and Europe. Alexandria was a base of operations which might be kept with surety against the enemy, while its port would always be open to supplies of men and means of warfare from the West. A footing once obtained, Egypt could better support the army of Christendom than any other country. Its perennial wealth had been the mainstay of the Arabs in their marvellous conquests over Syria and Northern Africa. Moreover, while the renown of Egypt was spread throughout Islam and Christendom alike, the enemy could be more advantageously fought in the densely-populated delta than in the wide and thinly-peopled regions of Syria.

Probably too it was known in Europe that the Egyptian Arabs had lost their early vigour, that the climate had told upon them, and that they were already becoming an unwarlike race. The occasion, however, in 1201 was peculiarly favourable for an attack on that country. Saladin had conquered it, had abolished the Egyptian Caliphate in 1171, and had done all that he could to exhaust its resources. On his death, in 1193, his two sons had quarrelled about the division of his empire. The one ruling in Egypt asked the aid of the Christians in Syria against his brother.

The civil war which followed had still further weakened Egypt. But an exceptional and remarkable circumstance rendered an attack upon Egypt still more opportune. During five successive years the Nile had ceased to fertilise the country. The result of this unprecedented calamity had been famine and distress. The population had been largely reduced. The wealth and strength of the country had been greatly diminished. To these considerations have to be added the fact that if Egypt were once in the hands of a Crusading Army, it could be held against all invaders, and its wealth turned against Islam. Every Mahometan country would feci the loss of Egypt. A wedge would have been driven into the long stretch of Moslem territory between the Atlantic and India. Islam would have been cut in two and its wealth used to reconquer and hold Syria.

The desirability of striking at Islam through Egypt, the very centre and fulcrum of Moslem power, had been recognised from the time of Godfrey by a succession of warriors and statesmen. Innocent the Third was especially impressed with the necessity of making the attack through Egypt. He called particular attention to the exceptional opportunity which the time presented from the accidental or, as he believed it, the providential impoverishment of the richest country in Islam, from the failure of the Nile to overflow, and from the division of its rulers. Even without these accidental advantages no other spot offered so many advantages for the attack.

No other country, if conquered, would be so great a loss to Islam. These considerations, in fact, seem to have been so generally recognised that it is doubtful whether any other plan was seriously considered. It was to Babylon, as the Crusaders generally called Egypt, that the expedition was to go, because, says Villehardouin, 'one could more easily destroy the Turks there than in any other country.'

The choice having been made, it will become necessary to ask why the original plan was abandoned How did it happen that an expedition prepared with great care, and proposing under such favourable circumstances to strike at the heart of Moslem power, turned away from its object and attacked the capital of Eastern Christendom? The question is one which was asked by all Europe at the time and has never been altogether satisfactorily answered, although in our own time the laborious industry of German and French scholars has succeeded in bringing to light a mass of evidence hitherto unknown bearing on the question. The conclusion to which this evidence appears to me to point will, I hope, become clear in subsequent pages.

The agreement between the delegates of the Crusaders and the Venetians was ratified, as we have seen, in May 1201. (In the same month Innocent had invited the dignitaries of the Venetian Church to contribute towards the crusade from the church revenues.) The Crusading Army was to arrive in Venice not later than the 24th of June, 1202.

In the interval between these dates many events happened. Theobald, Earl of Champagne, the young noble who had taken the Cross on the preaching of Fulk, who had probably been induced to do so partly in order to escape the vengeance of Philip of France, who had been elected leader of the expedition, and in whom all had confidence, died in May 1201. His loss was the more serious that his great wealth was no longer available for the purposes of the crusade.

A payment in advance which had been promised to Venice could not be met. The leaders were divided as to the course to be adopted for the conduct of the expedition. None among them possessed either position or ability sufficient to indicate him as the leader. After considerable delay the leadership was offered to the Duke of Burgundy, and on his refusal to Count Theobald of Bar, who also refused. Then a parliament of the Crusaders met at Soissons, and Villehardouin proposed Boniface, Marquis of Montferrat. The proposal was finally though reluctantly accepted.

From the first it was evident that Boniface had not the confidence of the Crusaders, and his election was the first severe blow given to the success of the expedition. Fulk himself affixed the Cross to the shoulders of Boniface in the church of Our Lady at Soissons, and, as the great preacher died in May 1202, he disappears from this history, (Villehardouin, c.) The appointment of Boniface was in August 1201. Two months later he was at the court of Philip of Swabia, (*Gesta Inno. III.* c.), on the invitation of that sovereign. What was the object of his visit may never be accurately known. But subsequent events raise the presumption that Philip either had the design of an attack upon Constantinople before this visit, or formed such a design at, and in consequence of, his interview with Boniface.

Philip, the head of the house of the Waiblings, or, as the name was now beginning to be spelt in Italy, Ghibelins, had married the daughter of Isaac Angelos, the Emperor of the New Rome, who was at this moment a prisoner in Constantinople deprived of his eyesight, though allowed to go about the city of which he had once been the ruler, (*Gesta Inno. III.* c.) The son of Isaac and heir to the throne—whom we may conveniently call after the fashion of the time young Alexis, to distinguish him from the reigning usurper Alexis in Constantinople—had made his escape from the capital. (One author states that the wife of the Emperor Alexis pitied the young man, and gave him notice that her husband determined to kill him.) He left the imperial city in the spring of 1201, arrived in Sicily and sent messengers to Germany announcing his safe arrival.

Allowing three months for the news to reach Philip, there was ample time for the messengers of Philip to reach the Marquis of Montferrat, and for the latter to have been at the Swabian court in October. Boniface remained with Philip until January or February 1202, and then left with an embassy for Rome, sent thither in order to induce Innocent the Third to take up the cause of young Alexis, (*Gesta Inno. III.* c.) In the spring of the year the latter received letters of recommendation to the Crusaders from Philip. (Nicetas says 'from Philip and the Pope,' but the latter is doubtful.) It therefore appears clear that, from the beginning of 1202, the leader of the expedition had become aware of the facts connected with the claims of Alexis. Subsequent evidence indicates that even at this time he had promised Philip to aid him.

At the time appointed—namely, the 24th of June, most of the leaders of the expedition had arrived, according to the arrangement, in Venice. Baldwin of Flanders, Hugo Count of St. Paul, Geoffrey of Villehardouin, perhaps Boniface, and many also from Germany were present, while the Abbot Martin and others from that country were on their way thither.

★★★★★★★★

M. Jules Tessier contends that the Crusaders could never agree upon the destination of the expedition. He admits that the most intelligent of its leaders proposed to attack Egypt, but he insists that the majority of the army were in favour of going to Syria. In support of this contention he (1) calls attention to the fact that the charter-party made with the Venetians makes no mention of either Syria or Egypt; (2) he quotes Villehardouin and claims that the 'grant peril' of which the Flemings stood in fear was of going to Egypt, and (3) he quotes the reply given to the speech of the Abbot of Citeaux (Villehardouin),' In Syria you can do nothing.' The first of these arguments is inapplicable if the contention is well founded, that it was intended to conceal the destination of the expedition. Later on I give a different interpretation to the 'grant peril' phrase, while the argument founded on the reply to the abbot appears to me to fall when connected with the surrounding circumstances. Gunther's statement that the resolution to attack Egypt was adopted unanimously is probably too sweeping. See *La Diversion sur Zara et Constantinople, par* Jules Tessier. (Paris, 1884.)

★★★★★★★★

Chapter 2

Arrival in Venice

Many of the pilgrims had only left home between Easter and Whitsuntide, 1202. The ordinary road taken was over the Mont Cenis and through Lombardy to Venice.

Meantime a fleet had left Flanders for the Mediterranean with a great number of Crusaders. The leaders of this detachment had sworn to Baldwin that they would join the division coming from Venice at the first convenient place after hearing of its whereabouts. Baldwin and the other leaders of the crusade who had already arrived at Venice soon learned with dismay that many pilgrims had gone by other routes to other ports, and that thus it would be impossible to provide the number for whose passage the delegates had undertaken to pay the Venetians. Those present were unable to raise the amount agreed upon. They did their best by sending messengers here and there to persuade the pilgrims to come to Venice, and to point out to them that Venice was the only port from which they could start with a fair prospect of success.

Villehardouin was himself sent on such an expedition, and succeeded in persuading Count Louis with a great number of knights and men-at-arms to come to Venice from Padua, where they had been encountered. Others were also brought in to Venice; but a considerable number had already left by other routes before they could be overtaken. Never, says Villehardouin, has a finer army collected than that which was at length gathered at St. Nicolo di Lido, the island where the Crusaders were lodged by the Venetians. No man had seen a finer fleet than the Venetians had prepared. The only fault to be found with it was that it could take an army three times as large as that which had assembled. The Venetians had kept their part of the bargain. The marshal exclaims:—

What a misfortune, that so large a portion of the Crusaders had sought other ports! Had they come to Venice the Turks would have been put down; Christendom would have been exalted.

The Venetians, having done their part, now asked for payment of the passage money according to the terms of the contract. This, however, could not be raised. Many pilgrims had come without money; others were already sick of the enterprise, and, according to Villehardouin, hoped that the money would not be found. Baldwin of Flanders, Earl Louis, and the Marquis and the Earl of St. Paul did their utmost by borrowing to raise the amount promised. But when all was done, when many a beautiful vessel of silver and of gold had been taken to the *doge's* palace, when two collections had been made, 34,000 *marks* out of the 85,000 stipulated for were still wanting.

So far, we are on safe ground. All contemporary accounts agree that the contract with the Venetians was broken; that a large amount was wanting to complete the sum agreed upon to be paid as freight; and that, even after every effort had been made to raise this sum, about 35,000 *marks* still remained due. From this time forward we are upon doubtful ground. The authorities upon whom we have to rely differ widely. The account given by Geoffroi de Villehardouin, Marshal of Champagne, may be taken as the type of what has been aptly called the official versions of the expedition, and of these it ranks undoubtedly the first.

Besides these versions, the labours of a number of historians, from Du Cange in the seventeenth century down to Count Riant, who has ransacked, and is ransacking, the libraries of Europe in search of evidence relating to the fourth crusade, have brought a large amount of evidence to light which may be conveniently classed as that of the unofficial versions. The official version of what passed in Venice is that which has been generally received by modern historians until our own time. Villehardouin states in few words that the *doge*, when it had become clear that the Crusaders could not pay the stipulated sum, proposed that they should agree to assist the Venetians in recapturing Zara, in Dalmatia, from the King of Hungary; that the Crusaders were divided as to whether this proposition should be accepted; that those who were tired of the enterprise opposed, but that the majority accepted it.

So far, the official account given by Villehardouin and followed by others. The diversion of the enterprise was due solely, according to these writers, to the simple fact that the Crusaders could not pay

34,000 *marks*. Villehardouin, whose history of the crusade is much longer than that of any other contemporary writer, skips over in a few short paragraphs the events which happened between the arrival in June and the alliance to attack Zara. The transaction was, according to him, the simplest possible. The Venetians had completed their part of the contract; the Crusaders were unable to pay their fare; the *doge* made a proposal which was accepted.

At this point it becomes necessary to examine such other testimony as exists, in order to learn whether the diversion was due to the simple cause which is assigned for it by the great apologist for the crusade. The intention was, as we have seen, to go to Alexandria.

Gunther says:—

> But this praiseworthy design was hindered by the fraud and malice of the Venetians.

Rostangus says:—,

> The Crusaders were received treacherously,' 'by those to whom they had come, who would not allow them for a long time to pass beyond sea. They refused to carry them beyond sea or to allow them to leave St. Nicolo di Lido unless they paid the uttermost farthing.

The leaders and the Crusaders generally appear, as we have seen, to have done their best to pay. But the number for which the city had furnished transport was largely in excess of that which had been brought together by the end of June. Out of 4,000 knights and their attendants, only 1,000 had assembled. Of the 100,000 foot soldiers provided for, there were not more than 50,000 or 60,000 on the Lido. The Crusaders argued that those who had come and were ready to pay ought not to be forced to pay for those who had not come. The Venetians claimed their pound of flesh. Resistance was useless; the Crusaders were prisoners.

The *doge*, according to Robert de Clari, (*La Prise de Constantinople*), told the Crusaders plainly, 'If you do not pay, understand well that you will not move from this island, nor will you find anyone who will furnish you meat and drink.'

It was upon this threat that the leaders had borrowed what they could to pay their jailers. It was after a second collection for payment, in July 1202, that there was still about one third of the freight, or, according to Robert de Clari, 36,000 *marks*, unpaid. Shortly afterwards the Crusaders were persuaded to accept a compromise, which on the whole could not be considered as unfair. Dandolo was understood to have proposed that out of the share of the first spoil which fell to the Crusaders in fighting the common enemy—that is, the Moslems—the sum due to the Venetians should be deducted. This proposition was gladly accepted.

Subsequently this promise was changed into a proposal for an attack upon Zara. This city lies on the opposite coast of the Adriatic to Venice, was the capital of Dalmatia, and belonged to the King of Hungary, who had himself sent aid to the Crusaders. It had been rising in importance for many years. The Venetians alleged that its inhabitants had often of late made piratical attacks upon their ships. Possibly the charge was true, but the real reason of the hostility felt towards it was a jealousy of its commercial prosperity.

The nonofficial versions represent the Zara expedition as forced on the Crusaders. The official versions represent the Crusaders as' gladly consenting to pay the Venetians out of the spoils taken at Zara falling to their share. The story of Villehardouin is not at variance generally with those of other contemporary writers. Its chief fault is a suppression of disagreeable facts. His object in writing the story of the crusade was to show that the expedition had not been so complete a failure as a crusade as the world had taken it to be. We must look to others for the unpleasant facts. The author of the *Devastatio*, states that the troubles of the Crusaders began even before their arrival in Venice. The Lombards charged them heavy prices for victuals. When they reached the city, they were cast out of the houses and compelled to go to Lido. The Crusaders were there treated in every respect as captives. Provisions were sold to them at famine prices. A *sistarius* of corn cost 50 *soldi*.

The Venetian rulers gave orders that no one should ferry any of the foreigners out of the island. The want of provisions and the sense of their helplessness created a panic among them. Those who could escaped. Some went home; some hastened to other ports in the hopes of finding ships for Egypt or Syria. The summer heats caused a terrible mortality among the crowded host, so that, according to the same author, the living could scarcely be found to bury the dead. According to Robert de Clari, the *doge* himself came to recognise that the Venetian policy of pushing the Crusaders in their distress too far was mischievous. Addressing his council he said:—

Sirs, if we let these men go home, we shall be looked on as rogues and tricksters. Let us propose to them that, if they will pay us the 36,000 *marks* out of their share of the first conquest they make, we will transport them beyond sea.

There was no proposal here to take Zara or to attack Constantinople. The *Outre-mer* to which they were to be transported was understood to be the land of the *infidel*. The conquests they were to make were to be the lawful spoils of a crusading war. There was nothing whatever in the suggestion to make it unacceptable to the Crusaders who gave heed to their vow. Hence, when the *doge*, having obtained the consent of the Venetian council, submitted the proposal to them, they accepted it gladly. A way had been found out of their difficulty. They were to leave the fever grounds of the Lido, were to go over the sea to fight the *infidel* and to fulfil their vow. On the announcement of the proposal their camp was illuminated and there were other manifestations of joy. (Robert de Clari.)

It is difficult to determine precisely when this proposition was made. Probably it was in the last week of July 1202. The 24th of June was the latest time appointed for the arrival of the pilgrims. The second attempt to collect the balance due had been made probably in the middle of July. Shortly afterwards came this proposal, which was joyfully accepted. Villehardouin speaks only of one proposal, namely, that to help the Venetians to capture Zara. If his account is to be reconciled with that of the non-official writers, the explanation is that the attack upon the Christian city was at the time carefully concealed from the mass of the Crusaders, a policy which was continually pursued throughout the expedition.

Robert de Clari, as we have seen, represents the proposal quite otherwise, and the fact that it was joyfully welcomed shows that the Crusaders were told nothing of an attack upon a Christian city as part of it. Another writer (*Anon. Suessionensis*), states that the Venetians kept the Crusaders prisoners for three months, and would not allow them to return home, and when after that time their substance was nearly consumed, then they were compelled to go to Zara. We learn from a German writer (*Anon. Halberstadt*), that after much complaint, both on the side of the Venetians and on that of the Crusaders, it was at length agreed that the Venetians should go with the pilgrims, and that whatever was gained should be equally divided, but that from the part going to the pilgrims the balance due for freight should be deducted for the Venetians.

We may rest assured that the pilgrims did not accept joyfully the promise to go to Zara, because, as we shall see, the crusading spirit was far too strong in the army for them yet to tolerate the idea of an attack upon a Christian city.

The conclusion at which I arrive after a comparison of the authorities is either that there were two distinct proposals, one made in July for the payment out of the proceeds of lawful spoil, and a subsequent one made some weeks later for payment out of the spoil to be taken at Zara; or that, if the proposal to attack Zara were made in July, it was made only to the leaders, and was carefully concealed at first from the mass of the Crusaders.

Robert de Clari's account points to the existence of two proposals. After speaking of the illuminations on the Lido when the *doge's* first proposal was made and accepted, he states that the *doge* afterwards went to the camp and declared that the winter was lost, and that it was too late to go to *Outre-mer*. Then the secret was let out.

> Let us do the next best thing. There is a city near here called Zara, which has often defied us, and which we are going to punish if we can. If you will listen to me, we will pass the winter there until Easter, and then we will go to *Outre-mer* at Lady Day. Zara is full of provisions and riches.

Then this author adds:—

> The barons and leaders of the Crusaders assented to the *doge's* proposal. But this proposal was not known to all the army.

Robert probably believed that there were two proposals, and that even the last was kept secret from the host.

The account of Robert is borne out by the evidence to which I have already called attention. Assuming that the portion of the proposal made during the last week of July, referring to an attack on Zara, was kept secret, as to which there can be little doubt if it be admitted that Zara was mentioned in July, the next month was spent in negotiations. There was a party opposed to its acceptance as soon as the attack was mentioned. Here again we are on solid ground. Villehardouin tells us that discord sprang up as soon as the Venetians refused to carry them beyond sea until they paid. He says that those who declared they wanted to leave Venice to go to other ports did so because in reality they desired that the army should break up, and therefore struggled against the acceptance of the proposition. The unofficial writers tell us why they did so. Gunther says:—

> In truth, the proposal to attack Zara seemed to our princes cruel and iniquitous, both because the city was Christian and because it belonged to the King of Hungary, who, having himself taken the Cross, had placed himself and his, as the custom is, under the protection of the Pope. While the Venetians were constantly urging us to accept the proposal, and we on the other hand were earnestly refusing, much time was lost.

Why was time lost? The same writer answers:—

> Because our men thought it altogether detestable and a thing forbidden to Christian men that soldiers of the Cross of Christ should march to pillage Christian men with slaughter and rapine and fire, such as usually happen when a city is attacked, and therefore refused their consent.

There was no idea of abandoning the crusade. The expedition to Zara was probably, though by no means certainly, regarded even by the leaders who were in the secret merely as a means of payment, in order that when it had been captured the Crusaders might go about their proper business. The third great mistake of the campaign had, however, been made; the second being the failure to bring sufficient men to comply with the terms of the charter-party entered into with the Venetians. The third blunder was the more serious.

The leaders of the first great crusade had declared under the walls of ancient Nicaea that it was no part of their business to fight Christian princes, that their work was to fight the *infidel*, and they had readily given that city into the hands of Alexis. The enthusiasts of the fourth crusade, who had left their homes in order to fight against Christ's enemies, had no heart for the new undertaking, and though they did not know all the adventures it would lead them into, we can see from Villehardouin himself that they would have preferred to return home rather than violate their vow.

On the 22nd of July (*Devastatio*), Cardinal Peter Capuano, the Pope's *legate*, arrived in Venice from Rome. Bishop Conrad, and probably others, required that the propositions of Dandolo should be referred to him. He at first protested against the proposal, (*Gesta Inn*. i.), because, as Gunther says, he thought the attack upon Zara 'a lesser evil than the abandonment of the crusade, the vow of the Cross unfulfilled, and the return home with ignominy and sin.' Cardinal Peter sent away all the sick, the useless hangers-on, and the women. (*Devastatio*),

The dissatisfaction among the Crusaders was at that time daily increasing. Some were for abandoning the expedition altogether. Many poor men who had brought but little with them and had nothing left for the journey quitted the army and went home. Gunther says:—

> Certain powerful and rich men, not influenced by poverty, so much as frightened by the horror of committing such a crime (as attacking a Christian city belonging to a crusading king), hesitated, and much against their will turned back.

Some of these went to Rome in order that they might be absolved from their vow or have its execution postponed. Others wished to leave Venice in order that they might embark for Alexandria or Syria from other ports.

Cardinal Peter's protest was followed by an earnest request that the expedition should be sent off as early as possible to Alexandria. His mission as *legate* was to accompany the army, to urge it to leave for Alexandria, to prevent it from going to Zara, to settle the differences between the Crusaders and Venetians, and generally to represent Innocent the Third. The Venetians, however, received him coldly. The *doge* and the council told him that if he wished to accompany the Crusaders in order to preach to them, he could do so: if he wished to go as envoy of the Pope he had better stay behind. (*Ep. VII.; Gesta.*)

News of what had been done in Venice reached the pilgrims who had not yet arrived in that city, and created consternation among them. Many of the German pilgrims in particular declared the expedition against Zara iniquitous and went home, and all further supply of Crusaders was thus cut off. (Gunther.)

Meantime the leader of the expedition, the Marquis Boniface of Montferrat, who had left Venice during July, returned to the city. Probably the treaty with the Venetians was concluded in the middle of August. The cardinal again protested, and, having committed the German pilgrims to the care of Bishop Conrad and the Abbot Martin, the latter of whom had avoided Venice when he learned the proposal of the *doge*, left for Rome.

The cardinal, however, seems to have vacillated. He protested but yielded. When he found that the Venetians would not give way unless the Crusaders would go to Zara, he seems, according to Gunther, to have considered it more venial and less inexpedient to accept the Zara proposal than to allow the expedition to be abandoned.

He, therefore, insisted on the promise that the Venetians would not only transport the army to Alexandria after the Zara expedition but would themselves join in the crusade. The author of the *Halberstadt MS.* confirms the version of the cardinal's conduct. The cardinal, in reply to Bishop Conrad, declared that the Pope would rather the terms of the Venetians were accepted than the expedition should be abandoned. He advised Conrad to bear with the insolence of the Venetians, and appointed him, together with four Cistercian abbots, to go with the army to represent the Pope. In the same way Abbot Martin was advised by the cardinal to remain with the army.

Gunther says that when the abbot saw that the expedition would necessitate the shedding of Christian blood, he was at a loss what to do. He begged the cardinal to absolve him from his vow and to allow him to retire to the quiet of his cloister. The cardinal, however, flatly refused, and ordered him in the Pope's name to take charge of the German pilgrims. He was further enjoined by the cardinal to go with the army wherever it went, and to use his influence with that of the other religious leaders to prevent all attacks upon Christians and their territory.

On Sunday, the 25th of August, there was an imposing ceremony in Saint Mark's, the object of which was probably partly to delude the pilgrims into the belief in the good faith of Dandolo and the Venetians, and partly to give a pretence to them to join the expedition. At the Mass, which was of unusual solemnity, Henry Dandolo ascended the pulpit and addressed the Venetians:—

> You are allied with the bravest men on earth. I am old, and weak, and infirm; as you see, I have need of rest; still, I know of no one more capable of taking command of your undertaking than I. If you wish that I should take the Cross and that my son should remain here to replace me, I will go with you and the pilgrims for life or death.

The assembly cried, 'Come with us, for God's sake.' Many in the congregation, both Venetians and pilgrims, shed tears as the old man was led to the altar, and a cross, made especially large so that it might be seen by all, was affixed to his breast. Dandolo from this time became, perhaps, the most conspicuous actor in the fourth crusade. His personal influence was immense. We have already seen that his hatred of the New Rome was intense, that he had to revenge private injuries as well as the wrongs of Venice. From the moment when he took the Cross, he towers above all the leaders in the great host which his fleet was shortly to transport to the Bosphorus. The venerable figure of the old man at the altar pledging himself to go with the Crusaders and to share their fortunes imposed on many.

Others, however, reflected that he had not entertained the idea of going with the army until the proposal to attack Zara had been accepted, and such distrusted his new-born enthusiasm for Christianity. A brave man—'*de bien grand coeur,*' says Villehardouin—but one also who knew the interests of Venice and cared for nothing else; a statesman of the Italian type before Mazzini and Cavour had taught or shown a more excellent model. Capable of venturing upon bold and dangerous enterprises, he had all the ability necessary to carry them through. Self-reliant to the last day of his long life, he was yet able to avoid arousing the easily-awakened jealousy of the Venetian oligarchs.

He was virtually dictator of Venice, and possessed the entire confidence of the Republic through his successful management of its affairs. He intrigued, kept his plans secret from his countrymen, deceived the Crusaders, and yet always succeeded in his designs. Lying and intrigue were indeed held to be fair by the rules of that Italian statesmanship which Machiavel reduced to a science. The best Italian statesman was the one who could best succeed in the purpose he had taken in hand. That faith should be broken, that craftiness should be continually necessary, were merely the incidents necessary to success. In Venetian politics, right or wrong had no meaning, except in the sense that everything which advanced Venetian interests was right, everything which made against them was wrong.

Dandolo never appears to have felt himself under any obligation to tell the truth, or to respect either his oath as a Crusader or his pledged word to the pilgrims. Provided the Republic could be benefited, all means were lawful. If a man '*de bien grand Coeur,*' yet also a statesman without conscience and an unscrupulous man.

The arrangements having been definitely made in conformity with which the Crusaders and the Venetians were to attack Zara, the preparations for sailing were rapidly pushed forward. For the moment discontent appears to have been hushed. The Crusaders even, who had objected to making war upon a Christian city, were delighted at any change which would get them out of the steaming and fever swamps of the Lido.

CHAPTER 3

Departure to, Conquest of, and Stay in Zara

The expedition against Zara left Venice in two divisions, one which started on the 1st and the other on the 8th of October. The whole fleet consisted of four hundred and eighty sail. The departure of the second and great division, containing the army of Crusaders, was one of the most picturesque sights which even Venice can ever have seen. The Republic of the lagoons has always cherished a love of artistic display, and nowhere can any spectacle be set amid surroundings which more completely enhance its beauty than amid the waters where the Queen of the Adriatic rises from the sea. The time had not yet come when her rulers thought it necessary to check lavish display of colour and undue extravagance.

The dwellings and storehouses of her people were already palaces. Her citizens had already grouped themselves into guilds, each with its own characteristic dress, so that brilliancy of colour was already a striking feature of a Venetian crowd. The silks and velvets of the East were set off with precious stones and jewellery, while over all the southern sun shed a light which, reflected from the waters, did not make their gorgeousness seem out of place. Robert de Clari describes with evident enjoyment the scene as Dandolo and the Crusaders left. Each of the nobles had a ship for himself and his esquires, while attending it was the sailing barge for the horses.

Each ship was girt around by the bucklers of the knights, and looked as if it had a belt of steel. The *doge* had fifty galleys, which 1 had been fitted out at his own cost or at that of the city. The one in which Dandolo voyaged was vermilion coloured, like that of an emperor. Four trumpeters with trumpets of silver attended him from his vermilion tent to his galley, and with the bearers of cymbals contributed to the popular demonstration on the departure of the expedition. The priests and monks were stationed in the castles at the cross-trees of the vessels, and solemnly chanted the *Veni, Creator Spiritus*. So beautiful a sight as this departure, says Robert, had never surely been seen.

A hundred trumpets with many other instruments of music gave the signal for sailing. When the vessels were in the open sea and had spread their sails, when the rich banners and *gonfalons* of so many earls and nobles were unfurled by the wind, while as far as the eye could reach the Adriatic was covered with ships, the beauty of the spectacle was at its greatest. It was remarked, and truly, says Robert, that never were there so many such beautiful ships assembled together.

★★★★★★★★

Rhamnusius estimated the fleet to consist of 480 vessels, composed of 50 galleys, 240 transports for troops, 70 for provisions, and 120 *huissiers* for the horses. Nicetas says 240, composed of no *huissiers*, 60 galleys, and 70 transports for provisions. I suspect the larger estimate is obtained on the fair supposition that there must have been an equal number of transports for the troops.

★★★★★★★★

Even here, however, he is careful to point out a jarring note. Very many, both great and small, deplored the sin which was being committed and the great joy which prevailed. They crossed the sea, says another writer, (Gunther), with great speed but with sad hearts.

On the 20th of October Dandolo made a triumphal entry into Trieste. Both divisions united a few days afterwards at Pola. The united fleet arrived off Zara on November II. On the same day the harbour was captured and the army landed. The city was the wealthiest on the eastern shores of the Adriatic, and the metropolis of Dalmatia and Croatia. It is situated on a peninsula, and was well fortified. It had formerly owned allegiance to Venice, but had shaken off her rule, and was now under the protection of the King of Hungary.

On the 12th a deputation proposed to surrender everything to Dandolo if the lives of the citizens were spared. While the proposal was being considered some of the Crusaders, at the head of whom was Simon de Montfort, told some of the deputation that they had only to fear the Venetians. He said:—

> I am not here to do harm to Christians. I wish you no ill, and, on the contrary, would rather protect you against those who would hurt you. (Petri, *Val. Cern. Hist. Albig.*)

The well-meant interference proved mischievous. The deputation returned to the city. The negotiations were interrupted, and the terms on which the people of Zara had proposed to surrender were withdrawn. The Venetians proposed to attack the city, and lest the Crusaders should make further delays in what Gunther calls this hateful and detestable business, the Venetians commenced the siege at once. The people of Zara, in anticipation, probably, of this attack, had obtained letters from the Pope, excommunicating any who should do them damage. These they sent to the *doge* and the leaders of the army. The *doge* declared his intention to disregard the threat, and most of the barons expressed their determination to follow his example.

The discontent and indignation of the better part of the Crusaders found at length a mouthpiece. A council was held. The Abbot of Vaux, a Cistercian monk, could no longer control his indignation. In the council held in Dandolo's tent he suddenly rose, and in a bold, clear voice said:—

> I forbid you in the name of the Pope to attack this city. It is a city of Christian men, and you are Crusaders. You have another destination.

The Venetians would have murdered him if he had not been protected by Simon de Montfort and by other nobles. Dandolo was greatly annoyed. He charged the Crusaders with having prevented him from taking possession of the city, and claimed the fulfilment of their promise to aid him in conquering it. The majority of them thought themselves bound to help Dandolo, and promised to do so. Simon de Montfort, however, and many other pilgrims declared that they would not act against the apostolic command, and that they had no intention of being excommunicated. Notwithstanding these protests, the letters of the Pope, and the threats of the Pope's representatives, the city was attacked.

It was captured in five days, namely, on the 24th of November, 1202. The pilgrims and the Venetians entered into it, and Zara was mercilessly plundered. Its churches were pillaged and many houses destroyed. The inhabitants were barbarously treated. Some were beheaded, others were banished, while a great number fled to the mountains to save their lives. Dandolo was not content with punishing the citizens of Zara. His intention was to bring it again under the rule of the Republic, and for this purpose considerable time was necessary. Hence, shortly after the conquest, he proposed that the army should winter in Zara. He said to the leaders:—

> The winter is coming on. We cannot budge from here until Easter, because we shall not be able to find provisions in any other place. The city is rich and well supplied with everything. Let us divide it. (Villehardouin, ch. xviii.)

The proposition was accepted; the spoil was shared, and the Venetians and Crusaders took up their quarters for the winter in different portions of the city, the Venetians near the harbour, the Crusaders inland.

Meantime the dissatisfaction between the Venetians and the leaders on the one side and the great body of Crusaders on the other was daily increasing. The latter had persuaded themselves that when Zara was taken, they would at once be permitted to go on their pilgrimage; They had violated their vow, and had fallen under the sentence of excommunication. The religious portion of the army in particular was greatly embittered against Dandolo and their own leaders. Within three days of the capture of the city the Venetians and the Crusaders were fighting against each other in a quarrel which lasted several hours, (a day and a night, says Robert de Clari), and in which a hundred persons were killed and many were wounded.

There was not a street where the fight was not going on. As fast as the leaders stopped the fighting in one quarter their attention was called for in another. Everywhere the Venetians had the worst of it. All the authority of the leaders of both sides was required to put an end to this quarrel. What was its immediate cause it is perhaps impossible to learn. The author of the *Devastatio* says that the barons kept the spoil to themselves, and did not share it with the poor men of the army. The explanation is possible, and is in accordance with the policy which was followed throughout the expedition until its end.

The leaders were in league with the Venetians, while the mass of the Crusaders, who had set their minds on pilgrimage, saw only that they were being made use of to benefit the Venetians and their own leaders. What is certain is that the army was already considerably demoralised, and that some at least of the leaders joined with a large body of the pilgrims in distrusting the Venetians. The quarrel increased the bitterness of feeling between the opposing sections. A large number of the Crusaders were anxious to leave for Egypt or Syria; a large number, Villehardouin says, were tired of the expedition and wished to return home.

During the weeks which followed there was great and continual dissatisfaction between the Venetians and the Crusaders. Possibly there is truth in the statement of Villehardouin that many wished the army to break up and were anxious to return home. They had not come out to fight either the King of Hungary or the Emperor of Romania, as it began to be whispered they were to be called upon to do. They had no desire to give their services to the traders of Venice. The great French chronicler wishes to leave the impression that the disaffection was merely wanton and without just cause.

The narrative, however, of every independent contemporary, and especially of the 'poor knight,' Robert de Clari, shows that abundant cause existed. The expedition had already fallen under the expressed censure of the Church. Each man knew without such official censure that in taking part against a Christian city he had violated his oath, and had been untrue to the pledges he had given and the convictions which had led him to join the enterprise. The treatment the Crusaders had received on the Lido, their loss of the autumn, their journey across the Adriatic, 'with great speed but with sad hearts,' in the interests of Venice, had been borne in the hopes that on the capture of Zara a way might be found for a speedy departure *outre-mer*.

But the pilgrims now saw that their allies cared nothing for the object of the pilgrimage, and were mainly bent on recovering territory and destroying a rival, while they believed that their own leaders were bent upon amassing the largest possible amount of spoil from a Christian people. They themselves were suffering much from cold and hunger, (*Devastatio*), and would have been content so to suffer if it were in the execution of their vow. Now, however, both their spiritual and their temporal interests were being sacrificed. Those who thought most of the first found themselves under the ban of excommunication, and those who might have been disposed to disregard spiritual censure found that they were being used to benefit the Venetians while others obtained the spoil.

Hence there were daily desertions. The strictest orders were given that none should leave the camp. These orders, however, were insufficient to check the evil. A thousand went without leave. The clamour for permission to go away was so great that the leaders judged it well to give permission to another thousand. Many merchant ships went away filled with soldiers. One had five hundred on board, who were all drowned. Another detachment tried to return home through 'Slavonia'—that is, through Dalmatia and Styria—but after being badly assailed by the peasants had to return to the army.

It should be noted also that this anxiety to leave the army was mainly caused by the desire of the deserters to be about the business for which they had left home. The object of most of those who left the camp was to get to Syria or Egypt.

CHAPTER 4

The Plot

PART 1

Thus, the winter of 1202-3 passed slowly away, in discontent among the Crusaders, in smouldering suspicion against their chiefs, and in animosity towards the Venetians. Suspicion was in the air—suspicion by the Crusaders that they were to be made the tools of Venice in the future as they had already been in the immediate past—a new suspicion also that Philip of Swabia, King of the Romans, was about to unite with Dandolo against the Pope of Rome, that their own leader, Boniface, had already betrayed them, sold them as an army to assist his kinsman Philip in fighting against the head of the Church.

The proof of treachery was not complete, but sufficient was known to justify the suspicion and to account for the uneasiness. The soldiers who had been carried away from their native countries on a wave of religious enthusiasm, who had come out to fight for God and His cause, had already violated their oaths, and felt themselves powerless to get out of the trap into which they had been led.

Leaving the Crusaders at Zara, I propose now to narrate the facts which justified the suspicion of the army, and to attempt to point out what was the plot against the object which the Crusaders had in hand.

Before doing so it is necessary to call attention to the reasons which are assigned by contemporary writers for the two circumstances which marked the diversion of the fourth crusade from its intended purpose. The two circumstances were, first, the attack upon Zara, and, second, the expedition to Constantinople.

These circumstances are described, as we have already seen, by two sets of contemporary historians, who may be classified roughly as official and non-official writers. In the first class I have already stated that the graphic and singularly interesting account written, dictated, or revised by Villehardouin takes the highest rank. The writer describes what he saw or heard. All the official accounts are open to the objection that they are the work of men who were either themselves leaders or were under the influence either of the leaders of the expedition or of Philip of Swabia. They are all pleas of men writing for the defence. Their testimony is therefore not impartial, and may fairly be examined with suspicion.

When they wrote, the crusade from which Europe had hoped so much had failed miserably in its object, had begun by destroying a Christian city, and had ended by destroying a Christian instead of a Moslem state. The Pope had indignantly condemned the conduct of the Crusaders, and in doing so had probably expressed the opinion of the conscience of Western Europe. The writers in question had to explain the change of a crusade into a buccaneering expedition as best they could.

The reason they assign for the diversion of the crusade to Zara is, as we have seen, that many of the Crusaders having taken ship elsewhere or having refused to leave home, the number of those who reached Venice was far below that which the delegates had contracted for; that the Venetians insisted upon their bargain, until at length they made a fair proposal by means of which the Crusaders would be able to pay the 34,000 *marks* which were still due to the Republic under the contract for transport. These writers add that those who opposed this proposal did so because they wished to break up the enterprise.

The chief of them, Villehardouin, begins his excuses for the failure of the expedition with the departure of the Flemish fleet already mentioned. He tells us that this fleet was a very fine one, was very well provided, and contained a great number of well-armed men. Baldwin of Flanders, however, did not go with it, but went overland to Venice. The command of the fleet was given to Jan de Neele and two others. (Villehardouin, x.) The pilgrims had great confidence in the fleet, because, says Villehardouin, the greatest number of their sergeants-at-arms were on board. (*Knights of the Cross* by Leonaur contains *Chronicle of the Fourth Crusade* and *The Conquest of Constantinople* by Villehardouin, and *Chronicle of the Crusade of St. Louis* by Joinville.)

Jan de Neele and the other officers in command had promised Baldwin that after they had passed the Straits of Gibraltar, they would join the army which had collected at Venice in whatever place they learned it had gone to. Villehardouin says that they had broken their word to their lord 'because they were afraid of the great peril in which those at Venice were engaged.'

The meaning of the phrase is doubtful. It probably signifies that those in the fleet descried the enterprise in order to avoid the peril to which those in Venice seem to have exposed themselves. (This is the meaning which Du Cange gives.) If the writer meant the peril or danger of being delayed in Venice, then a comparison of the dates at which the troubles in Venice began with that of the arrival of this fleet at Marseilles will show that no such fear could have influenced the fleet. The messengers announcing the arrival of the fleet in Marseilles reached Venice probably in January 1203. They declared that the fleet proposed to winter at Marseilles and asked for orders. Baldwin, after consultation with the *doge*, sent word to them to leave at the end of March and to proceed to Methroni, at the south-east of the Peloponnesus, to meet the Venetian fleet. Villehardouin says:—

> Alas! they acted so ill that they did not keep their word, but went away to Syria, where they knew that they could do no good.

The truth probably is that they had heard how the Crusaders had been tricked and turned away from their purpose, and therefore decided that they at least would go forward to fight the Moslem. If they were not strong enough to make an attempt on Egypt, they could at least give aid to the Christians who were in Syria. If Villehardouin's suggestion means that the Flemish fleet could have been of use to the army for the purposes of the Crusade, it is dishonest. The bargain for the attack on Zara was concluded before the fleet reached Marseilles. The capture of Zara had been made in November. The contract to attack Constantinople was made at latest before the fleet reached the Adriatic. The fact is that Villehardouin seizes upon the very slightest shadow of evidence to afford proof of the necessity of abandoning the expedition to Egypt.

The story of Villehardouin and his school, which attributes the diversion of the crusade to the want of men and to the pressure of the Venetians, is in the main true, but it is not the whole truth. We have to turn to the non-official historians of the expedition in order to supplement and check the narrative of the official writers. The former are less open to suspicion than the latter. They had fewer motives for misrepresentation. But even they were disposed to make the best of a bad business. They had no sympathy either with the Zarans or the Venetians.

At the same time, they were themselves Crusaders or derived their information from Crusaders, and were desirous of showing that the crusade had done something useful, if it were only the punishment of a nation which had refused to recognise the supremacy of the Pope. One advantage, however, they undoubtedly possess over the official writers. They do not consider themselves bound to conceal the conduct of Venice.

The explanation they give of the diversion of the enterprise is that it was due solely to the conduct of the Republic. Enough might have been gathered from a careful search of the authorities known to exist even in the time of Gibbon to raise a strong presumption against the good faith of Dandolo, Boniface, and Philip of Swabia. But it has been reserved to our own time to complete the evidence against them; to prove almost already to demonstration that the expedition was diverted from its purpose through the cupidity and treason of Venice, and that from this cause the army was converted into a band of robbers, who were to commit the great crime of the Middle Ages by the destruction of the citadel against which the hitherto irresistible wave of Moslem invasion had beaten and had been broken.

Bearing in mind the difference in weight to be attached to the two classes of witnesses, it becomes necessary to put together their evidence.

The messengers of the Crusaders arrived in Venice in the middle of February 1201. (Villehardouin.) Their treaty with the Venetians for the transport of an army to Egypt was made in the middle of March. (*Ibid.*) News of the signature of this treaty reached Malek-Adel, the Sultan of Egypt, very shortly afterwards, and filled him with alarm. The weakened condition of his country, due to natural causes and to the divisions in his own family, made it of the utmost importance that the Crusading Army should be diverted from Egypt.

An army very much inferior to the great hosts of the last expedition would inevitably conquer Egypt. Accordingly, Malek-Adel set to work not only to repair his defences but to buy over the Venetians. In the autumn of the same year two envoys were sent from Venice to this *Sultan*, possibly at his request, were received by him with great distinction and occupied themselves at once with framing terms of peace, which later on took the form of a commercial treaty.

Meantime the Crusaders had been collecting. According to their contract with Venice, they were to be in that city and the transports were to be ready by St. John's Day, the 24th of June, 1202. On the 13th of May, 1202, the envoys of Venice had concluded their treaty with

Malek-Adel. This treaty assured to the Venetians, in addition to many other privileges, a district or quarter in Alexandria, and to the pilgrims who visited the Holy Sepulchre under Venetian protection safety for their lives and goods. The *Sultan* sent an *emir*, named Sead Eddin, to Venice to secure its confirmation. His mission was successful, and the treaty was secretly ratified in July 1202. (Carl Hopf.) The signature of this treaty gives the explanation of the diversion of the Fourth Crusade from Egypt and of its subsequent failure.

Venice was henceforward playing a double game. She had signed her agreement of March 1201 with the Crusaders, in accordance with which she was to transport the army of the West to Egypt. She now signs a secret treaty with the enemy who was to be attacked. The successes which Pisa and Genoa had obtained over her in Constantinople were to be compensated by her successes over them in Egypt. The price of her triumph was the betrayal of Christendom. It was impossible to keep faith both with the Crusaders and with the Arabs. The signature of the treaty with the Sultan of Egypt meant that faith was to be broken with the followers of the Cross, and was therefore the immediate cause of the diversion of the enterprise from Egypt.

The Crusaders at the time and for years afterwards suspected treachery, and some of the contemporary writers did not hesitate to accuse Venice of betraying the expedition. But there is no evidence to prove that even any of the leaders had any certain knowledge that a treaty had been signed, by which the services of the Venetians in carrying the army to Egypt had become impossible. The presence of Sead Eddin in Venice, in July 1202, possibly gave rise to doubts as to the good faith of the Republic, though the presence of an envoy from the *Sultan* may have been concealed or may have been disregarded amid the multitude of visitors to the great centre of Eastern trade in Western Europe. If such doubts arose, the conduct of the Venetians to the Crusaders while at Lido increased them, while the attack upon Zara brought conviction into the minds of a large body of the army that they were not being fairly dealt with by the Venetians.

It is probable that the belief that Venice was not acting fairly was one of the causes of the ill-feeling which showed itself in the riot between the Venetians and the Crusaders within a week after the occupation of the city. But the secret of the treaty was well kept. The interest of Dandolo was, on the one hand, not to allow its provisions to transpire, and, on the other, to take advantage of every circumstance in order to divert the attention of the Crusaders from Egypt. Henceforward, and without any explanation being suggested, we find that the Crusaders speak rather of going to Syria than to Egypt.

The arrival of a smaller number of Crusaders in Venice than had been contracted for gave a plausible excuse to Dandolo, first, to delay the departure of the expedition, then to divert it towards Zara, and afterwards to keep it there during the winter. We have seen that he entirely succeeded. From the ratification of the treaty with the Sultan of Egypt, in July 1202, the intention was to divert the expedition from its intended attack upon Egypt, the weakest and at the same time the most important point under Moslem sway.

The evidence in support of an understanding between Venice and the *Sultan*, by which Venice was to prevent an attack upon Egypt, is already weighty, and will probably be conclusive when a more careful examination has been made of the Venetian archives. Charles Hopf, the greatest of German authorities on all that relates to the history of the East during the Middle Ages, and who had amassed large stores of materials for his historical works, appears to have had a copy of this treaty in his possession. (Unfortunately, on his death his collection was either dispersed or at any rate has not been made available to historical students.)

The treaty is mentioned by one of the earliest historians of the crusade. Arnold of Ibelino, the probable author of the *Continuation of the History of William of Tyre* gives an account which is full of detail and which there is no reason to regard as seriously inaccurate. He says that when the Sultan of Babylon, as the ruler of Egypt was then generally called, from the fortified town on the Nile which he usually occupied, heard that a great fleet had been chartered by the Christians to proceed to Egypt, he sent for the cadis and priests to take council with him how he should save his country from the Christians who were coming.

He made various proposals for the defence of the country. Then he sent messengers to Venice with rich presents to the *doge* and the inhabitants. The messengers were charged to ask for the friendship of the Venetians, and to promise that if the Christians were diverted from their plan of an attack upon Egypt the Venetians should receive great treasures and large privileges in the port of Alexandria. The messengers went to Venice, and, as we have seen, succeeded.

The explanation, therefore, of the diversion of the Crusading Army from Egypt is to be found first and mainly in the treason of Venice. In order to obtain advantages of trade over her Italian rivals she had accepted a treaty which made it impossible for her to conduct the army of the Cross to Egypt. The Crusaders grumbled, suspected treachery, and did all they could to fulfil their vows, but all in vain.

Venice had a fixed and definite purpose. Circumstances enabled her to force the Crusaders to go to Zara, and the winter once lost it became easier to divert the expedition from its original purpose than it had been a year previously. We shall now have to examine how it came about that Dandolo was enabled again to prevent the Crusaders leaving for Egypt, and in so doing to carry out at once his part of the treaty with Egypt and to revenge his own wrongs and those of Venice against Constantinople.

Part 2

It now becomes necessary to examine one of the most interesting intrigues that have ever influenced the course of European history. During the winter at Zara the discontent of the Crusaders increased daily. The pilgrims saw their chance of being landed in Syria or Egypt rapidly diminishing. Apart even from the suspicion of Venetian treachery, they remembered that their contract with the Republic was only for a year, and expired in June. They had already seen that the Venetians adhered to the strict letter of their agreement in regard to payment. They would be equally exacting in regard to time. The expenses of the expedition had moreover exhausted the provisions and money they had brought with them. Even the money which the barons had been able to borrow was nearly spent. It was already difficult to obtain provisions. (Robert de Clari, xvi.) If a further demand should be made for extra payment after June the army would be unable to meet it.

Villehardouin insists that many attempts were made in presence of these difficulties to break up the expedition. Many of the Crusaders wished to return home; many more wished to leave for Syria in order to accomplish the vow which they believed would be impossible of execution if they remained with the Venetians. But while Dandolo was well content that the attack upon Egypt had been temporarily avoided, he had his own reasons for preventing the break-up of the army. So far, he had been successful. But his own work was only half done. The expedition had been diverted from Egypt. Venice had gained time.

Still, if the Venetians kept their part of the bargain, it was quite possible that the army should be landed in Egypt, and should be able to fight its way to sustenance and victory. If the army broke up, the

Crusaders might reunite, and, with the aid of the Genoese and Pisans, the great rivals of the Venetians, still attack Egypt. Such a result would be the humiliation of Venice and the discomfiture of Dandolo. The great *doge* had long since provided against any such mishap. There is reason to believe that even before the expedition left Venice, he had determined to make use of the crusading host against Constantinople. A conspiracy had already been formed between Dandolo, Boniface, the commander-in-chief, and Philip of Swabia, which was to result in the greatest blow yet given to Christendom.

In order to understand how this conspiracy had been formed, we must recall briefly what had been passing in the imperial city. The reigning emperor was Alexis the Third. He had deposed his brother Isaac in 1195, and after putting out his eyes had imprisoned him in the dungeons of the *Diplokionion*, or in the tower of Anema. Isaac's son, Alexis, was allowed his liberty. At a time when Alexis the Third had apparently determined to kill young Alexis, his nephew and the lawful heir to the throne, the wife of the usurper warned Isaac of the contemplated crime. Isaac, according to the same authority, counselled his son to leave the city at once, and to escape to his sister, the wife of Philip of Swabia.

Young Alexis, either disguised as a common sailor or hidden in a box carefully disguised, (*Chron. Novgorod*), fled from Constantinople in a Pisan ship, and escaped the diligent search which was made for him by the imperial police. This was in the spring of 1201. Contemporary Western writers, who have been followed in this respect by all historians until the present day, speak of young Alexis as the son of Isaac by Margaret, daughter of Bela of Hungary, his second wife.

This marriage took place in 1185. Alexis, therefore, in 1200, could not be older than fourteen or fifteen. (Two facts are opposed to the accepted statement that Margaret was the mother of Alexis: 1, that the reigning emperor wrote to Innocent the Third that the youth was not *porphyrogenetos*; and 2, that, according to Nicetas, Margaret was only ten years old in 1185.) He had sent messengers to his sister (or more probably his half-sister), the wife of Philip, imploring the help of her husband.

He made his way, according to Villehardouin, to Ancona, in Italy. His movements, however, after leaving Constantinople, are doubtful. The balance of the evidence of contemporary writers seems to show that he went direct to Philip of Swabia, after calling at Sicily, and possibly taking Ancona on the way. According to one writer, he was in

July at Warzburg, where Philip held his court. (Böhmer, *Register Imperii*.) Apparently he continued with Philip until the end of the year, where, as I have already mentioned, he would have seen Boniface. In the summer of 1202 he was in Hungary, (*Continuatio*), probably on his way to the Pope with a request for aid. In August, or the beginning of September, he was at Verona. (Villehardouin.)

In order to understand why he had returned to Italy, we must trace the events which had happened in the interval between his flight from Constantinople and his arrival in Hungary. Young Alexis had appealed, as we have seen, to his sister and her husband Philip. The Swabian king wished for many reasons to help him. Philip, who claimed to be King of the Romans, was the head of the party opposed to the Pope.

On the death of the Emperor Henry the Sixth, the Pope and other princes had refused to recognise his infant son Frederic as his successor. Philip, brother of Henry, on failing to have his nephew recognised, had succeeded in having himself elected emperor by one party, while Otho of Brunswick had been selected by the Guelfs.

The Pope opposed the pretensions of Philip, and had carried his opposition to such an extent that in March 1201 Philip had been excommunicated. The result to the pretender had been very serious. His subjects were absolved from their obedience. Many nobles and ecclesiastical princes had withdrawn from or were wavering in their allegiance. Others, like the Bishop of Halberstadt, had joined the crusade in order to avoid the necessity of choosing between their temporal and their spiritual lord.

Philip was a delicate, fragile-looking man of the blond German type, whose appearance suggested weakness. The physical weakness at least was more apparent than real. He could hold his own in the manly pursuits of his time. He had been brought up by his father for the Church, and had been carefully trained in the monastery of Adelsburg, founded by a vassal of the House of Hohenstaufen. His education or natural temper made him a narrow churchman, a man ready for intrigue and for persistent petty opposition—a man, too, full of ambition. His great chance of recovering influence was to show that notwithstanding the Pope he could hold his own. If in so doing he could thwart the great object of the Pontiff's life, not only would he have succeeded in triumphing over his rival, but he might expect that those who had deserted him would return to their allegiance.

The arrival of messengers from Alexis corresponding with the collection of the Crusading Army appears at a very early period to have suggested the idea to Philip that the crusade might be made use of, under the pretext at least of assisting his brother-in-law. Philip had, however, selfish reasons which disposed him to help young Alexis. He seems to have persuaded himself that he had a right to the imperial throne of the East through his wife, and one of his dreams was that it might be possible to unite the two empires of the New and the Elder Rome in his own person.

Thus, the indignation which he had a right to feel at the deposition and imprisonment of his wife's father urged him to a course which coincided with that which his own ambition would dictate. Add to this that the disastrous result of the last crusade had been most keenly felt in Germany, and that any movement against the empire in the East was sure to be popular with his own subjects, and we see that the motives which urged Philip to assist young Alexis were exceedingly strong. If he could help him by turning the crusade into a weapon against the reigning Emperor in Constantinople, he would at the same time succeed in recovering the allegiance of those of his own subjects whom the Pope's excommunication had caused to waver. He could let the Pope see that he was more powerful than his rival, and even Innocent might think it well to side with the stronger claimant. His own power would be enormously increased. He might be not only the triumphant leader of the Ghibelin party, but lord of the East and of the West.

Impelled by such motives, the appointment of Boniface, Marquis of Montferrat, to the command of the Crusading Army on the death, in May 1201, of Theobald of Champagne, supplied the instrument he required. If Boniface could be induced to act with him, a successful attack might be made on Constantinople, and his plans appeared assured of success. Boniface, as Robert de Clari is careful to point out, was a relative of Philip. His father was William of Montferrat, who had played an important part on the Ghibelin side. This William had married Sophia, daughter of Frederic Barbarossa, and sister or half-sister of Philip. In the contest for the imperial throne, which had commenced on the death of Henry the Sixth in 1197 between Philip and Otho of Brunswick, Innocent himself had sent Boniface with the Archbishop of Mayence to try to arrange their differences.

The mission had, however, failed. Not only was Boniface acquainted with the affairs of Philip, but he had occasion to be well versed in what was passing at Constantinople. The family of Montferrat was well acquainted with the East. Six of its members had contracted marriages with the imperial family. William, the father of Boniface, had four sons, each of whom connected his name with the history of the crusades, and three of them very closely with that of Constantinople. These sons were William, surnamed Longsword, Conrad, Reynier, and Boniface.

The eldest was for a time the hope of the Crusaders. The family was related to those of the Roman Emperor in the West, the King of France, and other powerful princes. He married in 1175 the daughter of Baldwin the Fourth, the King of Jerusalem, and received in dowry the earldoms of Jaffa and Ascalon, but died two months afterwards.

The second son, who became Marquis of Montferrat on the death of William, was that Conrad whom we have seen in Constantinople, aiding the Emperor to resist the attack upon the city by Branas. We have seen also that after his marriage with Theodora, sister of Isaac, he refused to follow the emperor to Adrianople, was dissatisfied with his honours, and went to Palestine in 1187, where he played a most important part during the next four years, and especially distinguished himself in the siege of Tyre. After marrying Isabella, to the disgust of the Archbishop of Canterbury and other churchmen, and after having quarrelled with Richard, and having been named King of Jerusalem, he was killed by one of the assassins in 1192.

Robert de Clari alleges that Isaac behaved treacherously to Conrad even when he had organised an army of Latins to oppose Branas; that when the marquis went out of the city to meet the rebel the emperor shut the gate upon him instead of following with his own troops. Nicetas distinctly contradicts this statement, and states that the emperor himself commanded the right wing and Manuel Camyzes the left wing. It is not improbable that the story of Clari is one which only passed into circulation about the time of the capture of Constantinople, when the family and partisans of Montferrat found it convenient to find grievances against that of Isaac.

Reynier, the third son of William of Montferrat, younger brother of Conrad and elder brother of Boniface, had married Maria, daughter of the Emperor Manuel. He was at the time a beardless boy, and she a woman remarkably robust, and thirty years of age. (Nicetas.) The Western writers declare that he received as dowry the kingdom of Salonica, though no Greek writer mentions a fact so important. He died without children after the murder of Conrad, and his only surviving brother was Boniface. (A charter of 1204 states that Boniface sold to the Venetians his rights to the fiefs given by Manuel to his *father*, probably a mistake for his brother; *Tafel et Thomas, i.*)

Thus, the leader of the expedition, if we are to judge by narratives which were written by men whose object was in most cases to find an excuse for the conduct of Boniface, had family grievances which made him hostile to Constantinople. He considered himself *de jure* King of Salonica as inheritor of the dowry of Reynier. He had also, if Clari is to be believed, to revenge the attempt upon the life of his other brother Conrad. Philip and he had therefore each his own reason for wishing to attack the Emperor Alexis. It is by no means improbable that they had discussed and decided upon a plan of attacking the empire during the time that Theobald of Champagne was still alive.

The election of Boniface had taken place in June 1201. In August he took the Cross and was solemnly invested with the title of Captain of the Christian Army. Shortly afterwards, as we have already seen, he left Burgundy for the court of Philip of Swabia, which was then at Hagenau, where he arrived at the end of the year, and where he probably found young Alexis. It is in the highest degree probable that he had taken this long journey on the invitation of Philip, and it is equally probable that the object of Philip was to urge him to make use of the crusade to restore the Emperor Isaac, or to place his son Alexis on the throne.

It is, however, impossible to do more than surmise what passed during the weeks which Boniface spent at the court of Philip. The *Gesta* of Innocent the Third state that a treaty was concluded between them by which the Crusading Army was bound to place young Alexis on the throne at Constantinople. The existence of such a treaty is not improbable, but as no mention is made of it by other contemporary writers, such an agreement either never existed or was kept secret, or, what is more probable, was merely an understanding which it was unnecessary and undesirable either to disclose or to reduce to definite form in writing.

While there is nothing in the subsequent story of the crusade to indicate that Philip and Boniface had not a complete understanding, there is a large amount of evidence to suggest that they had. It is especially noteworthy that several contemporary writers speak of Philip having assumed the direction of the expedition from the time he was visited by Boniface.

The struggle between the Pope and Philip in regard to the use to be made of the fourth crusade began with the opening of the year 1202. Well knowing that the object dearest to the heart of Innocent after the success of the expedition was the union of the Eastern and Western Churches, Philip sent Alexis to Rome to ask for aid, and to put this union now, as always in these and all subsequent negotiations, in the front as the chief advantage to be gained in return for such aid.

In January or February 1202, Boniface himself left the court of Philip with an embassy for Rome. His mission from the King of the Romans was twofold, to urge the Pope to assist Alexis and to present the protest of the German nobles against the Pontiffs support of Otho. By putting in the front the promise of young Alexis to aid in bringing about the union of the churches, the Pope might be induced to support him. If he did so he could hardly continue to support Otho, since Philip's influence with the army would then be too powerful to be disregarded. If the Pope refused, it remained to be seen what could be done through Boniface with the Venetians and the Crusaders.

Boniface reached Rome early in March 1202. (March 11, Winkleman.) Alexis had already been received in solemn audience by the Pope, the cardinals, and the Roman nobility. He had asked for justice against his uncle. He urged that the whole city desired that he should become Emperor, and he insisted much upon his power to bring about a union of the two churches. The Pope seems to have hesitated as to the answer which he should give.

The offer was tempting, and especially perhaps because Alexis insisted that he had a large party devoted to his interests in the New Rome which would be ready to rise on his approach. (Chron. Novgorod.) The Pope concluded by distinctly refusing to promise any aid to Alexis. On the arrival of Boniface, the proposals were again submitted, but with a like result. Shortly afterwards the latter left Rome in deep disappointment, having altogether failed in the accomplishment of his and Philip's, designs.

From the moment of the failure in Rome, Boniface turned his attention to the execution of his designs by means of the army under his command. After a short visit made by himself and Alexis to Boniface's domains at Montferrat, we find the Pretender at Verona, the city which commands the Brenner pass, by which the German pilgrims came, as well as the road through Lombardy along which the Crusaders coming from France must needs travel.

On August 15, 1202, Boniface arrived in Venice. He found the army, as we have already seen, on the Lido in a state of the greatest distress. Forbidden to leave the island, plague-stricken, in need of provisions, wishing to be about their sacred business, they regarded the

Venetians as the cause of all their ills. But they could hardly look upon Boniface with great affection or confidence. He had been chosen only after the command had been refused by several others. He had seen less of the army than Baldwin of Flanders and others who had done their best to lessen the troubles of the Crusaders, and who had at least shared them.

Early in September an embassy arrived in Venice from Alexis in Verona. A meeting took place between the messengers of Alexis and the leaders of the army. The proposals of Alexis were submitted. A reply was given that a message should be sent to Philip with Alexis, who had sent word that he was going to his uncle. The message to Philip was in these words:—

> If Philip will aid us to recover the land *d'outre-mer* we will help Alexis to recover his own land. (Villehardouin.)

It is clear that the mass of the Crusaders knew little or nothing of this embassy or of this message. Probably Dandolo on the part of the Venetians, Boniface the commander-in-chief, and three or four of the leaders, including Villehardouin himself, were alone in the secret. It did not suit the conspirators yet to reveal their project, and we shall see that when it was made known to the army it was made to appear that the proposal to go to Constantinople was a quite recent suggestion, due to the necessities in which the Crusaders found themselves after wintering at Zara, instead of part of a well-planned conspiracy.

Still no definite agreement with the Crusaders and with Venice was yet arrived at. The project of Alexis had been favourably received; had been accepted in principle by the leaders. Almost immediately afterwards, and probably in September, Boniface again left the army, and remained absent until after the conquest of Zara. During a part at least of this time he was at Rome, where also was Cardinal Peter Capuano. Thus, while the Crusading Army was leaving Venice, its two chiefs, one in temporal and the other in spiritual things, were absent.

Boniface appears to have won over the Cardinal entirely to his views. In spite of the way in which Peter Capuano had been treated by the Venetians, he appears on this visit to Innocent to have made light of the expedition to Zara; to have spoken of it as a merely temporary incident, the punishment of a half heretical people by the occupation of their city, and as a punishment which would not entail the shedding of Christian blood. What is perhaps more remarkable is that in this visit to the Pope the Cardinal rather than Boniface seems to have been the chief advocate in favour of the proposal to help Alexis. (*Inno. III. Epist. viii.*)

It is easy to see what would be the arguments used. The Crusaders were short of money: had spent what they had, had been unable to borrow more, and, had been compelled to agree to the Zara arrangement in order to get rid of their obligations to the Venetians. Boniface would be careful to point out that the arrangement with Venice expired in June, and to urge that an expedition to Constantinople, with the object merely of restoring young Alexis, would be the only means of supplying money for the expedition; the only means of buying over the aid of the Venetians, without whom it could never reach either Egypt or Syria, and in short, the only means of preventing the crusade from absolute failure.

Innocent remained firm; refused to give any approval to the Zaran expedition; disavowed the *legate's* approbation, and sent to the army an injunction to restrain them from accomplishing their unrighteous purpose. In reference, however, to the project for giving aid to young Alexis, the arguments of Cardinal Peter and of Boniface made more impression. The Pope indeed formally refused to sanction the proposal. He did more. Knowing that the Cardinal agreed with Boniface, he forbade him to return to the army. But, notwithstanding this attitude of opposition, he appears to have thought it desirable at this time to keep the question in suspense. An embassy had been sent to Venice by the Emperor Alexis the Third to endeavour to bring about an alliance with the Republic. It was, however, too late, and was treated with ignominy. From Venice it appears to have gone to Rome.

The emperor seems from the first to have suspected the designs of Philip, of Boniface, and of Dandolo, and his embassy was the bearer of a golden Bull asking for the aid of the Pope against these designs. Innocent regarded the opportunity as favourable to his own plans. The great inducement which the young Alexis had offered to obtain the Pontiff's support was the union of the churches, an object only less dear to Innocent than the success of the crusade. While promising aid to Alexis, the reigning Emperor, he did so conditionally upon this union being brought about. At the same time, he sent word to the army distinctly forbidding the Crusaders to attack Romania.

The messengers sent to Philip by the Crusaders in Venice during September, to submit the proposition for assisting Alexis, arrived in Germany in October. Probably about the same time Philip would hear of the failure of the negotiations at Rome. This ill news would, however, be more than counterbalanced by the tidings of the great obstacle put in the way of the crusade by Venice, If the Republic could thus divert the expedition from its object, there was every reason to hope that with Dandolo's help he would be able to turn its energy to the accomplishment of his purpose.

Henceforward Philip acted more boldly, and was recognised by all as taking the leading part in the direction of the crusade. He negotiated the agreement that was to be made for aiding young Alexis. He acted at once as his guardian and guarantor. He sealed on his own behalf the treaty when concluded. In November the messengers of the Crusaders left Philip, accompanied by German plenipotentiaries. They arrived at Venice in the middle of December, and on the 1st of January, 1263, made their appearance at Zara, whither they had followed the army,

Alexis left the court of Philip probably at the same time as the messengers for Zara, but appears to have diverged in order to visit his uncle Emeric, King of Hungary.

In the middle of December Boniface had arrived at Zara. If the account of Robert de Clari is to be trusted, something like a comedy was arranged between him and Dandolo. The latter saw that the pilgrims were uneasy. The leaders were aware that they had not provisions enough for an expedition to Egypt or to Syria, and they had given out that even if they had they could do nothing when they reached either of these two countries. Dandolo therefore said to them:—

> Sirs, in Greece there is a bountiful supply of all things. If we can find a reasonable occasion to go there and to take provisions and other things, then we can easily manage to go *outre-mer*. (Greece and Romania are used as synonymous terms by many of the Western writers.)

Then uprose Boniface, Marquis of Montferrat, and explained that at Christmas time he had been in Germany at the court of Philip, where he had seen young Alexis, whose father had been treacherously driven from his throne. Boniface said:—

> Whoever has this young man can go into the land of Constantinople and take provisions and what is needed. (Robert de Clari, xvii.)

Hence, according to Robert, the messengers were sent to Alexis in order that by inducing him to come the Crusaders might have *boine acoison., rasnauvle ocaision,* to go to Constantinople.

On New Year's Day, 1203, the messengers returned from Philip, accompanied by those whom that king had sent. Henceforward it was impossible to keep the object of their mission secret.

The organisation of the Crusaders for the purpose of taking a decision was not unlike that which prevailed throughout most European states. (*Eclaircissements à Villehardouin*), Substitute the leaders and the great barons for the king, the lesser barons of the army and the knights for the lords, and the whole army for the commons, and the parallel will be complete. The leaders took the initiative. Then the parliament of lesser barons and knights had the proposition submitted to them, and lastly the commons of the army had to give their approval. The leaders had been consulted at Venice, and had accepted in principle the proposal to aid Alexis in return for his subsequently assisting the army. At Zara the proposition in a definite shape had to be submitted to the parliament of lesser barons and knights.

The day after the arrival of the two embassies from Germany, namely, on the 2nd of January, this parliament was held, to consider the proposals of Philip. The leaders of the expedition and their great barons—French, blemish, German, and Lombard—were present There were also as of right the bishops and abbots who were with the army.

It is probable, too, that Dandolo and his council also attended, since they, too, had taken the Cross. The five bishops were, with one exception, likely to be favourable to the plans of Philip. Of the four Cistercian abbots, two were partisans of the King of the Romans, and two believed that it was shameful to divert the crusade from its lawful object; one of the latter, the Abbot of Vaux and Cernay, as we have seen, had had the courage, at the risk of his life, to read the letters announcing excommunication against those who had taken part in the capture of Zara. The French barons were divided.

The most important, Baldwin of Flanders, Louis of Blois, and Hugues of St. Paul, were under the influence of Philip. The barons of Lombardy, as might be expected, were under the same influence through Boniface. The leader of those who were in favour of loyally carrying out the expedition as Innocent intended was Simon de Montfort, who appears to have exercised a considerable influence, but who was intemperate and rash. The German barons were divided. Those who had taken the side of Otho in his dispute with Philip were probably among the pilgrims who had gone to the Holy Land by other routes.

Those who had left Germany for the purpose of avoiding the excommunication which the Pope had pronounced against Philip, and had left, in most instances, against his wish, were unwilling to excite his anger by opposition to his designs. Those who were not under his *suzerainty*, like the great barons of Belgium and of Franche Comté, were more independent. The Venetians, under Dandolo, no doubt went into the parliament to accept a foregone conclusion.

The expedition to Romania would require an extension of time for the employment of the fleet chartered from Venice, and would therefore greatly enrich the Republic. Dandolo knew that its great advantage would lie in its enabling him to keep his promise towards the Sultan of Egypt, since, if the Crusaders ever fought against the *infidel*, it would be in Syria and not in Egypt All the Venetians hoped that the Republic would thus be enabled to punish Constantinople, and at least to obtain better concessions from the empire than any other Italian state; while, finally, the desire of Dandolo to be revenged upon the empire would be gratified.

The place of meeting was a palace occupied by Dandolo. The messengers were introduced, and explained that they had come from Philip. Villehardouin professes to give the words of their message:—

> My Lords, says the king, I shall send you my wife's brother. I put him in the hand of God and in yours. Since you are fighting for God, for right, and for justice, you ought, if you can, to restore to their inheritance those who have been wrongfully dispossessed. If you are willing, he, Alexis, will make with you the best agreement that anybody ever made, and will give you the most powerful aid for conquering the Holy Land. In the first place, if God allows you to restore him, he will place the whole of Romania under obedience to Rome, Moreover, he knows that you have exhausted your substance and are poor. He will give you, therefore, two hundred thousand silver *marks* and provisions to all in the army, small and great.
>
> He will personally go with you into the land of Babylon, or, if you prefer it, will send there ten thousand men at his expense, and will keep them there for a year; and for the rest of his life he will maintain, at his own expense, five hundred knights in the Holy Land as a guard. My Lords, we have full powers to conclude an agreement on these terms, provided you are also willing. And remember that so good an arrangement was never

offered, and he who refuses it will show that he has no wish for conquest.

These are the terms of the proposal as given by Villehardouin. There were other conditions which regarded the Venetians, and which may on that account have been omitted by the marshal. The advances made to the Republic were to be repaid. The contract for the freight of the Venetian transports was to be renewed for another year on its expiration in June, and the Republic was to receive one hundred thousand *marks*. (*Ernoul, Chron.*, Halberstadt. Robert de Clari and others mention the ships and victuals for another year.)

The messengers had brought with them letters from Philip, ordering the Germans under his rule, under strict injunctions, to support the proposal for the restoration of Alexis. He promised the French and Flemings that if Alexis should come to his own, he would always keep open a road through Romania safe and free. (Gunther.)

The meeting was adjourned until the next day. When it took place the division of opinion amongst the barons became at once evident. The Abbot of Vaux, who represented the party which Villehardouin insists was desirous of breaking up the army, declared that he and his friends would not agree to the proposal, though even this writer tells us that they gave as their reason that they had not left their homes for such work as that proposed, and that they wished to go to Syria.

Those, says Gunther, who were anxious for the success of the Cross earnestly dissuaded the rest from accepting the proposals of Philip. They urged that the restoration could not be effected without bloodshed. The plan, says this writer, seemed foolish and dishonest; foolish, because a few foreigners were not likely to take a city so well-fortified and so populous, and where there was sure to be much slaughter; dishonest, because they were departing from the holy purpose to which they had pledged themselves. I give the answer of the Venetian party in Villehardouin's own words:—

> *Beaux seigneurs*, you can do nothing in Syria, and you can see *that* by those who have left us and gone to other ports. Remember that it is either by the land of Babylon or by Greece that the Holy Land will be recovered if it ever be recovered. And if we refuse this proposal we shall be disgraced forever.

Feeling ran high. As I have already said, the Cistercians or White Friars were themselves divided. The Abbot of Loos and others spoke in favour of accepting the agreement in order to keep the army together, and as a means by which the expedition might best succeed in obtaining its object. The Abbot of Vaux replied that all this was wrong. Whether they succeeded or not, they were at least bound to do what was right. Boniface, Baldwin of Flanders, and others, declared that they would be ashamed to reject the offer. Their influence overwhelmed all opposition, and the result was that the agreement was accepted upon the conditions already mentioned. (Villehardouin.)

The two leaders mentioned, together with the Earl of St. Paul, swore to observe the treaty, and did their best to induce the French barons to do the same. Only eight, however, consented to sign. Among the whole of the leaders only the seals of sixteen could be obtained. (*Ibid.*)

Upon the signature of this agreement the messengers from Philip left Zara. They were accompanied on their journey homewards by two Crusaders, who were to bring young Alexis to the camp. Part of the arrangement was that the Pretender should join the Crusading Army within a fortnight after Easter, that is, not later than the 20th of April.

The news of this arrangement could not be altogether concealed from the Crusaders, and increased the dissatisfaction already felt. Only the barons, however, had any definite knowledge of the agreement The project, which had been approved in principle at Venice by the leaders, had now been advanced a great step further by its acceptance in the parliament of the barons and knights. It had not, however, been submitted or even published to the army, whose approval was nevertheless necessary.

Such particulars as had leaked out increased the number of deserters and raised a bitter opposition. Many of the people, says the author of the *Devastatio* assembled and conspired together and swore they would not go into Romania. The most notable opponent was again Simon de Montfort. He and his followers determined to refuse to follow Boniface, and when, a little later, the expedition left Zara, they went to Hungary, where they were well received by the king. (Gunther.)

Meantime the leaders of the crusade had become anxious to make their peace with Innocent. They had allowed themselves to be persuaded by the Venetians into an attack upon a Christian Army. They had violated their oaths, and had incurred the terrible penalties of excommunication. The strong party in the army which had protested against the attack upon Zara would naturally represent the facts in their own light to the Pope, while the King of Hungary would claim restitution of his territory, compensation for the injury done to him, and the punishment of the offenders. Accordingly, during the last days of December, the leaders of the expedition sent Nivelon, Bishop of Soissons, and John de Noyon to Rome to represent their case to the Holy See, and to ask for absolution. They were authorised to speak on behalf of the Crusaders only—not on behalf of the Venetians. They were accompanied by the German Abbot Martin, whose object was to obtain the Pope's permission to return home.

Innocent had been put on his guard, and could not be unprepared for the tidings which they were charged to convey to him. He knew enough of what had gone on at Venice to suspect Dandolo. The propositions which had been submitted to him in November by Boniface had warned him that the leader of the army would be ready to play into the hands of the Venetians, in return for their support of Philip's designs in favour of young Alexis. It is probable that the proposals for a truce among the Western princes made by Innocent at this time were due to his desire to place difficulties in the way of the execution of these designs.

If Otho could gain time by means of such a truce, he could form a league which might be sufficiently strong to occupy all the energy of Philip. Accordingly, when Bishop Nivelon and John de Noyon arrived in Rome, in the early part of February, the Pope was ready to hear their news. Before their arrival he had sent to Peter Capuano, who was in the neighbourhood of Zara, a solemn Bull of excommunication against the Venetians, together with a letter which he was directed to forward to the army:—

> Satan has pushed you to flesh your swords upon a Christian people. You have offered to the devil the first-fruits of your pilgrimage. You have not directed your expedition against Jerusalem or against Egypt. Loyalty to the Cross you bear, respect for the King of Hungary and his brother, and to the authority of the Apostolic See which gave you on this subject, precise orders, ought to have prevented you from doing such wickedness. We exhort you to put a stop to the destruction, and to restore all the plunder to the envoys of the King of Hungary. Unless this be done you will be liable to the excommunication which you have incurred, and you will be deprived of all the benefits of the crusade which have been promised you.

The letter further required that the Crusaders should give written declarations under seal that they would not again attack Christian nations. The pardon granted to them was to be conditional on such declarations being made and observed. In particular they were to pledge themselves not to attack Greece, either under pretext that they would thus be able to bring about the union of the churches or to punish the crimes committed by Alexis the Third.

When the messengers arrived from the army, they did their best to excuse the conduct of the Crusaders, but they spoke to a man who was their superior in intelligence, and who probably was to a considerable extent behind the scenes.

One of the knights who accompanied Nivelon and John de Noyon refused to explain the matter as the majority wished; in doing which, says Villehardouin, he perjured himself. The others excused themselves to the Pope by saying that the Crusaders had done the best they could under the circumstances. They laid all the blame on those who had not come to Venice, and had thus placed the army at the mercy of the Republic. They declared that to help the Venetians against Zara was the only way of keeping the army together, and that in so doing they believed they had been acting in conformity with the Pope's wish. (*Epist. vi.*) Innocent expressed to the deputies his deep grief at the conduct of the Crusaders.

Probably there were many interviews and much long and anxious consideration on the part of the Pope during the days which followed their arrival. They had left Zara, as we have seen, before the signature of the agreement for the restoration of Alexis (January 2), but they were probably aware that such a convention was contemplated. The conditional form of the absolution shows that the Pope had either heard from some other source of this pact, or believed it to be probable.

After some time, he addressed to the barons a second letter.

This was especially intended to influence the great body of the army. The Pope attempted indirectly to appeal to the rank and file against the leaders. The soldiers were not to be led away by any excuses. Innocent knew that they were not in the secret of the leaders. They at least had little to gain by the execution of Philip's projects, and cared nothing for political intrigues. Hence, the Pope's policy of making the absolution conditional upon their not again attacking a Christian country was likely to have, as we shall see that it had, a considerable measure of success. Pardon was to be granted provided they did not attack the Greeks.

The Pope, addressing the leaders, did not offer them the usual salutations. He was perforce compelled to grant them absolution if the expedition to which he had attached so much importance, and from which he hoped so much, were to have any chance of success. But even in doing so, he did not spare his reproaches. He admitted the excuse of necessity which the deputies had pleaded. But reparation was necessary, and this could only be made by restoring the whole of the booty. He declared that the absolution given by the bishops was not valid. Cardinal Peter was instructed to receive their oaths to be obedient henceforward to the Pope's orders, and Innocent again declared that it was only on such an oath being sworn and kept that the excommunication could be raised. Those who had offended must show their intention not again to invade a Christian country unless they were resisted, and must ask pardon from the King of Hungary for the wrong they had done him.

The sole concession which the Pope would grant was that in case of need the army might take provisions from the territory of the Greek Emperor. Alexis was, however, to be requested to give permission. (*Epist. vi.*)

At the end of March, Nivelon, Bishop of Soissons, left Rome, the bearer of this conditional absolution.

Meantime Boniface and the leaders became anxious to explain to the Pope why they had concealed from the army his Bull condemning their conduct. The messengers who had gone to Rome to ask for absolution would soon return, and would no doubt be aware of what the Pope had written. It would no longer be possible to conceal from the army the decision of the Pope, nor from the Pope the fact that his former letter had not been published.

The barons had argued, no doubt, that to have published it would have greatly strengthened the malcontents; that with daily desertions, with a desire openly expressed by many to break up the expedition, with the bitter feelings existing between the pilgrims and the Venetians, a statement of the Pope's solemn and formal condemnation would have put an end to the expedition. In the communication which Boniface and the other leaders sent to Rome they urged, by way of excuse, that everything had been done with the object of still carrying out the lawful designs of a crusade, and they protested that it was their intention to be obedient in the future to the pontifical orders.

When this communication reached Rome, the Pope knew the particulars of the plan to divert the crusade into an expedition against the New Rome. He knew that young Alexis had been sent for, and that his Bull of excommunication had been intercepted. Instead of the deeds under seal he had asked for, he received but vague promises. For the moment he was bewildered. (*Gesta Inno.*)

Both he and his Council saw the danger in which the crusade was placed of failing altogether. (Gunther, viii.)

The hesitation of Innocent was, however, of short duration. He declared that the Crusaders had no right to interfere in the internal affairs of Constantinople. (*Epist. viii.*) He warned them once more against being induced to attack Romania on the pretence of necessity. (*Epist. vi.*) The messengers from the army were sent back with letters from Innocent, in which the Crusaders were ordered to swear to be obedient, and were again warned that, if they refused, the absolution granted to them for their attack upon Zara was *de facto* null. A special clause in the oath to be taken contained a pledge that those who took it would not attack Greece.

Cardinal Peter Capuano was deprived of his post as papal representative with the expedition. The letters of the Pope to the army were given into the charge of John Faicete and John de Friaise. Among them was one ordering that the Bull which had formally excommunicated the Venetians should at once be published. John Faicete persuaded some of the leaders to send their written promises under oath to Rome. The influence of Boniface appears, however, to have been sufficient to prevent these promises from being generally made. A few were forwarded in an incomplete form during April.

Innocent was yet sanguine that the crusade would soon leave for Egypt. Though he had abundant evidence which showed him that influences were at work to prevent the crusade accomplishing its legitimate object, he did not know how strong these influences were. Though he had a profound distrust of Venice, and would not grant the Venetians his absolution, he could hardly have believed that she had become a traitor to Christendom. He had seen an army collected together with the utmost care, its plan of action carefully considered, submitted to himself, and adopted; and he knew of no reason why this plan should be abandoned. We have now to see the last step which had to be taken in order to divert the expedition from its purpose.

CHAPTER 5

From Zara to Corfu

In the beginning of April 1203, the bearers of the Pope's message arrived at Zara. That message consisted of two parts: first, a confirmation of the absolution which had been granted by the bishop; and, second, the formal order that the Crusaders were not to attack the Greeks except in case they refused to sell them provisions. (*Epist. vi.*)

The first part of the message was communicated to the army. There is no evidence to show that the second was, and there is much to suggest that it was not. It had been arranged that Alexis should join the army on the 20th of April. He might arrive at any day, and it would then be no longer possible to conceal from the great host the secret arrangement which had been concluded in January. His arrival would, therefore, be extremely inopportune. The disaffection in the army was great. The example of Simon de Montfort and others, whose departure I have already mentioned, had been largely followed by many who were unwilling to violate their oaths.

The Pope's order not to attack Greece, if, as I have suggested, it were kept secret, might become known. The ill-feeling between the army and the Venetians, which had shown itself by the rioting immediately after the capture, still existed. All were weary of inaction, and wished to be on their way to fight the common enemy. If Alexis should arrive the army would then learn that the leaders proposed to divert the enterprise from its lawful purpose. Accordingly, every effort was made to send the Crusaders a stage further before his arrival. On the 7th of April the army left the city of Zara, and prepared to embark. The Venetians destroyed its walls, towers, and palaces, and razed the city to the ground.

The army and its convoy set sail from Zara for Corfu on the 20th of April. Dandolo and Boniface had arranged to remain behind to await the arrival of Alexis. Two galleys were left for their use. The

Pretender arrived on the 25th of April, five days after the date which had been appointed. Without loss of time the two leaders and their charge embarked to follow the expedition. On their way they called at Durazzo, where a demonstration was made in favour of young Alexis. The inhabitants surrendered the city and swore fealty to him.

On May 4 they arrived at Corfu. They found the army already encamped before the town. Every opportunity was taken to impress the Crusaders with the importance of having with them the 'lawful heir,' as Boniface called Alexis. Every possible honour and mark of respect was shown to him. His tent was pitched in the midst of the army, near to that of Boniface, who assumed from this time forward the part of his protector and guardian.

The arrival of Alexis rendered all further attempts at concealment useless, because it was now necessary formally to submit the change of plan to the approval of the host. It was clear to every man that the leaders intended that the expedition to Egypt should be postponed till the young man now among them was placed upon the throne of the New Rome. The pretence was still kept up that after this was accomplished the army would go upon its appointed mission. The great mass even of those who approved, and even perhaps some of the leaders themselves, believed that such a course was possible. What was certain was that they must go first to Constantinople. The barons and Dandolo assembled, and before them Alexis solemnly ratified the convention of Zara.

He promised them 200,000 *marks*. He would pay the cost of the navy for a year, would himself accompany them on their pilgrimage as far as he could, would maintain during his life an army of 10,000 men in the Holy Land, and would provision the army of pilgrims for a year. (Robert de Clari, xxxii.)

The convention had, however, now to be submitted to the army, which had hitherto been kept as far as possible in the dark. When this was done the dissatisfaction among a large portion immediately broke out. There were many men, no doubt, in so large a host who were willing to go in search of adventure or of plunder, and who cared little whether this were to be found in Syria or in the rich capital of the world. The majority of the Crusaders had, however, left their homes in no such spirit, and were righteously indignant when they found they had been duped by their leaders and the Venetians.

They had been duped in many ways. They had taken up the Cross at the call of Innocent. The Pope, as they knew, believed the moment opportune for striking at Islam, and had thrown all his exceptional energy into the fulfilment of this the great design of his life. Innocent's influence had been cast against Philip of Swabia, and in favour of Otho.

Yet from the moment of the election of Boniface they suspected that they had been duped into opposing the Pontiff's great design, and into supporting Philip's cause in Western Europe against the Pope. They recalled that immediately after his appointment Boniface had visited his relation Philip, an excommunicated prince, the avowed enemy of Innocent, and had remained with him for many weeks. In the army were many partisans of Otho, the rival of Philip, and they could not but see that in the subsequent conduct of Boniface he was doing that which would be looked on favourably by Philip as well as severely condemned by the Pope. Others had been wiser than they.

Many Crusaders, as we have seen, had taken ship at Marseilles rather than trust themselves to the Venetians and to Boniface. Some of their German fellow pilgrims had refused to leave home, or had returned, because they foresaw that antagonism between Philip and the Pope was certain from the moment that Alexis was in Lombardy and Boniface in command.

They recalled the treatment of the army while on the Lido, by which they were duped into consenting to fight for Venice; the constant and ever-increasing rumour of an expedition into Romania, which was to be for the profit of the leaders and of Philip; the destruction of Zara; the fight between the Venetians and the Crusaders after the city was captured; the Pope's censures, which could not be altogether unknown; his absolution, strictly conditional upon their not repeating the offence; the opposition of Simon de Montfort and so many of the army, who were determined to find their way to the Holy Land by other routes, because they were convinced that Boniface and Dandolo had no intention of carrying out the great plan which Innocent had approved.

All their recollections showed them how completely they had been deceived, increased the discontent, and caused it now to culminate when all disguise was abandoned, and it became known to everybody that a convention had been entered into, by which, in spite of the Pope's express command, their destination had been changed from Egypt or Syria to Constantinople.

In the short time which passed between the arrival of Alexis with Boniface and Dandolo in Corfu and the agreement subsequently arrived at, probably many meetings and much discussion took place. The *doge* insisted much upon the necessity of obtaining the help which Alexis had promised, and pointed out that they had now a lawful excuse, a '*raisnauvle acoison*,' to go to Constantinople, because they had the rightful heir. The leaders of the opposition, however, took the view they had adopted from the beginning. They said:—

> Bah! what have we to do in Constantinople? We have to make our pilgrimage, and purpose to go to Babylon or Alexandria Our transports are only chartered for a year, and half of that is already past. (Robert de Clari, § xxxiii.)

Their duty was clear; they had not left home for plunder but for pilgrimage, and upon pilgrimage they would go. The same author gives the reply of the party of Philip:—

> What shall we do in Babylon or in Alexandria, when we have no provisions or means of getting them? Surely it is better to take the *raisnauvle acoison* to obtain meat and means for our journey than to go there and die of hunger.

The bishops were asked whether it would be a sin to go to Constantinople, and, as they were on the side of the marquis, replied that it would not, because as they had the lawful heir, they could help him to conquer his own and to be avenged of his enemies. (Robert de Clari.) Nothing was said at Corfu of the union of the Churches. This pretext had only been put forward so long as it was hoped that the Pope might be won over.

The malcontents, however, united together, and decided to leave the army and join Count Gautier de Brienne, who then held Brindisi. Villehardouin mentions by name twelve great chiefs who joined the popular party, and he asserts that there were many others who had secretly agreed to join them, and that they had with them more than half the army. (Villehardouin.) The malcontents had formed a parliament of their own, had separated from their brethren, and occupied a valley at some distance from the rest of the army. Their cry was '*Ire Accaron*,' (*Epist. H. S. Pauli*), a cry which probably indicates that the leaders of the dissentients recognised that with their diminished numbers it might be safer to go to Syria than to Egypt.

The danger was great. There was every appearance that the expedition would be broken up. The Marquis of Montferrat and the barons who were in his counsels were greatly troubled. The marquis said:—

If these men leave us, after those who have already gone on many occasions, our army will be ruined and we can conquer nothing. Let us go to them, and fall at their feet, and beg their favour; that, for God's sake, they will have pity on us, and will not dishonour themselves, and that they will not prevent us from delivering the Land of *Outre-mer*. (Villehardouin)

The leaders acted on the advice of the marquis. They went in a body to the valley in which the parliament of the malcontents was held, taking with them young Alexis and the bishops and abbots. When they arrived, the opposition barons were on horseback, but on seeing the leader of the expedition and the bishops approach unattended, dismounted and went to meet them. The barons fell at their feet, wept copiously, and declared they would not rise from their knees until the others promised that they would not leave the army.

Then, according to the melodramatic description of the Marshal of Champagne, there was a wonderful scene. Dandolo and Boniface and all with them wept. If Villehardouin is to be credited, there was never a greater flood of tears; those from Dandolo and the leaders being mostly of the crocodile sort. The opposition leaders were filled with pity, and wept sorely when they saw their lords, their relations, and their friends fallen at their feet. They withdrew, conferred together, and after some time returned with a proposal for a compromise. They would consent to remain with the army until Michaelmas Day., provided that the leaders would solemnly swear on relics that after that day they would provide them with a fleet, in good faiths at a fortnight's notice, with which they might go to Syria.

This proposal was accepted. The leaders swore to observe the conditions. Apparently, immediately afterwards the convention of Zara was adopted by the whole of the army. The authors of the *Continuation of William of Tyre* allege that, in addition to the terms accepted by Alexis at Corfu, there were secret conditions by which Boniface of Montferrat and Baldwin of Flanders were each to receive 100,000 *marks*, and others of the chief barons smaller sums. (Ernoul. This statement is confirmed by the fact that in the charter by which in 1204, Boniface ceded the island of Crete to the Venetians he includes the sum of 100,000 *marks* formerly promised to him by Alexis.)

In other words, they were bribed to divert the crusade to the support of the cause of Alexis. Henceforward, some of the chief opponents became the firm supporters of Alexis. (Villehardouin.) The pilgrim host had now been changed from a Crusading Army into a filibustering expedition, and its history in the future is that of their adventures in sacking the noblest and richest city of the Middle Ages.

As soon as the convention of Zara was ratified, the leaders lost no time in hurrying on the preparations for embarkation. The quicker the evil deed could be done the better.

CHAPTER 6

From Corfu to Constantinople

The expedition left Corfu on the 23rd of May, Whitsun eve. Villehardouin is again in raptures at the beauty of the spectacle presented by the fleet. It looked, says he, like one which could conquer the world. The sails of the vessels dotted the ocean from the shore to the verge of the horizon, so that the hearts of men rejoiced within them. All went well as far as Negroponte and Andros, at which latter island the leaders with young Alexis landed and received the submission of the inhabitants. The Marquis of Montferrat everywhere presented young Alexis to the population, and did his best to make the journey an imperial progress. On arrival at the Dardanelles the leaders and those vessels which had arrived with them waited a week until the galleys and the transports came up.

They occupied the time in plundering the neighbouring country and gathering in the harvest, their own stores having run short Then they sailed again, and on the 23rd of June anchored off the abbey of San Stefano, about twelve miles to the south-west of Constantinople and on the Marmora. The domes and churches, the walls and towers of New Rome were at length in sight The view from San Stefano is not the most picturesque which can be obtained of the imperial city, but even in these days it is sufficiently imposing.

The Crusaders were amazed at the sight before them. They could not have imagined, says Villehardouin, that there could have been in the world a city so rich as that which the high walls and higher towers now before them girt entirely round. No one would have believed that there could have been so many rich palaces and lofty churches if he had not seen it with his own eyes. Nor would he have credited that the city which was the sovereign among cities could have been so long or so broad.

Be sure there was not a man who did not tremble, because never was so great an enterprise undertaken by so small a number of men.

The *doge* and the leaders landed and held a parliament in the church of San Stefano. Dandolo advised that before any attack was made the fleet should sail some ten miles away to the Princes' Islands, and that a stock of provisions should be gathered from the neighbouring coast. The advice was accepted and the leaders embarked once more. In the morning, however, there was a southerly wind which made a journey to the islands dangerous, but which took them pleasantly right under the walls of Constantinople into the Bosphorus. The walls are built at the water's edge, and were crowded with spectators as the fleet passed. The ships anchored off Chalcedon, probably in front of the present (1885) English cemetery.

★★★★★★★★

This is usually spoken of as being at Scutari. It is, in fact, in a village between Scutari and Kadikeui, called Hyder Pasha, the latter being the name of a village, and not, as the Judicial Committee of the Privy Council stated recently (1885), the name of a 'respectable Turkish gentleman.'

★★★★★★★★

The army disembarked, and formed an encampment upon the Asiatic shore, the city of Constantinople being in full view and only a mile distant. The harvest in the neighbouring country had been gathered in, and was at once seized by the Crusaders '*comme gens qui en avaient grand besoin*.' The leaders took possession of a splendid palace belonging to the emperor. On the third day the fleet went a mile further up the Bosphorus to Scutari and there anchored.

The Crusaders waited nine days in order to take in provisions and make their arrangements for an attack. During this time a skirmish took place on the Asiatic shore with a small body of imperial troops, who were completely routed, and the Crusaders obtained a considerable quantity of booty.

Meantime the emperor was filled with alarm at the arrival of the Venetian fleet and the great Frank Army. On the tenth day after their arrival, he sent a messenger named Nicholas Roux, a native of Lombardy, across the Bosphorus with letters of credence to the leaders. The barons met in council. The messenger announced that he had been sent by the emperor to learn why they had come into his territory.

You are Christians and he is a Christian. He knows well that you are on your way to deliver the Holy Land. If you are poor and needy he will willingly give you provisions and what he has, but on condition that you leave his territory. He has no wish to do you any harm, though he can do it.

The statement implies that he had no knowledge of their intention. It may fairly be presumed that such knowledge as he had was of a very vague character. He certainly had officially no knowledge. It is possible, and indeed probable, that spies or others had hastened on to Constantinople as soon as the destination of the army had been made known at Corfu. It is unlikely that more than a suspicion of what was going on can have been communicated to him at any period before the arrival of the army in that island.

Canon de Bethune replied to the imperial messenger on behalf of the Crusaders. He denied that they had come into the land of Alexis, because the occupant of the throne was not the rightful emperor. The land belonged to his nephew, who was with them, the son of Isaac. The message he was to take back to his master was, that if Alexis would surrender his crown and empire to his nephew, they, the Crusaders, would ask young Alexis to pardon him and to give him enough to live upon luxuriously. If the messenger did not return with an answer accepting these conditions, he had better not dare to return at all.

The leaders seem to have been under the impression that there existed within the city a strong party in favour of Alexis. No doubt Philip, and possibly young Alexis himself, had done their best to persuade them that such was the case. The barons determined to give this party the opportunity to declare itself. The nephew of the emperor should be shown to the people of Constantinople.

Accordingly, they manned and armed all their galleys. Dandolo and the Marquis of Montferrat and young Alexis went on board one of them, and a crowd of barons and knights into the others. The walls of Constantinople then, as now, came down to the water's edge through two-thirds of their extent. The tideless waters of the Marmora and the Golden Horn are deep enough within ten feet of the walls to float larger vessels than the great galleys of the Venetians. The procession crossed the Bosphorus. The walls were crowded with spectators. The boats went quite near and then stopped. Someone on board the galley containing Alexis proclaimed:

Here, here is your rightful lord. We have not come to do you any harm. We will protect you if you do what you ought. He whom you obey rules you wrongfully against God and law. You know how disloyally he behaved to his lord and his brother, how he put out his eyes and usurped his empire. Here is the real heir. If you do not acknowledge him, we will do the worst we can against you.

The proclamation was received with laughter. The only answer given, and that in derision, was, 'We know nothing about him. Who is he?' (Robert de Clari, xi.)

The Crusaders returned to Scutari. Next day a parliament was held to consider what steps should be taken for attacking the city. It was agreed that the army should be divided into seven parts. Baldwin of Flanders was appointed to lead the van, because of the great number of archers and crossbowmen who were under his command. The Marquis of Montferrat was to bring up the rear with the Lombards, Tuscans, Germans, and men from the country between Mont Cenis and Lyons.

The business in hand was felt to be a serious one. There was apparently no longer any disaffection. The consciences of all had been quieted or their scruples overcome by the prospect of rich booty. All that remained was to fulfil their part of the contract and to receive their reward. But many a stout heart quailed at the prospect of the difficult undertaking before them. No Spaniards under a Cortez or a Pizarro ever had an apparently more hopeless task, and, to the credit of the filibustering host, it must be added that none ever succeeded more completely in the work of destruction before them. The bishops and clergy in the army exhorted the soldiers to confess and make their wills. Solemn religious services placed the army under the protection of the saints.

Then the embarkation commenced. The knights with their chargers went once more on board the *huissiers* or transports, which were so constructed that either large ports or a portion of the bulwarks opened readily, and could allow the knights to ride across the gangways while mounted. The rank and file, on board the larger ships, followed. The galleys were manned, the fighting men clothed in battle array, and the vessels themselves made ready for action. Alexis was attended by numerous troops, and was treated with every mark of respect. The next morning at daylight, everyone being in his place, the trumpets sounded; the signal for starting was given, and the expedition set out on the last stage of its journey to the imperial city.

The knights had their helmets laced, their armour on, while their horses were arrayed in battle gear. Each galley took in tow one of the *huissiers* with knights on board. The crossbowmen and archers went first to keep clear the coast for landing. (Robert de Clari, xli.) No other order of precedence was observed. The vessel which could get over first did so. The distance from Scutari is under a mile, and was soon covered. The knights, though in armour, leaped overboard while the water was still up to their waists, and, lance in hand, made for the shore. They probably landed near the modern Tophana, or between it and the mouth of the Golden Horn. Some of the troops of the emperor saw the fleet approach, but they turned and fled from the bowmen before the cavalry was landed. The disembarkation was allowed to go on without interruption.

The entrance to the Golden Horn, the harbour of Constantinople, was guarded by a chain thrown across from the city to Galata. On the Galata side, the end of this chain was protected by a tower spoken of by the Western writers as the tower or castle of Galata. (This must not be confounded with the present Galata tower, which is at the apex and highest point of the triangle formed by the walls of Galata, and was not built until two centuries later.) The slope of the hill behind it was the Jewry of Constantinople.

Near it also were probably Genoese and other Italian quarters, the whole forming already a wealthy suburb. The Crusaders encamped in the Jewish quarter, and prepared for an attack. It was necessary for the protection of the expedition that the ships should be brought within the harbour, and the Venetians urged that an attempt should be made next day to capture the tower within which the Galata end of the chain was fastened. (Robert de Clari, xlii.) The council of war agreed to this proposal, and of Galata? determined that such an attempt should be made immediately.

Fortune favoured them, and gave them their first success on the following day. In early morning the ordinary guard of the tower, assisted by a detachment which had crossed the harbour, instead of remaining on the defensive, made a foolish attack upon the invading army. The Greeks were far less numerous than the enemy, and were completely overpowered by the Crusaders. Many were killed; others were driven into the water and drowned. The remainder fled, and endeavoured to regain the protection of the castle which they ought not to have left. The enemy, however, pressed them so hard that they were unable to close the gates. A severe struggle took place, and the superior weight of the knights triumphed. The castle was captured.

While this attack on the watch tower had been going on by land, the Venetian ships were doing their best to break the chain which was stretched across from Galata to the city. The capture of the tower gave the army command over this chain. It was at once broken or loosened. The fleet entered swiftly into the Golden Horn, attacked the imperial galleys, captured some and sank the others. (Nicetas.) The surprise was complete; the victory, both by land and sea, brilliant and unexpected. It is hardly too much to say that it was the beginning of the end, because the weakest portion of the walls were those facing the Golden Horn and within the harbour. The Greeks scarcely realised at the time how great was their loss, but the elation among the Venetians and the Crusaders showed the importance they attached to the event. (Nicetas.)

Readers will remember that in 1453 the defence of the harbour was so strong, by means of the chain and the fortifications, that Mahomet, in despair of breaking through, had to obtain possession of the harbour by transporting his boats over the neck of land between the modern Tophana and the valley now known as Cassim Pacha. Galata was then, however, a walled city, and the Turkish ships were probably much smaller than those of Venice.

Venetians and Crusaders were rightly of opinion that the advantage they had gained should be immediately followed up by a general attack. No attempt at negotiations appears to have been made. A bold, sudden attempt was to be made before the emperor should have time to organise a defence Four days only were spent in Galata, and these were occupied in transporting their stores, in preparing for battle, and in determining upon the plan of attack. The Venetians were naturally in favour of making the principal assault by sea. Their proposal was to take their ships close up to the wall on the north side of the city, and throw out ladders from the ships to the walls—a feat quite capable of execution, as subsequent events showed.

The Crusaders as naturally preferred fighting on land. The difficulty was overcome by the arrangement that the Venetians should attack by sea, while the army endeavoured to effect an entrance through the landward walls. The army passed round the head of the Golden Horn, crossing by a stone bridge which the Greeks had destroyed, but which the Crusaders were able, by working day and night, to repair in time for the attack.

On the fifth day after the capture of the port, the army took up its position opposite the palace of Blachern, which was at the north-west corner of the walls, facing on one side towards the Horn, on another landwards. (Nicetas.) This was the one position where fleet and army could bring their forces to act simultaneously on contiguous portions of the defences. The palace occupied the corner, had many outworks, and, though it had no fosse, it was strongly fortified. The position taken up by the army was at Gyrolemna. No camping-ground could have given the Crusaders a better idea of the wealth and strength of the capital. The hill behind them enabled them to have, perhaps, the most picturesque view of the beautiful city they were about to attack.

Point beyond point stretched out, under the July sun, into the blue waters of the Golden Horn. In the immediate foreground were the new walls which Manuel had built to fortify Blachern. (Nicetas.) Behind these walls rose the superb palace of the emperors, which had now, rather than the palace of Bucoleon, or, as the Crusaders called it the Lion's Mouth, on the side of the Marmora, become their favourite dwelling-place. Churches, the great law courts, columns, and towers rose one behind the other in infinite confusion, until, on the last hill, was the church of the Divine Peace, adjoining that which was at once the richest and most beautiful building of all, the great temple dedicated to the Divine Wisdom of the Incarnate Word.

The strength of the city might be judged from its landward walls, which were immediately before them. The wide moat, except on the immediate descent to the Golden Horn, was well filled with water, though this had to be kept up by a long series of dams, while a wall immediately behind it could only be assailed from the bed or the waters of the moat itself. When these obstacles were passed, there remained a second and a third wall, each higher than the former. The short distance between the towers with which each of these walls are studded enabled the occupants to have an enemy well within range even of the simple machines with which, in that age, stones could be hurled upon an invader.

All that the best mechanical science of the most civilised nation in Europe could do towards making the triple walls strong had been done. Nor were these fortifications untried. Again and again in the history of the city they had proved stronger than the power of any invader. Not to speak of less important sieges, it may possibly have been known to some of those who now sat down before these walls that the great horde of Arab invaders which had been checked in its hitherto irresistible progress had been encamped on almost precisely the same spot which Boniface and Baldwin now occupied. The site is among the most interesting in the world. Occupied, within a half-century, by two invading hosts of Arabs which had spent their strength before the virgin city, and which had been as completely defeated by the Romans as were the Moors who had crossed the Pyrenees by Charles Martel, it was destined to be the place from which the city was to be destroyed by Western Europeans. (See *Charles Martel & the Battle of Tours: the Defeat of the Arab Invasion of Western Europe by the Franks, 732 A.D* by Edward Creasy, G. L. Strauss, Charles King & Walter Copland Perry. Leonaur; 2018.)

Two centuries and a half later it was to witness a greater triumph over the city—a victory which was to inflict upon the Balkan peninsula four centuries and a half of barbarism. The army of Mahomet, the second of the Ottoman house, was encamped on the same corner, and effected its entrance at a point very little outside the grounds which were enclosed within the palace walls of the Blachern. On a portion of this historical site the mosque of Job, or Eyoub, now marks the supposed burying-place of the great leader of the chief Arab attempt upon the city. The mosque is regarded with more sanctity than any other now in the city. No unbeliever is allowed to enter it. Within it is kept the sacred banner of the prophet, and no *Sultan* is considered invested until he has been girt with the sword of Osman, which is treasured within its sacred walls.

As soon as the Crusading Army had taken up its position at Gyrolemna, the Greeks within the city sought to harass them. Their efforts, however, were feeble. Several sorties were made under the command of Theodore Lascaris, son-in-law of the emperor. (The sorties were made most commonly from a gate above the palace of Blachern, probably therefore from the very same gate which in 1453 was the first to fall into the hands of the Ottoman Turks.) The Crusaders enclosed their camp with palisades until their preparations were completed. In the meantime, the Venetians had drawn up their fleet in such a manner as best to co-operate with the army.

On the 17th of July everything was prepared for an assault. Three out of the seven divisions guarded the camp under the leadership of Boniface, while the remaining four made the attack under the orders of Baldwin. The outside wall, an outwork of the imperial palace, near if not actually on the sea, was defended partly by Pisan auxiliaries, but mainly by the Waring guard, *les Anglois et les Danois*, as the Western historians call them. This was the position first attacked by the army.

Two scaling ladders, or probably wide platforms, were thrown against the wall.

The assault was '*fort et bon et dur*,' and by sheer force fifteen of the boldest among the Flemings managed to win a position on the wall. There they fought shoulder to shoulder with their swords against men of their own race armed with Danish *bills*. The struggle on the wall was fierce. The Warings steadily recovered ground, drove their daring assailants back, and captured two of them. The Crusaders were not able again to gain even a temporary foothold on the walls. The first attack had failed on the landward side.

On the seaward side the Venetians were more successful. The brave Dandolo, old and blind, the *gonfalon* of St. Mark flying proudly over his head, directed the attack from his own galley. No precaution that long experience could suggest was neglected by him. The ships had been carefully cased and covered with raw hides so as to resist the famous Greek fire. Scaling ladders, or rather bridges, had been provided in great numbers, which could reach from the ships' cross-trees to the walls. These were formed of the ships' yards, with sails and skins, so completely protecting the fighters that it was almost impossible for arrows to reach them. They were so wide that three knights could advance abreast. (Robert de Clari.)

The fleet was drawn up in line three crossbow shots long opposite the walls. The order was given to advance as near the shore as they could get. This was done under a tremendous discharge of stones from *mangonels* placed on the towers. In spite of this opposition the ships pushed boldly ashore. Their stems were moored to the land, and anchors were thrown out from their sterns. Each *huissier* had a *mangonel*. The stones thrown in immense quantities by the Romans were returned by the Venetians, and the return shots were better aimed. The Venetians succeeded during the attack in destroying the outer wall of the palace with a battering-ram. (Nicetas.) The bolts came in abundance from the crossbows. The scaling-ladders thrown out from the ships' tops were so close to the walls that the contending soldiers fought together with lance and sword.

A fierce hand-to-hand fight went on for some hours without interruption. The galleys had at first not ventured to run their bows on to the land, but had remained astern of the transports. Dandolo determined that everything should be dared. He commanded his own crew to put him on shore on the narrow strip of land a few feet broad, between the walls and the water, and threatened his followers with death when they hesitated to obey. The old man and those with him leaped on shore. When the men in the other galleys saw the *gonfalon* of St. Mark carried on shore over the head of their fearless leader, they rushed to defend him. The enthusiasm spread throughout the fleet. Numbers of men from the transports and the barges leaped into their boats or into the water and landed. The order was given that a general attack of all the Venetians should be concentrated upon a short distance of the walls.

A battering ram was brought to bear against one of the towers. Those who worked it were defended by a crowd of crossbowmen. While this thundered at the walls below, hundreds of men were fighting from the scaling-ladders, and trying to win or to hold a position on the walls. Presently the *gonfalon* of St. Mark was seen flying from one of the towers. For a while the defenders were panic-stricken and fled. Immediate advantage was taken of this success. Twenty-five towers were captured by the Venetians before the Greeks could rally. The invaders pushed beyond the walls, but a new detachment of the imperial troops, consisting of Warings and Pisans, (Nicetas), came up and drove them back to the towers, but from the latter even the Warings were not able to dislodge them.

In order to render their hold on the fortifications less liable to attack, or perhaps, as Villehardouin asserts, in order to cover their retreat, the Venetians set fire to the neighbouring buildings. The fire spread rapidly, and burnt a large mass of buildings.

While this fighting about the seaward towers was going on, a sortie of the imperial troops took place from the gate of St Romanos, at a considerable distance from the camp. The Crusaders immediately abandoned their attack, and drew themselves up behind their palisades. Villehardouin alleges that against their six battalions the imperial troops were forty, and an even greater discrepancy is represented by Robert de Clari. The former adds, however, that they could only be attacked in front. The tidings of this incident were at once conveyed to Dandolo, who immediately withdrew his forces from the towers and hastened with as many men as he could muster to help the Crusaders. The emperor brought his troops opposite to the pilgrims.

Neither side dared to begin the attack. After considerable marching and countermarching the imperial troops commenced to retire. The Crusaders rode slowly after them, but no fighting took place. (The account of this sortie given by Robert de Clari represents it as occupying a considerable time and engaging much more attention than the reader of Villehardouin would suppose.) This movement was watched by the ladies of the palace, who crowded the windows and walls.

The results of the general attack had on the whole been and fails, in favour of the defenders. The army of the Crusaders had been beaten back. The Venetians had indeed obtained possession of twenty-five towers, but they had not been able to hold them. The great loss to the citizens was occasioned by the fire lighted by their enemies.

CHAPTER 7

Flight of the Emperor Alexis and Restoration of Isaac—Revolution in the City

The most useful ally of the invaders was the spirit of indifference and discontent which reigned within the city. While this spirit paralysed the efforts of the defenders, there was probably also a small but active, although secret, party in favour of Isaac and of young Alexis. The latter had made many promises to his friends within the city, and had urged them to assist him. (Gunther, xiii.)

The dissatisfaction with the ruling emperor was great, and was doubtless increased by this party. The enemy without had not asked for possession of the city. There was nothing said even about an occupation. All that was demanded was that a young prince, who undoubtedly had claims to the throne if his father were dead, should replace Alexis the Third. There was indeed a payment to be made, though it is doubtful whether the terms of the convention with Alexis were at this time known within the city, and even if they were the payment might perhaps be avoided, or at least levied on the provinces. At any rate, it was better to come to an arrangement with the enemy when his demands were so reasonable than to fight. (Nicetas.)

Moreover, there was now a distinct threat that if an arrangement were not made the city would be destroyed. (Gunther, xiii.) Accordingly there was considerable murmuring within the city. The many dynastic troubles within the experience of the inhabitants made them think lightly of a change of rulers. Alexis the Third had done nothing to make himself respected. He was now informed that if he did not deliver his subjects from the enemy, they would declare for the younger Alexis, and would make him Emperor. (Robert de Clari.)

In spite, however, of these threats, I am disposed to think from the narrative of Nicetas, who knew better what went on within the city than any of the Western chroniclers, that the great mass of the inhabitants of Constantinople were indifferent rather than hostile to the emperor. The majority of the inhabitants had long lost all interest in dynastic changes. The experience of the last generation had accustomed them to see one sovereign deposed and another placed on the throne, until they had come to look on depositions or attempts to obtain the throne as matters with which they had little concern. Apathy in regard to political changes very closely resembled that which exists now in Constantinople.

I have been present in the city during the deposition of two *Sultans*. The most striking characteristic in the circumstances attending these depositions was the utter indifference of the great body of the native, and especially of the Moslem, population to the change which was being made. There was a small but active party which took action, but beyond this there was comparatively very little excitement; no resistance, no rioting, no expression of dissatisfaction. When newspaper correspondents and foreigners generally were aware that a revolution was in preparation, it is impossible to believe that thousands of Turks and rayahs were in ignorance of the fact.

The general feeling among the *Sultan's* subjects was one of indifference. If the conspirators failed it would go hardly with them. If they succeeded it would go hardly with the *Sultan*. *That* business only regarded the parties concerned. Beyond a vague belief that any change could hardly be followed by a worse condition of things than had existed, there was no public sentiment on the matter.

In 1203 the frequent dynastic troubles and the influences of Asia had brought the people to the same indifference to any mere change of government. The inhabitants in the besieged city knew that a few years before Isaac Angelos, who was still in prison, though his eyes had been put out, had been deposed by the present ruler, Alexis, just as the Turks of today, (1885), know that a deposed *Sultan* is imprisoned somewhere on the Bosphorus, but in neither case did they regard the matter as of any consequence.

The besieged in 1203 knew that the son of Isaac, the young Alexis, had persuaded the Venetians and a body of Latins, through the influence of his sister's husband Philip, to assist him to regain possession of the empire, and that he and his friends were now outside the city wails. The Latins did not wish to capture the city. Even if they did, stronger armies than this had tried to do so and had failed. If the invader won there would be a new Emperor—that was all. Indeed, why should the citizens care? They had no love for the reigning sovereign nor he for them. When he heard that young Alexis was coming with a band of Venetian pirates, he made no preparations for resistance. He was a mere idle lover of luxury, an Eastern Charles the Second, who thought only of the ills of today; an essentially weak man, too sentimental to be a successful ruler. He shrank from inflicting the cruelty of ordinary punishments, and still more from that which was necessary to make him a strong despot.

Though he had not hesitated to depose his brother, he was either conscience stricken or pretended to be so, and continually upbraided himself. The eunuchs, says Nicetas, who guarded the royal forests with as much care as the Destroying Angel guarded Paradise, threatened to kill anyone who ventured to cut timber for the construction of vessels. The emperor's brother-in-law had sold all the navy stores. Those who thus robbed the public seemed rather thereby to gain in the estimation of their sovereign.

The emperor appeared more amused than frightened with the preparations of which he heard, and it was only after he learned of the proclamation of his nephew which had been made at Corfu—and this he could only have learned a few days before the arrival of the expedition in the Bosphorus—that he concerned himself with the means of defence. But even then, the voluptuary and the drunkard could not set himself with sufficient energy to meet the danger.

When the expedition had arrived and the Crusaders were encamped opposite the imperial palace, he wished to withdraw from the city. His relatives, however, and the ring which always surrounds an Eastern despot urged him to resist on their account. It was they who forced him to make a show of defence. The bravest among them was the emperor's son-in-law, Theodore Lascaris. When, as we have seen, the seaward towers around Blachern were taken, and a part of the city set on fire, his subjects openly reproached him with cowardice, and it was then, probably, that the threats of which Robert de Clari speaks were uttered.

Perhaps it was under the influence of these threats that he had been induced to lead his army outside the walls on the occasion mentioned. Lascaris begged hard to be allowed to attack the Crusaders. (Nicetas.) The emperor, however, was either afraid or possibly believed that as the city never had been captured it never could be. (Nicetas charges the emperor with cowardice, and is probably right; but he is so continually unfair, not only to Alexis but to all the Comneni, that his account has to be received with caution.)

The retreat, according to Nicetas, encouraged the Latins. It strengthened the party of Isaac within the city. Even indifferent men argued that if there were no arrangement there should at least be fighting, and if an army more numerous than the invaders had yet been forbidden to attack, it was time to change their sovereign. The cowardly voluptuary had, however, no intention of making resistance. The same night he fled ignominiously from the city. He told Irene, his daughter, and several other women of his intention; took ten thousand pieces of gold, a number of precious stones and imperial ornaments, (Nicetas), and embarked, deserting his wife and children, his throne and people.

The flight of Alexis filled the city with alarm. Constantine, the minister of finance, however, assembled the troops and declared for Isaac. The blind old emperor was led, or rather carried, out of prison, placed upon the throne, and once more treated as the Emperor of Rome. As soon as he understood the situation he sent the news of his release to his son, to the leaders of the Venetians, and to the Crusaders. His great anxiety was to hear once more his son's voice.

The Venetians and Crusaders could scarcely believe the tidings of the flight of the emperor and the restoration of Isaac, and suspected treachery. Boniface of Montferrat called a council. The news had been brought during the night, and the leaders immediately armed themselves, as Villehardouin says, *'parcequ'els ne croyent pas beaucoup les Grecs.'* Boniface and the Venetians had apparently never contemplated that such a step as a restoration of Isaac would have been taken. In the negotiations directly with Philip, in the pact of Zara, in the proceedings at Corfu, no writer gives the slightest indication that a thought had ever been given to the possibility of the restoration of the old emperor.

If the design of Philip and of Boniface had not been to join the imperial dominions of the East and West, as I venture to think that it was, the Swabian king at least intended to keep his hold over Constantinople through the young Alexis. The desertion of the Emperor Alexis was a gain to the party of Philip, but the resurrection of Isaac from the tombs of the Blachern was a severe blow. This party had posed before their deluded followers as the asserters of right. They had dwelt on the justice of punishing a usurper who had deposed and blinded the anointed of God. They had pointed to young Alexis as the exile deprived of his rights and fleeing for his life; the bishops had expressly authorised the siege on the ground that the Crusaders might punish a wrong and defend the right. Boniface and Dandolo had urged the importance of having with them 'the rightful heir.' The very existence of Isaac seems to have been ignored.

Perhaps even there were doubts whether he still lived. If he did, he was blind, and by a well-recognised practice could not be emperor. The sentiment of chivalry to help the weak against the strong, the oppressed against the oppressor, had been roused, but always in favour of Alexis and not of his father. In a night all this was changed. The oppressor had fled. The Crusaders learned that one who had been oppressed far more than the youth among them had been brought out from his dungeon, and was now occupying the throne of which he had been wrongfully deprived. The first order was to arm, the first thought probably to snatch the prize out of the hands of Isaac.

Reflections, however, soon convinced the party of Philip that this could not be done at once. For the moment they would have to acquiesce in the settlement which had been arrived at. The simple-minded Crusaders would be unable to find fault with the citizens for placing the father of Alexis on the throne, of which he undoubtedly was, according to Western notions, the rightful occupant. The only pretext for remaining in Constantinople would henceforward be that they wished to be paid according to their bargain. Isaac had sent word, says Villehardouin, that he was willing to ratify the promises that had been made by his son.

Boniface was probably unwilling to allow Alexis to escape from his influence, but replied that the heir to the throne would not be permitted to enter the city until these promises had been formally confirmed by the father. Accordingly, Villehardouin himself and Matthew of Montmorency, chosen to represent the Crusaders, with two Venetians, were sent to convey a reply to this effect to Isaac. At the gate of the city the messengers dismounted, and passed through a lane guarded on each side by Warings, *les Anglois et les Danois*, with their axes, to the palace of Blachern.

When they entered, they saw before them Isaac and his wife, the sister of the King of Hungary. The messengers, after being received with every honour, told the emperor that they wished to speak to him in private on behalf of his son and the leaders of the army. Accordingly, the emperor, his wife, the chancellor, and the interpreter, with the four messengers, passed into a private room. It had previously been arranged that Villehardouin should speak on behalf of the messengers, and he gives us the substance of what he said. He called attention to the service which the army and the Crusaders had rendered to his son, and to the fact that they had kept their part of the bargain.

As to his son, he would not be allowed to enter the city until he had given security for the execution of the obligations he had undertaken. Young Alexis now asked through them that Isaac should confirm the contract which the youth had made, both as to substance and manner of execution.

'What is the contract?' said the emperor.

'I will tell you,' said Villehardouin:—

First and foremost, there is the promise to put the Empire of Romania under obedience to the Pope; afterwards to give 200,000 silver *marks* to the army, and provisions for a year to small and great; to transport 10,000 infantry and cavalry in the proportion that we shall designate in his vessels, and at his expense, into Egypt, and to keep them there for a year; and to maintain in the Holy Land, and at his expense, during his life, 500 knights to protect it. This is the contract which your son has made. He has confirmed it on oath by charters with pendent seals, and by the guarantee of King Philip of Germany, your son-in-law; we now ask you to confirm it.

The emperor replied:—

Of a surety, the convention is very hard, and I don't see how it can be carried out, but still, you have done so much for him and me, that if one gave you the whole of the empire you would have deserved it.

The result of the interview was that the father confirmed his son's agreement by oath, and by letters patent with the gold seal or imperial Bull. The messengers returned to the camp bearing the precious document. Probably the same day young Alexis was conducted by the chief barons into the presence of his father. The Greeks received him and his friends with great feasting and rejoicing, and with every mark of respect.

The revolution had been accomplished rapidly. Alexis the Third had fled on the night of the 18th of July. Next day Isaac had been placed on the throne, and had again been allowed to see his son. During the next ten or eleven days there appear to have been many negotiations between the emperor and his son on the one side and the leaders of the expedition on the other. The great result which Boniface obtained was that Alexis should be associated with his father as Emperor, and as a joint occupant (Villehardouin), of the throne. Apparently, before this decision was accepted by Isaac, and probably as a condition precedent, it was arranged that the Crusaders and Venetians should retire across the Golden Horn.

On the 1st of August, 1203, young Alexis was crowned Emperor together with his father Isaac in the Great Church with the usual pomp. He at once set about the payment of the 200,000 *marks* promised to the Venetians and Crusaders. Enough was received to enable each Crusader to pay back the price that had been paid for his passage at Venice. (*Ibid.*) The treasury, however, was empty. The drain upon the resources of the population in order to pay the foreign army was naturally unpopular. The young emperor was not secure of his throne, He accordingly proposed to the barons a new arrangement. The agreement between the Venetians and the army was to terminate at Michaelmas.

The new emperor declared with simple truth that he could not pay within so short a term, that he would lose his throne if the Crusaders left him, and would be killed by his own subjects; and that the Greeks hated him on account of his friends the Crusaders. If they would stay till the following Easter he would bear their expenses up to that time, and would pay the Venetians their freight for the fleet for a year. If these terms were accepted, his revenues after harvest would have come in from the provinces, he would be able to pay what he had promised, to preserve his throne, and to go with them, or at least to send an army.

Then the old trouble once more broke out. The party of the marquis recognised, says Villehardouin, that the emperor's statement was true, and that his proposal was the most advantageous one possible under the circumstances. On the other hand, the bargain at Corfu had been that after Michaelmas those who had come out for Holy War, and had no wish to join in an expedition against a Christian city, should be free to go, and should have a fleet provided for their transport to Syria. The compromise had been confirmed by the most solemn oaths. This party now claimed its fulfilment '*Baillez-nous les vaisseaux, ainsi que vous nous l'avez juré; car nous voulons aller en Syrie.*'

Dandolo and Boniface readily accepted the imperial proposal. The first, because of the treaty with Malek Adel, not to introduce the Crusaders to Egypt, for though Syria was spoken of it was by no means clear that the original plan would not be adhered to; the second, with the object of serving Philip and himself. They could now use stronger arguments than at Corfu. They had begun the business and must finish it. It was dangerous to go down to Syria or to Egypt in winter. They could do nothing at that season even if they were there. The cause of the Lord would be lost. 'Wait till March, and we can then leave the emperor in a good position. We can 'then go with plenty of money and of provisions.' Again, and again Villehardouin insists that the aim of the malcontents was to break up the army:—

> They cared neither for better nor for worse, provided that the army should be divided.

Once more it is worth recalling that his object is to explain why the Army of Crusaders did not accomplish its object The Venetians accepted the proposal, and bound themselves to hold the fleet in readiness for a year from Michaelmas. The opposition, feeble now in comparison with what it had been at Corfu, found itself in far too small a minority to prolong its resistance, and thus the proposal of Alexis was accepted by the Crusaders also.

In truth, the position of the young emperor was exceedingly critical. He had gone himself to Galata to make his proposal, and although he probably wished that it should not be published, it is pretty certain that its tenor would be known within the city. If he indeed stated that his subjects. hated him on account of his having been brought there by the Crusaders, and would kill him if he were left without their help, he probably told the truth. Nicetas says that the new emperor had changed the ancient faith, and had renounced the ancient rites of the Romans to follow the new laws of the Pope.

The Crusaders had probably been cajoled into the belief that to bring the Greeks into subjection to Rome would be a success which would ensure for them the Pope's absolution. The hint of such an intention had become known, and was of itself sufficient to arouse the hostility of every member of a Church as jealous of foreign interference as that of Rome. But the great cause of hatred towards Alexis was, no doubt, because he was associated with the enemy. So long as the question had been merely one of a change of ruler, public opinion had hardly existed. There is no reason to suppose that the citizens had known of the agreement which had been made by Alexis.

Now, however, that he was on the throne, and had made unheard of demands for money, with which to pay his supporters, now that the process of robbing the churches and extorting large sums from the wealthy citizens had commenced, and now that one of the conditions which this youth had accepted was that he was to place the Church of the New under that of the Elder Rome, popular sentiment was altogether against him. If the invaders were to be bought off at once, it would have to be with money raised in the city itself. If the payment could be postponed, a large portion might be raised in the provinces.

It is possible also that Boniface saw that he had blundered in consenting to allow Alexis to enter the city. The latter was a weak youth, who, so long as he had been with the Crusaders, had been under the influence of his guardian. Now that he had become Emperor, Mourtsouphlos and a few others, who took the lead among the citizens, became his advisers. From them he soon learned how difficult was the execution of the contract which he had signed. It became important to Boniface to place the young emperor again under his own guardianship and influence. After all Isaac was weak, blind, and old. He could not last long. He might probably easily be deposed.

Provided that young Alexis would do what was wanted, the designs of Boniface and of Philip might yet not miscarry. With the object, partly of recovering his lost influence and partly of preventing his falling under that of the popular leaders within the city, Boniface and a portion of the army agreed to go with Alexis to Adrianople, in order to pursue the late emperor, Alexis the Third, who had fled to that city, and to help also young Alexis to reduce his subjects to submission.

Boniface probably recalled the influence which he had obtained at Corfu and in the islands of the Aegean, while accompanying Alexis as guardian. It might be hoped that again he would have the youth entirely in his power, and that thus the design of Philip to obtain either direct sovereignty over the empire, immediately or at some later period, could be carried into effect. Accordingly, the proposition to accompany Alexis was accepted, by the advice, says Villehardouin, of the Greeks and the French. Baldwin of Flanders remained behind in command of the remainder of the army.

During the absence of Alexis, a second fire, more destructive than the first, broke out within the city. The fire deserves to take rank among the great historical conflagrations of the world. Even Constantinople, which has always been particularly liable to great fires, never saw its like. In the value of the wealth consumed, in the influence of the fire in striking terror into the population and exasperating them against the invaders, and in thus influencing the fate of the empire, few similar disasters can compare with it in interest. The circumstances attending it are also remarkable, as throwing light on the relations existing during the joint reign of Isaac and Alexis the Fourth between the citizens and foreign invaders.

Shortly after the arrival of the Crusaders, the mob attacked the wealthy Pisan quarter within Constantinople and on the shores of the Horn. It was not surprising that they should have done so. Nicetas says that the untaught masses did not distinguish between friend and foe. They knew that the invaders were all Latins—that is, members of the Western Church, that the fleet which was in the harbour was from Venice; and it was natural that a mob should not make the distinction between the inhabitants of one or another Italian city. Many houses belonging to the Pisans were destroyed. The wealthier portion of the population did what they could to assist the Pisans to save their property, and to explain to the mob that though Italians they were not allies of the Venetians.

On the other hand, it is, to say the least, highly probable that a considerable number of the Pisans had fraternised with the Venetians, and had thus awakened the hostility of the Constantinopolitans. Greek and Frank writers agree in saying that Crusaders and Venetians went over in considerable numbers from Galata to see the rich palaces, the richer churches, and the other marvels of the imperial city. (Pera and Galata are always confused by the Western writers, or rather the present distinction did not exist. All was Pera *across* the Horn.

The immediate slope was Galata.) The Italians and Burgundians in the army spoke the same language as the Pisans, and it is probable that even the Frenchmen did not find much difficulty in making themselves understood by them. This alone would tend to make them sympathise with the Italians, and when it is remembered that they were all of the Church of the Elder Rome, and that the people among whom they were living had long been jealous of their commerce, it is easy to see that there were many common sentiments and interests which worked towards bringing the Latin inhabitants and the invaders together.

Nicetas tells us expressly that the Pisans and Venetians were reconciled, and adds that the reconciliation was the work of Isaac. The consequences of the attack made upon the Pisan quarter were twofold: first, this understanding with the Crusaders was improved; and, second, many of the Pisans were so alarmed that they fled across the Golden Horn to Galata, and took up their residence with their fellow-countrymen and co-religionists. Meantime, whilst constant and daily visits were paid by the foreigners to the Great Church and the marvels at the east end of the city, the old emperor was receiving daily visits from the Italian and crusading chiefs at the Blachern palace in the west. They were received, to the disgust of the Romans, says Nicetas, as saviours of the empire and as benefactors. The emperor melted down the statues and even the sacred vessels of the churches, in order to supply their insatiable greed.

For a few days the growing hostility between the citizens and the invaders was restrained. But on the 19th of August an incident occurred which gave the spark necessary to cause an explosion. Some of the Flemish soldiers, accompanied by Venetians and Pisans, crossed the harbour in order to pillage the Saracens. Under the system of capitulations, which has always prevailed in Constantinople, these Arab and other Moslem traders were allowed to have their own quarters and their own mosque even within the city. This building stood near the Pisan quarter, on the northern slope, and between the church of the Divine Peace (Nicetas), and the sea.

Probably the Crusaders regarded the existence of such a building as a cause of offence, just as a London mob in the seventeenth century so regarded the existence of a Roman Catholic chapel in their midst. We may fairly conjecture also that the Pisans regarded it as a special object of detestation, because it had been built in the neighbourhood of their *khans* for the use of rival traders as well as miscreants. The Flemings and Crusaders looked upon the wealth of the Moslems as their lawful prey.

The Saracens were found in their mosque and were surprised. The Christian mob rushed in upon them, and at once, at the point of their swords, made them give up all the property that could be found. Their Roman neighbours came, however, to their assistance. A disgraceful riot took place, in the course of which the robbers set fire to the city in several places. The fire commenced near the mosque, and was carried by a strong north wind (Nicetas), across the peninsula to the Marmora. Then the wind changed, and a new district was devastated. The fire lasted two days and nights.

★★★★★★★★

So, says Villehardouin. Others say eight days, and the continuator of William of Tyre nine days. All accounts agree that the fire was of a terrible character. Nicetas implies that it occurred before the departure of Alexis with Boniface. This may be so, but he is always so violent against the emperor that it is impossible to trust his statement. For example, in this place he affirms that while Isaac was greatly troubled at this sad accident, Alexis, who had a face like that of the greatest incendiary, the Destroying Angel himself, would have liked to see the whole of the city reduced to ashes. The statement of Villehardouin that the fire was during the absence of Alexis is confirmed by the *Chronique de Munic*. See also Eracles, *Recueil*.

★★★★★★★★

A large portion of the richest and most thickly populated quarters of the city was entirely destroyed. A wide belt across the peninsula from the harbour to the Marmora was left a heap of ruins. The width of the fire was at one time, according to Villehardouin, half a league. The inhabitants of this burnt strip lost everything they had. The houses, says Nicetas, were enriched with many precious ornaments, and were full of various kinds of valuable property. No one, says the Marshal, can estimate the amount of the wealth which was destroyed, while many men and women perished in the flames. (Villehardouin.) The barons and leaders regretted the fire, '*furent bien tristes et eurent grand pitie,*' (*ibid*), when they saw these beautiful churches and splendid palaces being consumed and the great commercial streets burning, but they could do nothing.

The natural result of the fire was to intensify the ill-feeling which existed between the Latins and the citizens. The brutal soldiery of the West had caused the fire, and had been brought into the city by Italian colonists. It was not surprising that the citizens no longer cared to protect any Italians within their walls. None of the Latins, says Villehardouin, dared remain any longer in the city. They escaped with their families and such property as they could save from the fire, and, crossing the harbour, took up their abode with the Crusaders. Fifteen thousand thus fled.

On the 11th of November the Emperor Alexis returned to Constantinople, and was welcomed by the Crusaders, and, according to Villehardouin, by his own subjects. The old friendly relations between the young emperor and the host which had accompanied him from Corfu continued for a time. Alexis, however, soon lost the respect of both his own subjects and the pilgrims. He had come into his empire. His one idea was to enjoy it. But the condition of the city made this impossible within its walls, and for enjoyment he had to return to his old comrades. He passed days and nights in drinking bouts with the invaders and at play. He was 'hail-fellow, well met' with all. He allowed those who were at the gaming table with him to take off his imperial diadem, and to replace it by one of their own woollen caps. He soon became despised, says Nicetas, by every honest man, both among the Romans and among the Crusaders.

Meantime his wretched father was filled with jealousy at the honours accorded to his son. Isaac appears to have been almost entirely ignored by the Western host—partly, no doubt, because of his feeble condition, and partly because Boniface and Dandolo found a readier instrument in Alexis. He complained that he was not treated with sufficient respect, that his son was intriguing against him. Probably his long imprisonment, his sufferings as a common prisoner, and the loss of his eyesight combined to make him ill-tempered, and had injured his health. He became more than ever the victim of superstitious fears. The monks by whom he was surrounded promised that he would become the lord of a great empire, that he would recover his eyesight, that he would be cured of gout or rheumatism, to which he was a martyr, and Isaac was weak enough to believe them. (Nicetas.) The astrologers persuaded him to transport into the Great Palace from the hippodrome a statue of the Calydonian boar, under the belief that by so doing his enemies would be destroyed, as the enemies whom the original boar was sent to attack had been rent in pieces.

Since the fire the condition of the city had been one of confusion. The Romans hated Crusaders and Venetians as the cause of all their ills, especially of the heavy taxation and of the two fires. A trivial incident, mentioned by Nicetas, shows how great was the irritation. The mob broke up one of the finest statues in the city, a representation of Minerva in bronze, which stood in the great square of Constantine. The statue faced to the West, and in the imagination of the people appeared to be beckoning the natives of the West towards New Rome.

The Crusaders were still encamped in Galata, and after the flight of the foreign residents do not appear to have entered the city. They were becoming impatient to be paid. Alexis let them have what he could. But the money only came in driblets—'*pauvre petits payements,*' as Villehardouin calls them. Alexis was doing his best to satisfy his former friends. Their protection had become as dangerous as their enmity, and Alexis would probably now have been glad to get rid of them. The two emperors endeavoured again to levy a tax upon the city, but the people rose against it. They therefore did their best to raise the sum necessary from the wealthy class of the population, and by melting down the gold and silver vessels, chandeliers, and other valuable metallic furniture of the churches.

Meantime the Crusaders were helping themselves. They were naturally, says Nicetas, the enemies of every kind of beauty. They went about in bands, and plundered the beautiful villas of the wealthy nobles and the rich churches which were on the neighbouring shores of the Marmora. It pleased them even to burn and destroy many of the villas. The inhabitants resisted, and sent to the city for soldiers to defend their homes. No help was, however, there to be obtained. The monk-ridden and imbecile old emperor was powerless. The worthless and inexperienced youth was unable or unwilling to assist them. Reproaches were addressed almost daily by the Crusaders to the Emperors, but without effect, except to bring in new '*pauvre petits payements*.'

****

> Villehardouin says Alexis commenced to pay immediately after the coronation (1st August, 1203). The payments to the army enabled those who had not paid to repay what had been paid for them at Venice.
>
> Robert de Clari states that 100,000 *marks* were paid, of which half went to the Venetians, together with 34,000, balance of unpaid freight, while the rest—*i.e.* 16,000 *marks*—repaid the Crusaders who had advanced money to the Venetians for their poorer brethren's passage.
>
> Gunther declares that half of the promised sum was ordered to be paid.
>
> Nicetas says that, in conference between Dandolo and Mourtzouphlos in St. Cosma, the *doge* demanded immediate payment of fifty *centenaria* of gold, or about 120,000 *marks*.
>
> One-fourth, therefore, of the promised sum of 400,000 *marks* agreed to at Zara appears to have been paid almost immediately after the coronation, 1st August. Then came in the '*pauvre petits payements*' during September, October, and December. Probably in all there was little if anything short of 200,000 paid by the end of the year.

****

Indeed, during November and December 1203 and January 1204 the confusion within the city and the anxiety without were of a kind which we, who have seen Paris besieged, may fairly realise. The rule of the city was rapidly slipping out of the feeble hands of Isaac and those of his son. The imperial orders were disobeyed. The demoralisation of the populace, caused by taxation, by the interruption of commerce, though the city was not yet besieged, and by the fires, had ruined half the traders, and increased daily. The foreign residents had left. The ordinary business of life was at a standstill. The troops were divided in their allegiance; the Warings remaining faithful to the emperors, the Greek troops being some on the side of those who were clamouring for the deposition of Isaac and Alexis, some probably willing to recall Alexis the Third, and some few willing to remain faithful to the reigning sovereigns.

Across the Golden Horn the condition of the invaders was one of extreme anxiety. The opposition wanted to be gone about their lawful business. Their provisions were running short, and had to be replenished by raids upon the surrounding country. Dissension and dissatisfaction were increasing daily. Alexis had declared that it was impossible for him to execute his promises, and the Crusaders knew that what he said was true. The citizens dared, says Gunther, to forbid the emperor to take from his own property and give it to foreigners. The Crusaders, on the other hand, he declares, were loath to attack the city because they had no hope of success. They were in such danger that they were not safe around the city, nor could they leave without great risk. Hence it came to pass, says this writer, that 'our men determined to besiege the city from which they could not flee.' (Gunther.) Another author describes the situation of the army in equally striking terms. The Franks were between the hammer and the anvil. (Rostangnus of Clugny, *Exuviae Sac.*)

The invaders, however, had the great advantage over the citizens that they had two leaders who knew precisely what they wanted, and who intended to make every sacrifice in order to succeed. Though the chiefs and the soldiery might be restive, there was yet a military and a feudal discipline. There never appears to have been a murmur of discontent among the Venetians. Gunther again and again insists on the determination of the Venetians, 'who drove us earnestly this way, partly because of the promised reward, and partly from their desire to obtain the dominion of the sea.' The expedition, which, he adds, had been undertaken to please King Philip, was now solely directed by Boniface and Dandolo.

The brave old leader, whose tenacity of purpose it is impossible not to admire, ruled the host by his nod, and, in spite of want of provisions, of secret disaffection among the troops, and of open opposition, was neither to be frightened nor weaned out of the accomplishment of his purpose. Boniface had blundered, had lost his hold over Alexis, and seems, since his return in the beginning of November from Adrianople, to have been gradually losing ground. Still he, too, had his object, for which he was prepared to make every sacrifice, and so long as Dandolo was willing to hold out he, too, would defy disaffection and opposition.

Ostensibly, all that Boniface wanted was to be paid. In reality, nothing was further from his desire. No other grievance remained. (This reason is assigned in Villehardouin, Gunther, the *Halberstadt Chron.*, and Rostangnus.) No other pretence is alleged by any writer. The great chance of making payment impossible was to insist upon its being made at once. The emperors were doing their utmost, and Isaac had scandalised the Greeks by selling church ornaments to raise money. (Nicetas and *Chron. Novgorod*.) The revolution within the city might result in the substitution of a strong man in lieu of the two feeble occupants of the throne.

In such case, not merely would the great conspiracy of Philip and Boniface fail, but payment itself might be altogether lost, or terms might be offered to the Crusaders which the malcontents would have sufficient influence with the army to cause to be accepted. Whether payment were made or the latter alternative adopted, the invaders would have no pretence to remain longer before the city. There were, therefore, many reasons, some of which weighed with the army, while others had especial influence with Boniface, in favour of demanding immediate payment and of precipitating a struggle.

The barons, therefore, held a parliament, at which Dandolo was present, and determined to send a deputation to the emperor, in order to bid him pay or to publicly insult him by defying him to battle. The Venetians and the barons each chose three of their number for this bold mission. Among the latter was Villehardouin himself. The six rode round the harbour to the palace of Blachern girded with their swords. The marshal points out that they adventured much and went in great peril on this enterprise. They descended at the palace gate, and were admitted into the imperial chamber. The emperors, seated on their respective thrones, side by side, together with the empress, Isaac's wife, and a large assembly of nobles, received them. The messengers reminded the emperors of their oaths. Conon de Bethune, addressing apparently only Alexis, said:

> We come to summon you in the presence of your barons to fulfil the agreement made between you and us. If you fulfil it, well; if not, take note that the barons will recognise you neither as lord nor as friend, but they will consider themselves free to take that which belongs to them in any way in which they can

get it. They give you notice that they will do you no harm till they have defied you. They will not betray you; it is not the custom in their country so to do. You have heard what we have said, and you will take counsel upon the matter as you like.

The noise which this public challenge made in the city was great, as no doubt Boniface and Dandolo intended that it should be. The messengers returned to the camp, thinking themselves fortunate, as Villehardouin admits, that they had escaped with their lives. It is hardly necessary for him to add, that the Greeks took this defiance as a great insult, and remarked that no one had hitherto dared to challenge the Emperor of Constantinople in his own palace.

There was now open hostility between the inhabitants and the invaders, and each side prepared to oppose the other. The Greeks made a night attempt to burn the Venetian fleet. They prepared seventeen boats, set fire to the wood and various combustibles with which they had been loaded, and at midnight on New Year's Day, when a strong southerly wind was blowing, turned them adrift. The attempt, however failed. A few persons were injured, and a Pisan merchantman was burnt with her cargo; but the Venetians with their boat-hooks managed to push the burning ships away from them to the mouth of the harbour, where the strong current which is always running soon carried them out of the way of doing harm. A week after the Greeks made a sortie with their cavalry, but were repulsed.

Within the city the confusion increased daily. The people were convinced that they had nothing to hope from either emperor. They had at length awakened to a sense of danger. The question was no longer one of a mere change of rulers, but one of fulfilling a contract to which they were no party, of paying a band of robbers who were without the walls for a service which their young emperor had requested, but which they had not desired, and for which they certainly had no reason to be grateful. What they wanted was a ruler who would not allow them to be plundered. They saw an enemy which had already done them grievous wrong, and were burning to be delivered from him. The policy of Alexis seemed to the citizens to be to sacrifice everything in order to keep on good terms with their enemies. Even the Crusaders admitted that he was doing what he could for them. He was divided between loyalty to his own subjects and fear of displeasing Philip of Swabia and his late companions. (Gunther.)

The leaders of the citizens had asked the emperors to take the offensive, to attack the Crusaders, and make an end of the matter, but these emperors were either unwilling or afraid to do so. The attempt on the ships was apparently the result of a popular impulse. The same popular sentiment urged the party to get rid of their imbecile rulers. The impulse seems to have been general, for amidst the popular movement no attempt appears to have been made to suppress the rising which took place against the government. During some time, the people were undecided as to the course they ought to adopt.

Meetings were held in the Great Church, and each day saw the confusion increase. As day by day passed, however, one man was steadily coming to the front. A certain Alexis Ducas, a member of the imperial family, and nicknamed Mourtzouphlos, on account of his meeting eyebrows, headed the discontented party, and became the leader of the revolution. He had for a long time been known as the bitterest opponent of the Latins. (Villehardouin.)

On the 25th of January, 1204, an extraordinary meeting of the inhabitants was held in Hagia Sophia. The senators were there, and the members of the college of pontiffs and other high dignitaries of the Church. The senate was a survival of the early days of the New Rome, and had long since ceased to exercise any real authority. In the midst of the anarchy which now prevailed public opinion turned for support to its mere semblance of power, and senators and pontiffs were forced by the threats of the multitude to deliberate on the election of a new emperor. They wished to temporise, but the multitude protested that they could not and would not live under the actual government.

The names of the members of the reigning family and of other nobles were gone through, and apparently submitted to the public assembly of the citizens. The meeting, however, could not agree upon a choice. Those who were selected refused to act. Some of the magistrates present were themselves asked to become emperor. A second and a third day were spent in these meetings. Finally, the choice fell upon a young man named Nicolas Kanabos, who was, however, chosen against his will.

Alexis and Isaac knew what was going on, but were powerless. Isaac was ill. Alexis, alarmed for himself, seeing that whoever the next emperor might be the citizens were at least determined that he should no longer reign, feeling that power was rapidly slipping away from him, and that but for the presence of his foreign guards his own life would be in immediate danger, took what under the circumstances was perhaps a natural act, but what was nevertheless justly regarded by the citizens as an act of treason. He sent to the Marquis of Montferrat, and invited him to fill the palace of Blachern with Frenchmen and Italians, in order to defend his life and maintain him on the throne. This treason to the city cost him both his throne and his life.

On hearing of what Alexis had done, Mourtzouphlos decided that the time had come for him to act. The minister of finance was in his favour, but the imperial guard of the Warings, who knew that their duty was to defend the emperor, constituted a serious obstacle to any attack on the occupant of the throne. It is probable that, as foreign mercenaries, they were by no means favourably regarded by the people, The very fidelity for which, as we have seen, they were so justly esteemed by the imperial family, even in the time of Anna, made their opposition on the present occasion the more probable. The object of Mourtzouphlos was now to secure the person of Alexis, either by inducing him to leave the palace or by withdrawing the Warings themselves.

The latter course was found to be the easier. The Warings were therefore deceived, and led to believe that in leaving the palace they were to fight for Alexis. The guards being thus withdrawn, Mourtzouphlos undertook to secure Alexis. As *Protovestiarios*, he had the right of entrance to the palace. This he made use of, entered, and, according to the narrative of Nicetas, told the young emperor that there was a mob coming to the palace and ready to tear him in pieces on account of his proposal to introduce the Crusaders into the city.

Alexis fell into the trap. His only thought was to save himself, and instead of remaining in his palace and awaiting the return of the Warings, he wrapped himself up so as not to be recognised, and followed Mourtzouphlos out of the palace walls. When he reached the tent of the leader he was immediately put in irons and sent to prison. Mourtzouphlos seized the imperial insignia, assumed the vermilion buskins, and was saluted as Emperor.

****

Vermilion and not purple was the imperial colour in the New Rome. The *Œcumenical Patriarch* still signs with vermilion ink, maintaining in this as in several other matters the traditions of the empire. The Western writers generally speak of vermilion, though sometimes also of scarlet, tents, &c., as if no distinction were made between the two colours.

****

Kanabos was abandoned, and the elect of the citizens was crowned with the usual formalities in Hagia Sophia. Isaac, already very weak, died on hearing the news of his son's arrest. Alexis did not survive him beyond a few days. He was imprisoned, and on the 1st of February he also died. Whether his death was a natural one, as his successor affirmed, or whether, as Nicetas and Villehardouin declare, he was strangled, it is impossible and immaterial to say.

The new emperor, Mourtzouphlos, had an impossible task to perform, but he set himself to work in a vigorous manner to organise the defence. The treasury was empty. Everything was in confusion. The army was disorganised. Such navy as had existed had already been destroyed. A large portion of the city was in ruins from the fires. He at once ordered a heavy contribution from the wealthy classes, and insisted upon the money being paid. He immediately set energetically to work to improve the defences. Men worked day and night in heightening the walls on the harbour side, and in fortifying the gates on the landward side. The emperor encouraged citizens and soldiers by his presence, now at the works, now in leading the attacks that he organised upon the foraging parties of the enemy.

His conduct confirmed him in the confidence of the people. He was hampered, however, by the old aristocratic spirit of the wealthy nobles. To them he was objectionable because in such a time he refused to recognise their privileges. He insisted on their help, and subjected them together with the rest of the inhabitants to the severity of discipline of a city in a state of siege. They feared his voice, says Nicetas, like death. His energy seems to have entirely won the confidence of the imperial guard. They probably resented his conduct in withdrawing them from the palace while he obtained possession of Alexis; but when they subsequently learned that the emperor had proposed to bring in the enemy, they consented to join Mourtzouphlos. (The author of the *Chronicle of Novgorod* charges Alexis, when the Greeks sent their fire-ships against the Venetians, with having given notice to the Franks beforehand.)

There were doubtless men among them who had left England rather than endure Norman tyranny, and such men had now no wish to treat Normans and Frenchmen as friends. Had the Gambetta of this revolution been able to have delayed the attack upon the city, it is possible, and even probable, that he would have saved it. The writers on the side of the Crusaders and Venetians speak of the new Emperor in a manner which shows that they believed they had now a much more formidable opponent to deal with. His great object was to save time. The enemy also saw, however, that in their interest no time should be given him.

The deposition of Isaac and Alexis gave Boniface and Dandolo the excuse they wanted. So long as the 'right heir' and his father were reigning within the city, the only pretext which the leaders could put forward for remaining before it was the merely mercenary one that they were waiting to be paid. Now, however, that they were deposed, that Isaac was dead, and Alexis, their late guest, a prisoner, and now murdered, as they believed, the leaders could again pose as the defenders of the right, as the avengers of the injured. Villehardouin says:

'Never was so horrible a treason committed by any persons as the deposition and imprisonment of young Alexis.'

All agreed, he adds, that the murderer had no right to reign, and that all who had consented to the deposition were accomplices in the murder. The clergy once more used their influence at the bidding of Boniface, and preached to the Crusaders that war in such a case was lawful and right; and added that if they intended to conquer the land and place it in obedience to the Pope, they would have the Pontiff's indulgence. Crusaders and Venetians alike appear to have been content with this assurance. We shall see presently that, while some were appealed to on the ground that it was their duty to punish murderers, a more substantial inducement was held out to all by the prospect of a rich harvest of plunder.

The city was divided. To understand its division, it must be remembered that the citizens knew little or nothing of the plans of the enemy. Boniface appears, on the death of young Alexis, to have been regarded in the city as a candidate for the imperial throne which his ward had lost. The death of the latter would probably increase the resentment of his friends; and the nobles, who formed the bulk of his party in the city, never worked heartily for Mourtzouphlos. This was, no doubt, the party which hailed Boniface as king. Mourtzouphlos had had as yet insufficient time to organise his forces, but meantime was acting bravely, was superintending and pushing on the repairs, and was harassing the enemy. The Crusaders and Venetians, on their side, were equally active. During the days which followed the accession of the new emperor, and before the death of Alexis, an incident occurred which is worthy of note.

★★★★★★★★

Gunther says that Mourtzouphlos did his utmost to conceal the death of Alexis, and sent messengers continually, in the name of the young emperor, asking the leaders of the army to enter the city, but that

Dandolo persuaded them not to go.

****

Fighting was going on daily. The neighbouring country was scoured in order to lay in a stock of provisions preparatory to the attack and the siege. One of these raids was made during the end of January as far as Philies, (possibly Kilios), near the Black Sea entrance of the Bosphorus, where Henry, the brother of Baldwin, Earl of Flanders, led an expedition and captured great quantities of cattle and provisions. Mourtzouphlos, hearing of their departure, endeavoured to surprise them. A sharp skirmish took place, in which he was defeated and narrowly escaped being taken prisoner. The imperial *gonfalon* was captured, and a banner which represented the Virgin, by which the Greeks set great store.

****

Codinus says that the emperors had twelve ensigns which were used in public ceremonials, one or two only of which were employed when the emperor took the field. The emblem of the city has always been the crescent, probably derived from the horns of a bull, which was the symbol of the Turanian race, as that of the lion was of the Arian. Each regiment had its own flag whence we still speak of a band of soldiers.

****

Profiting by the occasion presented by this defeat, Boniface appears to have entered into negotiations with the emperor in order to save the life of Alexis. All hope of carrying out the design of Philip of Swabia was not lost so long as the life of Alexis was safe. The message may even have been given in the form in which the Russian monk reports it: 'Give us Alexis, and we will depart and allow you to remain Emperor. We have been forced to come here through necessity.'

The answer was that the application was too late. Alexis was dead. It is impossible to tell what was the full signification of this message, but, read in the light of the surrounding circumstances, it appears to me to point to a distinct divergence between the Crusaders and the Venetians. Boniface and Dandolo found themselves forced to work together, but each distrusted the other and was jealous of him.

At this moment the great object of the first was to save the life of his pupil; that of the second was to make an arrangement with Mourtzouphlos impossible. A mission had arrived from the Holy Land, with which was Abbot Martin, urging the Crusaders to lose no time in going to the aid of those who were fighting the Saracens. The old spirit of dissatisfaction was once more showing itself. Possibly already some news of the intention of the Pope, as shown by a letter ordering them to leave for the business of the crusade, had reached them.

The design of placing Alexis on the throne was at an end with the death of the young man, and even if Boniface had knowledge of the arrangement made between the Venetians and the Sultan of Egypt, he had no interest in prolonging the stay before Constantinople. The failure of the object of the expedition had added largely to the number of the malcontents, and it may well be that Boniface felt inclined to give way to them. If this were so we can well understand the jealousy which undoubtedly soon displayed itself towards Dandolo. But the latter was now master of the situation. The Crusaders were almost as much at the mercy of the Venetians as when they were on the Lido.

Provisions were short. January and February are in Constantinople cold and stormy months. The Venetians could urge the necessity of waiting for fine weather before they embarked. Their money was spent. They were to some extent as one writer says, between the hammer and the anvil, and were compelled to follow as Dandolo led. The next negotiation was therefore one in which there is no evidence that Boniface took any part, just as in the one already mentioned there is nothing to show that Dandolo had any share. Each leader was playing for his own hand. The common bond of union had not yet been found.

A meeting took place between the Emperor Mourtzouphlos and Dandolo in order professedly to discuss conditions of peace. The meeting was held at the monastery of St. Cosma, which was about half a mile without the walls of Blachern. The *doge* asked for immediate payment of fifty *centenaria* of gold, (Nicetas), and imposed other conditions which were exceedingly hard, among which probably was obedience to the Romish Church. Dandolo must have known that his conditions were certain to be refused.

While the two leaders were together, a detachment of the Crusaders' cavalry made a descent from an adjoining hill with the object of capturing the emperor, and would have succeeded if he had not fled. Some of his bodyguard were indeed captured. (Nicetas is the authority for this statement. It is not improbable, and indeed is likely enough, if Gunther's story is true that the emperor had tried to decoy the leaders into the city.)

No further attempt at negotiation appears to have been made either by the Venetians or the Crusaders. Boniface had failed, and had probably no wish to come to an arrangement when he learned that Alexis was really dead. He could no longer carry out the design of

Philip to unite the two empires. Two courses were open to him: to go with the Crusaders to Egypt or to Palestine, or to throw in his lot with Dandolo. His oath, the wishes of the better portion of his troops, the command of the Pope, the call from the messengers who had come from the Holy Land, urged him in one direction. But to leave Constantinople was to admit himself beaten, and to be submitted to the reproaches of the Crusaders for the failure of the expedition up to the present.

The chances of success against the *infidels* were now far less than they had been. Even supposing that Boniface knew nothing of the treaty between Venice and the Sultan of Egypt, the difficulties before a crusading host were largely increased. The expedition organised with so much care by Innocent had been divided, and all who had taken part in it had up to the present time been unfortunate. The messengers with whom Abbot Martin had arrived told how the Flanders fleet, which had wintered in Marseilles, and which had more Crusaders on board than those who were before Constantinople, had failed in Syria. Great numbers had been stricken down with country fever and had died. The rest had returned home. They related also how those who had gone to Prince Bohemund in Antioch, who was fighting for the Armenians against the Turks, had been slaughtered or captured to a man.

The Venetians, moreover, were not yet paid, and would never consent to transport the army. It would be necessary, if Boniface wished to lead his army against the *infidels*, either to pay the Venetians or to fight them. To do the one was impossible. To do the other was inexpedient. If the Crusaders defeated Dandolo, his army would be at the mercy of the Greeks. If Dandolo should succeed, he was equally ruined. The Crusaders at least were between the hammer and the anvil.

The second course, on the other hand, to throw in his lot with Dandolo, offered innumerable advantages. The richest city in the world was before them. Its inhabitants were divided. Its defences had already been proved to be vulnerable. Its soldiers had shown themselves less valiant than his own host. The Crusaders and Venetians alike would fight heartily in order to have the looting of such undreamt-of wealth as they had already seen. The disaffected in the army, who were uninfluenced by the bait of plunder, could be brought over under the plea that the dearest object of Innocent, after the defeat of the miscreants, was the union of the two Churches, and that in attacking the Greeks they were punishing them generally for their schism, and specially for their share in the deposition of their lawful ruler. The temptation of plunder, added to the excuse that they were in the path of duty and of obedience, would overcome the most scrupulous.

And then, the greatest inducement of all to Boniface presented itself. If the city were captured a new emperor would have to be chosen. Who so certain of success as he? He was the chosen leader of the Crusading Army. Baldwin of Flanders and the other princes of the army had never pretended to dispute his supremacy. He had hitherto carried everything before him. The malcontents at Venice, at Zara, at Corfu, and before the city had been powerless. He had but to triumph once more, and he would be Emperor of the New Rome. He had done his best, as even Philip must admit, for young Alexis. The Swabian king could not blame him if, after all his loyal efforts, he should now fight for himself. The prospect was too dazzling to admit of indecision. He threw in his lot heartily with Dandolo and declared for the siege.

In conformity with the practice followed throughout the expedition it became necessary to assemble a parliament to decide on the next step. This met probably in the early days of March. We have no information as to what went on in reference to the proposal to attack the city. What is certain is that the parliament agreed to it. We know also that the meeting was long and stormy. '*On y parla assez, en avant et en arrière,*' says the marshal. The result arrived at confirms the natural presumption that there were two, and probably even three, parties. The interest of the Crusaders was opposed to that of the Venetians. But the Crusaders were still, as they had always been, divided. The malcontents who had been opposed to the expedition to Constantinople distrusted and were disgusted with Boniface, and, though they were not able to have their own way, were sufficiently powerful at least to thwart his plans.

It was decided that if the city were taken six Venetians and six Crusaders should be elected to form a committee to choose an Emperor. (Robert de Clari says twenty were chosen, ten from each.) A proviso was, however, added that all the twelve delegates should solemnly swear on holy relics that they would elect the candidate whom they believed to be the best in the interest of the world. The other provisions show that the parties were pretty equally balanced. It was agreed that if a Frank should be elected Emperor the *Patriarch* should be chosen by the Venetians, and *vice versa*.

★★★★★★★★

The term 'Franchois' is used by all the contemporary writers to designate Frenchmen, Flemings, Germans, and Burgundians. The term 'Frank,' which is still used in the Balkan peninsula, in much the same sense, is therefore a convenient one.

****

The emperor was to receive one-fourth of all that should be captured within the city and throughout the empire, together with the two imperial palaces of Blachern and the Lion's Mouth. 'The remaining three-fourths were to be divided equally between the Venetians and the Crusaders. The gold and silver, the cloth, the silk, and all the rest of the booty captured were to be abandoned to the host, and to be collected together for the sake of a fair division. When this should have been accomplished a new committee of twenty-four, chosen by the Venetians and the Crusaders, was to be named to divide the empire into fiefs, and to define the feudal service which the holders should render to the new emperor.

It was further resolved that no one should lay hands on priest or monk nor plunder the churches or monasteries. The division of the spoils of the empire, including the carving out of the fiefs, was to be finished within a year, and therefore to be completed before the end of March 1205. After the capture of the city all were to be free to leave it who wished to do so up to that date. After it, however, all who remained were to be bound to accept the *suzerainty* of the emperor.

The bear's skin having thus been divided, it only remained to capture the bear.

The Crusaders and Venetians had been pressing on their works for the attack upon the city with all their might. Rewards were offered to those whose scaling ladders and covered gangways, to be thrown out from the ships' cross-trees to the walls, were first ready. The machines were prepared for hurling stones, Battering-rams, *balistae, mangonels,* and all the engines known to the military science of the time for attacking a walled city were got ready. There was no longer any question of leaving for the Holy Land. The lust of gain had fallen upon the whole of the army, and while they were making preparations for the attack, they were already planning out the best course for a division of the spoil.

CHAPTER 8

The Assault, Capture, and Plunder of the City

The preparations which the leaders had been pushing on during several weeks were completed by the 8th of April, and that day was chosen for an assault upon the city. A noteworthy change of plan had been made from that which had been acted upon nine months before. Instead of attacking simultaneously a portion of the harbour walls and a portion of the landward walls, Venetians and Crusaders alike directed their efforts against the defences on the side of the harbour. The horses were embarked once more in the *huissiers*. The line of battle was drawn up; the *huissiers* and galleys in front, the transports a little behind, and alternating between the *huissiers* and the galleys.

The whole length of the line of battle was upwards of half a league, (Robert de Clari says it was a league long—a statement which cannot be true), and stretched from the Blachern to beyond the Petrion.

★★★★★★★★

The Petrion, which is repeatedly mentioned by contemporary writers, was a district built on the slope of a hill running parallel to the Golden Horn for about one-third of the length of the harbour walls eastwards from Blachern. It had apparently been a neglected spot during the early centuries of the history of Constantinople, but had lately come to be the residence of numerous hermits, and the site of several monasteries and convents. A great part is now occupied by the Jewish colony of Balatia.—Du Cange, *Cons. Ch.* Dr. Mordtmann, of Constantinople, has carefully examined the question, and has published the result of his inquiry in Constantinople. Nicetas says that the ships reached from Blachern to the monastery of Everyetis. This monastery was near, and below the present mosque of Sultan Selim.

★★★★★★★★

The emperor's vermilion tent had been pitched on the hill just beyond the district of the Petrion, where he could see the ships when they came immediately under the walls. Before him was the district which had been devastated by the fire. On the morning of the 9th the ships, drawn up in the order I have described, passed over from the north to the south side of the harbour. The Crusaders landed in many places, and attacked from a narrow strip of the land between the walls and the water.

Then the assault began in terrible earnest along the whole line. Amid the din of the imperial trumpets and drums the attackers endeavoured to undermine the walls, while others kept up a continual rain of arrows, bolts, and stones. The ships had been covered with planks and skins so as to defend them from the stones and from the famous Greek fire, and, thus protected, pushed boldly up to the walls.

The transports soon advanced to the front, and were able to get so near the walls that the attacking parties on the gangways or platforms, flung out once more from the ships' tops, were able to cross lances with the defenders of the walls and towers. The attack took place at upwards of a hundred points until noon, or, according to Nicetas, until evening. Both parties fought well. The invaders were repulsed. Those who had landed were driven back, and amid the shower of stones were unable to remain on shore. The invaders lost more than the defenders. The heightening of the walls had made their capture more difficult than at the previous attack. Before night a portion of the vessels had retired out of range of the *mangonels*, while another portion remained at anchor and continued to keep up a continual fire against those on the walls. The first day's attack had failed.

The leaders of both Crusaders and Venetians withdrew their forces to the Galata side. The assault had failed, and it became necessary at once to determine upon their next step. The same evening a parliament was hastily called together. Once more, in the presence of defeat, the old differences showed themselves. Some advised that the next attack should be made on the walls on the Marmora side, which were not so strong as those facing the Golden Horn.

The Venetians, however, immediately took an exception, which everyone who knew Constantinople would at once recognise as unanswerable. On that side the current is always much too strong to allow vessels to be anchored with any amount of steadiness, or even safety. Villehardouin's irritation at the suggestion shows how bitter the opposition still continued. There were some present, he says, who would have been very well content that the current or a wind—no matter what—should have dispersed the vessels, provided that they themselves could have left the country and have gone on their way.

It was at length decided that the two following days, the 10th and 11th, should be devoted to repairing their damages, and that a second assault should be delivered on the 12th. The previous day was a Sunday, and Boniface and Dandolo made use of it to appease the discontent in the rank and file of the army. Once more, as at Corfu and before the first attack upon the city, the bishops and abbots were set to work to preach against the Greeks. They urged that the war was just, because Mourtzouphlos was a traitor and a murderer, a man more uisloyal than Judas; that the Greeks had been disobedient to Rome, and had perversely been guilty of schism in refusing to recognise the supremacy of the Pope, and that Innocent himself desired the union of the two Churches. They saw in the defeat the vengeance of God on account of the sins of the Crusaders.

The loose women were ordered out of the camp, and for better security were shipped and sent far away. Confession and communion were enjoined, and, in short, all that the clergy could do was done to prove that the cause was just, to quiet the discontented, and to occupy them until the attack next day. (Robert de Clari.)

The warriors had in the meantime been industriously repairing their ships and their machines of war. A slight, but not unimportant, change of tactics had been suggested by the assault on the 9th. Each transport had been assigned to a separate tower. The number of men who could fight from the gangways or platforms thrown out from the tops had been found insufficient to hold their own against the defenders. The modified plan was, therefore, to lash together, opposite each tower to be attacked, two ships containing gangways to be thrown out from their tops, and thus concentrate a greater force against each tower. Probably also the line of attack was considerably shorter than at the first assault.

On Monday morning, the 12th, the assault was renewed. The tent of the emperor had been pitched near the monastery of Pantepoptis, one of many which were in the district of the Petrion, extending along the Golden Horn from the palace of Blachern, about one-fourth of its length. From this position he could see all the movements of the fleet. The walls were covered with men who were ready again to fight under the eye of their emperor. The assault commenced at dawn, and continued with the utmost fierceness. Every available Crusader and Venetian took part in it. Each little group of ships had its own special portion of the walls with its towers to attack. The besiegers during the first portion of the day made little progress, but a strong north wind sprang up, which enabled the vessels to get nearer the land than they had previously been.

Two of the transports, the *Pilgrim* and the *Parvis*, lashed together, succeeded in throwing one of their gangways across to a tower in the Petrion, and opposite the position occupied by the emperor. (Nicetas.) A Venetian, and a French knight, André d'Urboise, immediately rushed across and obtained a foothold. They were at once followed by others, who fought so well that the defenders of the tower were either killed or fled. The example gave new courage to the invaders. The knights who were in the *huissiers*, as soon as they saw what had been done, leaped on shore, placed their ladders against the wall, and shortly captured four towers. Those on board the fleet concentrated their efforts on the gates, broke in three of them, entered the city, while others landed their horses from the *huissiers*.

As soon as a company of knights was formed, they entered the city through one of these gates, and charged for the emperor's camp. Mourtzouphlos had drawn up his troops before his tents, but they were unused to contend with men in heavy armour, and after a fairly obstinate resistance the imperial troops fled. The emperor, says Nicetas, who is certainly not inclined to unduly praise the emperor, who had deprived him of his post of *Grand Logothete*, did his best to rally his troops, but all in vain, and he had to retreat towards the palace of the Lion's Mouth. The number of the wounded and dead was '*sans fin et sans mesure.*'

An indiscriminate slaughter commenced. The invaders spared neither age nor sex. In order to render themselves safe they set fire to the city lying to the east of them, and burnt everything between the monastery of Everyetis and the quarter known as Droungarios. (It was the quarter about the gate in the harbour walls, now, 1885, known as Zindan Capou, near the dried fruit market.) So extensive was the fire, which burned all night and until the next evening, that, according to the marshal, more houses were destroyed than there were in the three largest cities of France. The tents of the emperor and the imperial palace of Blachern were pillaged, the conquerors making their headquarters on the same site at Pantepoptis.

It was evening, and already late, when the Crusaders had entered the city, and it was impossible for them to continue their work of destruction through the night. They therefore encamped near the walls and towers which they had captured. Baldwin of Flanders spent the night in the vermilion tent of the emperor, his brother Henry in front of the palace of Blachern, Boniface, the Marquis of Montferrat, on the other side of the imperial tents in the heart of the city.

The city was already taken. The inhabitants were at length awakened out of the dream of security into which seventeen unsuccessful attempts to capture the New Rome had lulled them. Every charm, pagan and Christian, had been without avail. The easy sloth into which the possession of innumerable relics, and the consciousness of being under the protection of an army of saints and martyrs, had plunged a large part of the inhabitants, had been rudely dispelled. The Panhagia of the Blachern, with its relic of the Virgin's robe, the host of heads, arms, bodies, and vestments of saints and of portions of the holy Cross, had been of no more use than the palladium which lay buried then, as now, under the great column which Constantine had built.

The rough energy of the Westerns had disregarded the talismans of the Greek Church as completely as those of paganism. In vain had the believers in these charms destroyed during the siege the statues which were believed to be of ill omen or unlucky. The invaders had a superstition as deep as their own, but with the difference that they could not believe that a people in *schism* could have the protection of the hierarchy of heaven, or be regarded as the rightful possessors of so many relics. During the night following its capture the Golden Gate, which was at the Marmora side of the landward walls, had been opened, and already an affrighted crowd was pressing forward to make its escape from the captured city.

Others were doing their best to bury their treasures. The emperor himself, either seized with panic or finding that all was lost—as, indeed, everything was lost so soon as the army had succeeded in obtaining a foothold within the walls—fled from the city. He, too, escaped by the Golden Gate, taking with him Euphrosyne, the widow of Alexis. The brave Theodore Lascaris determined, however, to make one more attempt. His appeal to the people was useless. Those who were not panic-stricken appear to have been indifferent. Some, at least, were apparently still dreaming of a mere change of rulers, like those of which the majority of them had seen several.

Theodore turned his attention to the Waring guard, but before any attempt at reorganisation could be made the enemy was in sight, and Theodore himself had to fly. The Crusaders had expected, according to the marshal, another day's fighting, and knew nothing of the flight of Mourtzouphlos. To their surprise, they encountered no resistance. The day was occupied in taking possession of their conquest. The Byzantine troops, including also the Warings, laid down their arms on receiving assurances of personal safety. The Italians who had been expelled took advantage of the entry of their friends, and appear to have retaliated upon the population for their expulsion.

Two thousand of the inhabitants, says Gunther, were killed, and mostly by these returned Italians. As the victorious Crusaders passed through the streets, women, old men, and children, who had been unable to flee, met them, and, placing one finger over another so as to make the sign of the Cross, hailed the Marquis of Montferrat as King, while a hastily gathered procession, with the Cross and the sacred emblems of Christ, greeted him in triumph. The people had known him as the guardian of Alexis. Besides those who yet believed that all the change which would be made would be that of the sovereign, there were some among the number who had been the partisans of young Alexis, and who believed that they were therefore entitled to share in the favour, or at least in the clemency, of Boniface. It was, therefore, natural that he should be hailed as king.

The marquis had led his division along the shore of the Horn round to the palace of Bucoleon. The occupants surrendered it. The ladies of the court, including one who had been the sister of the King of France and another the sister of the King of Hungary, had fled to the fortress of this palace on the capture of the city. While Boniface took possession of the Bucoleon, Henry, brother of Baldwin, occupied the Blachern.

Then began the plunder of the city. The imperial treasury and the arsenal were placed under guard; but with these exceptions the right to plunder was given indiscriminately to the troops and sailors. Never in Europe was a work of pillage more systematically and shamelessly carried out. Never by the army of a Christian state was there a more barbarous sack of a city than that perpetrated by these soldiers of Christ, sworn to chastity, pledged before God not to shed Christian blood, and bearing upon them the emblem of the Prince of Peace. Reciting the crimes committed by the Crusaders, Nicetas says with indignation:—

> You have taken up the Cross, and have sworn on it and on the holy Gospels to us that you would pass over the territory of Christians without shedding blood and without turning to

the right hand or to the left. You told us that you had taken up arms against the Saracens only, and that you would steep them in their blood alone. You promised to keep yourselves chaste while you bore the Cross, as became soldiers enrolled under the banner of Christ. Instead of defending His tomb, you have outraged the faithful who are members of Him. You have used Christians worse than the Arabs used the Latins, for they at least respected women.

An immense mass of treasure was found in each of the imperial palaces and in those of the nobles. Each baron took possession of the castle or palace which was allotted to him, and put a guard upon the treasure which he found there. The marshal says:—

> Never since the world was created, was there so much booty gained in one city. Each man took the house which pleased him, and there were enough for all. Those who were poor found themselves suddenly rich. There was captured an immense supply of gold and silver, of plate and of precious stones, of satins and of silk, of furs, and of every kind of wealth ever found upon earth.

The sack of the richest city in Christendom, which had been the bribe offered to the Crusaders to violate their oaths, was made in the spirit of men who, having once broken through the trammels of their vows, are reckless to what lengths they go. Their abstinence and their chastity once abandoned, they plunged at once into orgies of every kind.

The Greek eye-witness gives the complement of the picture of Villehardouin. The lust of the army spared neither maiden nor the virgin dedicated to God. Violence and debauchery were everywhere present; cries and lamentations and the groans of the victims were heard throughout the city; for everywhere pillage was unrestrained and lust unbridled. The city was in wild confusion. Nobles, old men, women, and children ran to and fro trying to save their wealth, their honour, and their lives. Knights, foot soldiers, and Venetian sailors jostled each other in a mad scramble for plunder. Threats of ill-treatment, promises of safety if wealth were disgorged, mingled with the cries of many sufferers.

These pious brigands, as Gunther aptly calls them, acted as if they had received a licence to commit every crime. Sword in hand, houses and churches were pillaged. Every insult was offered to the religion of the conquered citizens. Churches and monasteries were the richest storehouses, and were therefore the first buildings to be rifled. Monks and priests were selected for insult. The priests' robes were placed by the Crusaders on their horses. The icons were ruthlessly torn down from the screens or were broken. The sacred buildings were ransacked for relics or their beautiful caskets. The chalices were stripped of their precious stones and converted into drinking cups. The sacred plate was heaped with ordinary plunder. The altar cloths and the screens of cloth of gold, richly embroidered and bejewelled, were torn down, and either divided among the troops or destroyed for the sake of the gold and silver which were woven into them.

The altars of Hagia Sophia, which had been the admiration of all men, were broken for the sake of the material of which they were made. Horses and mules were taken into the church in order to carry off the loads of sacred vessels and the gold and silver plates of the throne, the pulpits, and the doors, and the beautiful ornaments of the church. The soldiers made the chief church of Christendom the scene of their profanity. A prostitute was seated in the *patriarchal* chair, who danced and sang a ribald song for the amusement of the soldiers. Nicetas, in speaking of the desecration of the Great Church, writes with the utmost indignation of the barbarians who were incapable of appreciating and therefore respecting its beauty. To him it was an 'earthly heaven, a throne of Divine magnificence, an image of the firmament created by the Almighty.'

The plunder of the same church in 1453 by Mahomet the Second compares favourably with that made by the Crusaders of 1204.

The sack of the city went on during the three days after the capture. An order was issued, probably on the third day, by the leaders of the army for the protection of women. Three bishops had pronounced excommunication against all who should pillage church or convent. It was many days, however, before the army could be reduced to its ordinary condition of discipline. A proclamation was made throughout the army that all the booty should be collected, in order to be divided fairly among the captors. Three churches were selected as depots, and trusty guards of Crusaders and Venetians were stationed to watch what was thus brought in.

Much, however, was kept back and much stolen. Stern measures had to be resorted to before order was restored. Many Crusaders were hanged. The Count of St. Paul hung one of his own knights with his shield round his neck because he had not given up the booty he had captured. A contemporary writer, the continuator of the history of William of Tyre, forcibly contrasts the conduct of the Crusaders before and after the capture. When the Latins would take Constantinople, they held the shield of God before them. It was only when they had entered that they threw it away, and covered themselves with the shield of the devil. (*L'Estoire de Eracles, Recueil.*)

I have already mentioned that the Italians resident in Constantinople who had returned to the city with their countrymen were conspicuous in their hostility to the Greeks. Amid this resentment there were examples, however, that former friendships were not forgotten. The escape of Nicetas himself is an illustration in point. He had held the position of *Grand Logothete*, but he had been deposed by Mourtzouphlos. (This office still exists, 1885, the principal duty of the person who holds it is to recite the Creed in great religious services when the *patriarch* officiates.) When the Latins entered the city, he had retired to a small house near Hagia Sophia, which was so situated as to be likely to escape observation. His large house, and probably his official residence, which he is careful to tell us was adorned with an abundant store of ornaments, had been burnt down in the second fire. Many of his friends found refuge with him, apparently regarding his dwelling as specially adapted for concealment.

Nothing, however, could escape the observation of the horde which was now ransacking every corner. When the Italians had been banished from the city Nicetas had sheltered a Venetian merchant with his wife and family. This man now clothed himself like a soldier, and, pretending that he was one of the invaders, prevented his countrymen or any other Latins from entering the house. For some time, he was successful, but at length a crowd, principally of French soldiers, pushed past and flocked within. From that time protection became impossible. The Venetian advised Nicetas to leave, in order to prevent himself from being imprisoned and to save the honour of his daughters.

Nicetas and his friends accepted the advice. Having clothed themselves in skins or the poorest garments, they were conducted through the city by their faithful friend as if they were his prisoners. The girls and young ladies of the party were placed in their midst, their faces having been intentionally smeared in order to give them the appearance of being of the poorest class. As they reached the Golden Gate the daughter of a magistrate who was one of the party was suddenly seized and carried off by a Crusader. Her father, who was weak and old, and wearied with the long walk, fell, and was unable to do anything but cry for assistance.

Nicetas followed and called the attention of certain soldiers who were passing, and after a long and piteous appeal, after reminding them of the proclamation which had been made against the violation of women, he ultimately succeeded in saving the maiden.

The entreaties would have been in vain if the leader of the party had not at length threatened to hang the offender. A few minutes later the fugitives had passed out of the city, and fell on their knees to thank God for His protection in having permitted them to escape with their lives. Then they set out on their weary way to Silivria. The road was covered with fellow-sufferers. Before them was the *patriarch* himself, Nicetas says:—

> Without bag or money or stick or shoes, with but one coat, like a true apostle, or rather like a true follower of Jesus Christ, in that he was seated on an ass, with the difference that instead of entering the New Sion in triumph he was leaving it.

A large part of the booty had been collected in the three churches designated for that purpose. The marshal himself tells us that much was stolen which never came into the general mass. The stores which had been collected were, however, divided in accordance with the compact which had been made before the capture. The Venetians and the Crusaders each took half. Out of the moiety belonging to the army there was paid the fifty thousand silver *marks* due to the Venetians. Two foot sergeants received as much as one horse sergeant, and two of the latter sergeants received as much as a knight. Exclusive of what was stolen and of what was paid to the Venetians, there were distributed among the army 400,000 *marks*, or 800,000*l.*, and 10,000 suits of armour. (Du Cange's version says *chevaucheures*, or beasts of burden. I adopt that of M. Wailly.)

The total amount distributed among the Crusaders and Venetians shows that the wealth of Constantinople had not been exaggerated. 800,000*l.* was given to the Crusaders, a like sum to the Venetians, with the 100,000*l.* due to them. These sums had been collected in hard cash from a city where the inhabitants were hostile, and where they had in their wells and cisterns an easy means of hiding their treasures of gold, silver, and precious stones—a means traditionally well known in the East—and in a city half of which had been recently burnt in three great fires. As we have seen, abundance of booty was taken possession of by the troops which never went into the general mass. Sismondi estimates that the wealth in specie and movable property before the capture was not less than twenty-four million pounds sterling.

The distribution was made during the latter end of April. Many works of art in bronze were sent to the melting-pot to be coined. Many statues were broken up in order to obtain the metals with which they were adorned. The conquerors knew nothing and cared nothing for the art which had added value to the metal. The weight of the bronze was to them the only question of interest. The works of art which they destroyed were sacrificed not to any sentiment like that of the Moslem against images which they believed to be idols or talismans. No such excuse can be made for the Christians of the West. Their motive for destroying so much that was valuable was neither fanaticism nor religion. It was the simple greed for gain. No sentiment restrained their cupidity.

The great statue of the Virgin which ornamented the Taurus was sent as unhesitatingly to the furnace as the figure of Hercules. No object was sufficiently sacred, none sufficiently beautiful, to be worth saving if it could be converted into cash. Amidst so much that was destroyed it is impossible that there were not a considerable number of works of art of the best periods. The one list which has been left us by the Greek *Logothete* professes to give account of only the larger statues which were sent to the melting-pot. But it is worthwhile to note what were these principal objects so destroyed.

Before doing so, however, let me again point out that Constantinople had long been the great storehouse of works of art and of Christian relics, the latter of which were usually encased with all the skill that wealth could buy or art furnish.

It had the great advantage over the Elder Rome that it had never been plundered by hordes of barbarians. Its streets and public places had been adorned for centuries with statues in bronze or marble. In reading the works of the historians of the Lower Empire the reader cannot fail to be struck alike with the abundance of works of art and with the appreciation in which they were held by the writers. First among the buildings as among the works of art, in the estimation of every citizen, was Hagia Sophia. It was emphatically the Great Church. Tried by any test, it is one of the most beautiful of human creations.

Nothing in Western Europe even now (1885) gives a spectator, who is able with an educated eye to restore it to something like its former condition, so deep an impression of unity, harmony, richness, and beauty in decoration as does the interior of the masterpiece of Justinian. All that wealth could supply and art produce had been lavished upon its interior —at that time, and for long afterwards, the only portion of a church which the Christian architect thought deserving of study. A great authority on architecture says:

> Internally, at least, the verdict seems inevitable that Santa Sophia is the most perfect and most beautiful church which has yet been erected by any Christian people. When its furniture was complete the verdict would have been still more strongly in its favour. (Fergusson's *Hist. of Arch.*, vol. ii.)

We have seen that to Nicetas, who knew and loved it in its best days, it was a model of celestial beauty, a glimpse of heaven itself. To the more sober English observer, 'its mosaic of marble slabs of various patterns and beautiful colours; the domes, roofs, and curved surfaces, with gold-grounded mosaic relieved by figures or architectural devices' are 'wonderfully grand and pleasing.' (*Ibid.*) All that St. Mark's is to Venice, Hagia Sophia was to Constantinople. But St. Mark's, though enriched with some of the spoils of its great original, is, as to its interior at least, a feeble copy.

Hagia Sophia justified its founder in declaring, 'I have surpassed thee, O Solomon,' and during seven centuries after Justinian his successors had each attempted to add to its wealth and its decoration. Yet this, incomparably the most beautiful church in Christendom, at the opening of the thirteenth century was stripped and plundered of every ornament which could be carried away. It appeared to the indignant Greeks that the very stones would be torn from the walls by these intruders, to whom nothing was sacred.

Around the Great Church were other objects which could be readily converted into bronze, and the destruction of which was irreparable. The immense hippodrome was crowded with statues. Egypt had furnished an obelisk for the centre. Delphi had given its commemoratory bronze of the victory of Plataea. Later works of Pagan sculptors were there in abundance, while Christian artists had continued the traditions of their ancestors in a style by no means so debased as Western writers have, until recently, believed it to be. The cultured inhabitants of Constantinople appreciated these works of art, and took care of them.

In giving a list of the more important of the objects which went to the melting pot, Nicetas again and again urges that these works were destroyed by barbarians who were ignorant of their value. Incapable of appreciating either their historical interest or the value with which the labour of the artist had endowed them, the Crusaders knew only the value of the metals of which they were composed. (The bronze, or 'Corinthian copper,' was formed of copper, gold, and silver. The stand of the tripod of Platæa still, 1885, remains in the hippodrome, and was probably spared on account of the inferior quality of its metal.)

The emperors had been buried within the precincts of the church of the Holy Apostles, the site of which was afterwards chosen by Mahomet the Second for the erection of the mosque now called by his name. Their tombs, beginning with that of Justinian, were ransacked in the search for treasure. It was not until the palaces of the nobles, the churches, and the tombs had been plundered that the pious brigands turned their attention to the statues. A colossal figure of Juno, which had been brought from Samos, and which stood in the forum of Constantine, was sent to the melting pot. We may judge of its size from the fact that four oxen were required to transport its head to the palace.

The statue of Paris presenting to Venus the apple of discord followed. The Anemodulion, or Servant of the Winds, was a lofty obelisk, whose sides were covered with *bas-reliefs* of great beauty, representing scenes of rural life, and allegories depicting the seasons, while the obelisk was surmounted by a female figure which turned with the wind, and so gave to the whole its name. The *bas-reliefs* were stripped off and sent to the palace to be melted. A beautiful equestrian statue of great size, representing either Bellerophon and Pegasus or, as the populace believed, Joshua on horseback, commanding the sun to stand still, was likewise sent to the furnace. The horse appeared to be neighing at the sound of the trumpet, while every muscle was strained with the ardour of battle.

The colossal Hercules of Lysippus, which, having adorned Tarentum, had thence been transported to the Elder and subsequently to the hippodrome of the New Rome, met with a like fate. The artist had expressed in a manner which won the admiration of beholders the deep wrath of the hero at the unworthy tasks set before him. He was represented as seated, but without quiver or bow or club. His lion's skin was thrown loosely about his shoulders, his right foot and right hand stretched out to the utmost, while he rested his head on his left hand with his elbow on his bent knee. The whole figure was full of dignity; the chest deep, the shoulders broad, the hair curly, the arms and limbs full of muscle.

The figure of an ass and its driver, which Augustus had had cast in bronze to commemorate the news brought to him of the victory of Actium, met with the same fate.

For the sake of melting them down into money the barbarians seized also the ancient statue of the wolf suckling Romulus and Remus; the statues of a sphinx, a hippopotamus, a crocodile, an elephant, and others, which had represented a triumph over Egypt; the monster of Scylla and others; most of which were probably executed before the time of Christ.

To the same period belonged the eagle struggling with a serpent, which was ascribed to Apollonius Tyanensis. Nicetas describes with glowing admiration the statue of Helen:—

> What shall I say of Helen, of elegant stature, with snowy arms and beautiful form? Why could she not soften the barbarians?— she who formerly had led all spectators captive; a statue clothed in a robe which graced rather than concealed her charms, her brow clear, her hair flowing gently to the wind, her graceful lips slightly opened as if about to speak, arched eyebrows; a figure full of harmony, elegance, and beauty; the joy of beholders, a pleasure to the eyes, such as makes it impossible to give an adequate description for posterity.

This statue was destroyed by men who knew nothing of its original. There must be added to these the graceful figure of a woman who held in her right hand the figure of an armed man on horseback. Then near the eastern goals, known as the 'reds,' stood the statues of the winners in the chariot races. They stood erect in their bronze chariots, as the originals also had been seen when they gained their victories, as if they were still directing their steeds to the goals. A figure of the Nile bull in deadly conflict with a crocodile stood near.

These and other statues were hastily sent to the furnace to be converted into money. We may judge of the value and artistic merit of the bronze statues which were destroyed by the specimens which remain. The four horses which the Emperor Theodosius had brought from Chios and placed in the hippodrome escaped by some lucky chance the general plunder, and were taken to Venice, where they still adorn the front of St. Mark's.

I have already alluded to the wealth of Constantinople in relics. As the city had become the storehouse of works of art, so also from the same causes it had drawn to it nearly all the relics of the Eastern world. There was even an additional reason why the relics should have flowed in greater number to the capital than did works of art, because faithful Christians felt bound to prevent them falling into the hands of the Moslem miscreant. This was a species of wealth which the Crusaders could much more readily appreciate than that which consisted merely in marble or bronze, to which the genius of the sculptor had added value.

Even among the more conscientious of the soldiers it seems to have been held that the surest way to compensate for the breach of their vow was to steal a relic for the use of the church in the neighbourhood from which they had come. I have already said that the relics were usually encased either in coverings of silver or gold, to which the best art of the time had added value, and the caskets were often set with precious stones. The coverings would, of course, be preferred by us to the contents, but that is because we do not believe in the genuineness of the relics. To understand the feelings of the Crusaders we must remember that doubt as to their genuineness scarce entered their minds.

Out of the great number of documents which have been collected together by the zeal of a recent writer, and which give minute accounts of the reception of these relics in the West, there are very few that speak of the value of the covering, and, even when they do so speak, it is only incidentally. The fragment of the true cross or the arm of the true saint was the gem; the silver or gold covering was only the suitable casket to contain it.

The pillage of the relics of Constantinople lasted for forty years. More than half of the total amount of objects carried off were, however, taken away between the years 1204 and 1208. During the few days which followed the capture of the city the bishops and priests who were with the Crusaders were active in laying hands on this species of sacred spoil; and the statement of a contemporary writer is not improbable, that the priests of the Orthodox Church preferred to surrender such spoil to those of their own cloth rather than to the rough soldier or the rougher Venetian sailor. On the other hand, the highest priestly dignitaries in the army—men, even, who refused to take of the earthly spoil—were eager to obtain possession of this sacred booty, and unscrupulous as to the means by which they obtained it.

The holy cross was carefully divided by the bishops for distribution among the barons. Gunther gives us a specimen of the means to which Abbot Martin, who had had the German Crusaders placed under his charge, had recourse. The abbot had learned that many relics had been hidden by the Greeks in a particular church. This building was attacked in the general pillage. He, as a priest, searched carefully for the relics, while the soldiers were looking for more commonplace booty. The abbot found an old priest, with the long hair and beard common then, as now, to Orthodox ecclesiastics, and roughly addressed him, 'Show me your relics, or you are a dead man.'

The old priest, seeing that he was addressed by one of his own profession, and frightened probably by the threat, thought, says Gunther, that it was better to give up the relics to him than to the profane and bloodstained hands of the soldiers. He opened an iron safe, and the abbot, in his delight at the sight, buried his hands in the precious store. He and his chaplain filled their surplices, and ran with all haste to the harbour to conceal their prize. That they were successful in keeping it during the stormy days which followed could only be attributed to the virtue of the relics themselves.

The way in which Dalmatius de Sergy obtained the head of St. Clement is an illustration of the Crusader's belief that the acquisition of a relic and its transport to the West would be allowed as a compensation for the fulfilment of the Crusader's vow. That knight was grievously afflicted that he could not go to the Holy Land, and earnestly prayed God to show him how he could execute some other task equivalent to that which he had sworn but failed to accomplish. His first thought was to take relics to his own country.

He consulted the two cardinals who were then in Constantinople, who approved his idea, but charged him not to buy these relics, because their purchase and sale were forbidden. He accordingly determined to steal them, if such a word may be applied to an act which was clearly regarded as praiseworthy. The knight, in order to discover something of especial value, remained in Constantinople until Palm Sunday in the following year. A French priest pointed out to him a church, in which the head of St. Clement was preserved.

He went there in the company of a Cistercian monk, and asked to see the relics. While one kept the persons in charge speaking with him, the other stole a portion of the relic. On leaving, the knight was disgusted to find that the whole head had not been taken, and, on the pretext that he had left his gauntlet behind, a companion regained admittance to the church, while the knight again kept the monk in charge in conversation at the door. Dalmatius went to the chest behind the altar where the relic had been kept, stole the remainder, went out, mounted his horse and rode away. The head was placed with pious joy in the chapel of his house. He returned disguised some days after to the church in order, as he pretended, to do reverence to the relic, in order really to ascertain that he had taken the right head, for there had been two in the chest.

He was informed that the head of St. Clement had been stolen. Then, being satisfied as to its authenticity, he took a vow that he would give the relic to the church of Cluny in case he should arrive safely. He embarked. The devil from jealousy sent a hurricane, but the tears and prayers before the relic defeated him, and he arrived safely home. The monks of Cluny received the precious treasure with every demonstration of reverent joy, and in the fullest confidence that they had secured the perpetual intercession of St. Clement on behalf of themselves and those who did honour to his head. (I have taken this account from Hurter, whose authority is Dalmatius de Sergy himself. *Bibl. Cluniac.*) The relics most sought after were those which related to the events mentioned in the New Testament, especially to the infancy, life, and passion of Christ, and to the saints popular in the West.

But the mass possessed by the imperial city ranged from the stone on which Jacob had slept, and from the rod which Moses had changed into a serpent, down to that of the latest opponents of heresy in Constantinople. Those connected with the life of Christ and His Mother existed in great number, and comprised objects supposed to be connected with almost every event of His life. There was the cross on which the Saviour had been crucified, the great drops of blood which He had shed in Gethsemane, one of His first teeth, and some of the hair of His childhood. The devout had venerated the purple robe, and could reverence also a portion of the bread which He had blessed at the Last Supper. But besides these there was hardly a disciple a saint, or a martyr of whom some relic did not exist.

The greater portion of these objects formed part of the plunder of the city which was collected during the first few days after its capture, and which was officially divided amongst the invaders. Three-eighths were allotted to the clergy and monks who accompanied the Crusaders; the remainder were bought or otherwise acquired subsequently, mostly by private persons. The officially certified relics first mentioned seemed to have come chiefly from the imperial palaces of Bucoleon and Blachern.

Many of those which were collected after the scramble of the first few days were certified with imperial golden Bulls. When they reached their destination, they were received with great honour and ceremony.

Princes attended and took part in the solemn procession which met them on their way to the church, where with solemn rites they were to be deposited. A sermon often followed, relating to the events with which the relic was supposed to be connected. In many instances an annual festival was appointed to celebrate the arrival of the relic, and occasionally the gift was made conditional upon the establishment of such annual festival in its honour. Lessons from the Old or New Testament appropriate to the saint, a relic of whom had been received, were selected for public reading on such festivals. Special services were framed to commemorate the event. Hymns were composed in honour of the relic. (Count Riant has found eighty-five of such feasts of the relics of 1204, seventy-four of which commemorate the reception of the relic.)

In the case of the monastery of Selincourt, where a sacred tear of Christ had been carried, the name was changed through the reception of this relic to that of the monastery of the Sacred Tear. A few of the more important objects of the same kind may be mentioned in order to show both the quantity which were received in the West and the honour with which they were regarded. The Venetians are accused by the author of the *Continuation of William of Tyre* of having taken an undue share of the spoil and of having concealed it in their ships. Many of the beautiful objects which bad adorned the church of the Divine Wisdom went to decorate St. Mark's. The high altar of that church, with its columns of marble and its bronze gates, was one of the most valuable acquisitions.

The Venetian church obtained also many pieces of sculpture, pictures, gold and silver vessels, and a mass of church furniture. The Venetians obtained the famous picture of the Virgin which was painted by St. Luke under the direct inspiration of the Holy Ghost. (Innocent III. apparently did not believe in the genuineness of this relic.) In 1205 there were received at Soissons from its bishop, Nivelon, who was at Constantinople, the head of Si. Stephen, the finger which St. Thomas thrust into the side of Christ, the crown of the head of St. Mark, a thorn from the crown worn by Christ, a large portion of the sleeveless shirt of the Virgin Mary, a portion of the garment with which the Lord girt himself at the Last Supper, the girdle of the Virgin and the arm of John the Baptist; and a few months after the arrival of these a further consignment containing the head of St. John the Baptist, the head of

St. Thomas, two great crosses made out of the true cross of our Lord, the head of St. James, with two other crosses made out of the true cross, the head of St. Thaddeus, and three other relics of lesser importance which are specified, together with a large number of others which are not specially mentioned, but which were distributed among the parish churches and convents mostly in the diocese of Soissons.

An anonymous account, probably written about 1208, by a clerk of Halberstadt, tells another story of the bringing of certain relics from Constantinople. The whole of the population, laymen and clergy, and an immense number of people even from adjacent dioceses, came together on the occasion of the reception of these relics, which were borne by Conrad the bishop, who had himself come from Constantinople. Such a concourse, says the chronicler, was never seen before, and the rejoicing at the reception of the relics was such as might have been expected, seeing that they were destined to bring peace and safety to the country.

If any relics could do this, surely those brought home by Conrad ought to have sufficed, since among them was some of the blood of Jesus from the true cross, from the sepulchre, from the crown of thorns, from His agony and bloody sweat, from His purple robe, from the sponge and reed, and from seven other sources; the head of James the brother of Christ, and thirty other relics which are specially mentioned, besides many others, says the narrative, of martyrs, confessors, and virgins, which it would take long to name.

By the side of such relics the further gifts of silk cloths in imperial purple woven with gold, and of a dress set with gold and silver and precious stones, seemed probably poor and almost unworthy of notice. (*Anon.* Halberstadensis, *Ex. Sac.*) Amiens was fortunate to obtain possession of the head of St. John the Baptist, which was sent by Peter the Walloon. (Richard of Gerberon, *Ex. Sac.*) Sens was even more successful, and received the crown of thorns worn by the Lord. Gunther tells us how the Abbot Martin, of Pairis in Alsace, transported many relics from Constantinople into that country, the principal one being a large portion of the true cross.

Other relics which went to the glorification of this diocese were a trace of the blood of Christ, a further portion of the wood of the true cross, an arm of St. James, and fifty others which are enumerated. (Guntherus Parisiensis, *Ex. Sac.*) The body of St. Andrew was taken to Amalfi. (*Ibid.*) The sacred tear already mentioned was taken to Selincourt, and the abbot was warned of the approach of the person bringing it by the ringing of the bells, a fact which could only be attributed to miraculous agency. (Count Riant has collected 145 documents relating to relics sent to the West.)

It would be tedious and unprofitable to attempt to give a list of other relics which were taken from Constantinople. Some of these found their way to our own country. Two documents apparently derived from the same source are inserted in the chronicles of Rauel or Rudolph of Coggleshall and Roger of Wendower which have special interest for Englishmen. They give an account of a relic surreptitiously taken away from Constantinople, and are in fact the confessions of the author of the theft. The relic was a small cross cut from the wood of the true cross, and the writer had seen it in the hands of Baldwin of Flanders. The writer having stolen it, took it to Norfolk, and subsequently gave it to Bromholm. The gift made what had hitherto been the 'poor little house' of Bromholm a richly-endowed house, and enabled the monks to put up new and handsome buildings.

****

> The story is told most fully by Roger of Wendower, and is illustrative of many similar stories. There appears to have been a practice in England like that which still prevails on the peninsula of Mount Athos. Pilgrims went from monastery to monastery to do reverence to the relics, and in each case they were expected to pay for the privilege of so doing. Such pilgrimages were, as they are still in the East, one of the chief sources of revenue for the monkish houses.

****

The Crusaders were not indifferent to the value of the coverings of these relics, and while they looked after objects of veneration, kept a keen eye also on the reliquaries—the gold and silver ornaments of the church, church furniture, golden embroidery, silk cloths, and the beautiful bindings set with precious stones of the gospels and liturgies. The treasury of St. Mark's at Venice was filled, in 1205, with costly reliquaries received from Constantinople. It is hardly possible to believe that the cunning workmen and traders of Constantinople did not palm off upon the Crusaders a good many relics which they knew to be fictitious. The objects could be manufactured so cheaply, and the critical spirit of the Crusader was so slightly developed, that it would be beyond the power of human nature to let such a chance of profit escape.

In the years which followed the conquest Latin priests were sent to Constantinople from France, Flanders, and Italy, to take charge of the churches in the city. These priests appear to have been great hunters after relics. Thus, it came to pass that there was scarcely an important church or monastery in most Western countries which did not possess some share of the spoil which came from Constantinople.

For some years the demand for relics seemed to be insatiable, and caused fresh supplies to be forthcoming to an almost unlimited extent. The new relics equally with the old were certified in due form to be what they professed to be. Documents duly attested and full of detailed evidence, sometimes doubtless manufactured for the occasion, easily satisfied those to whom it was of importance to possess certified relics. The 'poor little house of Bromholm,' which had been enabled from its possession of a cross made out of the sacred wood to become large and powerful, became the envy of many other poor little houses, and throughout the West the demand for relics which might bring profit to their possessors continued to increase.

At length the church deemed it necessary to put a stop to the supply, and especially to that of the apocryphal and legendary acts which testified to their authenticity, and in 1215 the fourth Lateran Council judged it necessary to make a decree enjoining the bishops to take means to prevent pilgrims from being deceived.

It is easy to ridicule the respect and veneration paid to the sacred tears, the numerous small crosses made from the holy wood, the heads, arms, and old garments of saints and martyrs. It is more difficult to understand how the men of the thirteenth century could have regarded these objects as genuine. It seems reasonable to suppose that many persons must have suspected their genuineness. The relics existed in such numbers, there were so many professing to be originals of the same object, the wood of the true cross was so abundant, and the legends relating to the preservation of such relics as, for example, the tear of Christ, were so extraordinary, that it is almost incomprehensible that men's suspicions were not generally aroused.

It must be remembered, however, that we are dealing with the ages of faith, and that relics in the East were not regarded with the same superstitious veneration as they were at the end of the twelfth century, and subsequently by the masses in the West. Neither earnestness in religion nor belief in its superstitions were, or are, so intense in the Eastern as in the Western Churches, In the East I doubt whether relics have ever been regarded with the same veneration as they were in the West. The Eastern spirit was less gross or more spiritual than that of the West. The tendency to drive a harmless and natural habit into a fetish worship was much more common among the earnest men of the West than among the more easy-going Christians of the East.

Probably the Greek could never hate idol-worship with the same amount of hatred as the Jew or the Western Christian, and mainly for the reason that he never realised how completely some races can fall into it. To St. Paul idol worship was devil worship. To our fathers, when they had once come to see that the articles were spurious, relic worship was idolatry. But the Greeks both of the time of St. Paul and their representatives of the Middle Ages regarded the creations of Greek art and the relics of the saints rather as symbols than as objects of reverence, and, speaking generally, were never in danger of converting the worship or respect due to the person or thing symbolised into fetish worship.

Just as the men of the West had transferred much of their ancient heathenism into the ceremonies and practices of the mediaeval church, so the Greeks had allowed their Christianity to become saturated with the ideas of old Greek religion. While there were probably gross and material views taken of the Olympic gods and of the other deities recognised by the ancient Greeks, it is doubtful whether there existed among them, to any considerable extent, statue, picture, or relic worship in the modern sense of the term. Asiatics might venerate a stone which had fallen from Jupiter, but such worship was alien to the Greek spirit.

But even while remembering these facts, anyone who is acquainted with the contemporary writings of the twelfth and thirteenth centuries is forced to recognise that even in the East in religious matters the spirit of inquiry can scarcely be said to have existed. For many years afterwards scepticism was unknown even in historical or geographical matters. The wonderful stories told by our early geographers are often scarcely more childish than those related by our early historians.

When a man of genius and learning, like Milton, writing a century after the Reformation, and contemplating even a reform of Reformation itself, could yet accept the fables concerning English history which he has transmitted to us, we may well cease to wonder at the spirit of credulity possessed by rough Crusaders three centuries before the Reformation. The time came when an Erasmus, enumerating the fragments of the true cross which he knew to exist, could fairly and properly turn relic veneration into ridicule, but at the opening of the thirteenth century we are far from such a period.

The Fourth Crusade
Dana Carleton Munro

1. THE PREPARATIONS FOR THE CRUSADE

Taught by the experience of the earlier crusaders, the barons resolved to go by sea. Venice was the city that seemed most able to furnish sufficient vessels. Accordingly, Ville-Hardouin and five other embassadors were sent to make a bargain with the Venetians. The official compact is given in full in Muratori: Rerum Italicarutn Scriptores, vol. xii, and in Bouquet: Rerum Gallicarum et Francicarum Scriptores, vol. xviii. The most important difference between that and Ville-Hardouin's version is that, according to the compact, the expedition was to start on St. Peter and St. Paul's day. For the events preliminary to the crusade, as well as for all the matters connected with it, consult Pears', The Fall of Constantinople, also reprinted in this edition.

The second extract relates to one of the most hotly debated subjects connected with the crusade. Did Venice treacherously make a treaty with the Sultan of Egypt? If she did, her conduct and the diversion of the crusade are more easily explained. (Pears) believes such a treaty was made, and quotes references to support his view. But Wailly, in a very able discussion, brings out the difficulty in reconciling the dates, and endeavours to show that this L'Estoire de Eracles is entirely untrustworthy. Consult also Heyd: Levantehandel, I.

The third extract is self-explanatory. Ville-Hardouin and Robert de Clari are the most important authorities for the fourth crusade. The first was one of the leaders and gave an official, "inspired" account. The second was one of the poorer knights and is especially useful as he told what the bulk of the army knew and thought, and enables us to check the statements of Ville-Hardouin.

1. The compact with the Venetians.
Ville-Hardouin: *Conquête de Constantinople.*

18. Sire, we have come to you in behalf of the noble barons of France who have taken the cross in order to avenge the shame of Jesus Christ and to reconquer Jerusalem, if God will permit. And because

they know no people who are as able to assist them as you and your people, they pray you, for God's sake, to pity the land of *Outre-mer* and the shame of Jesus Christ, and to endeavour to furnish them transports and ships of war."

19. "Under what conditions?" asked the *doge*.

"Under any conditions that you may propose or advise, if they are able to fulfil them," replied the messengers.

"Certainly," replied the *doge*, (to his associates) "it is a great undertaking that they have asked of us and they seem to be considering an important matter;" (to the messengers) "we will give you an answer in a week, and do not wonder if the time seems long, for such a great undertaking deserves much thought."

20. At the time fixed by the *doge*, they returned to the palace. I cannot tell you all that was said, but the conclusion of the conference was as follows:

"My lords," said the *doge*, "we will tell you what we have decided, if we can get the Grand Council and the people of the country to agree to it; and you shall decide whether you can fulfil your part.

21. "We will furnish *huissiers* (vessels having a door, *huis*, in the stern, which could be opened so as to take in the horses) for carrying 4,500 horses and 9,000 esquires, and vessels for 4,500 knights and 20,000 foot-soldiers. The agreement shall be to furnish food for nine months for all these horses and men. That is the least that we will do, on condition that we are paid four *marks* per horse and two *marks* per man.

22. "And we will observe all these conditions which we explain to you, for one year, beginning the day we leave the harbour of Venice to fight in the service of God and of Christianity, wherever we may go. The sum of these payments indicated above amounts to 85,000 *marks*. (According to Wailly, this sum would be equal to 4420,000 *francs* in silver.)

23. "And we will do still more: we will add fifty armed galleys, for the love of God; on the condition that as long as our alliance shall last, of every conquest of land or money that we make, by sea or land, we shall have one-half and you the other. Now deliberate whether you can fulfil these conditions."

24. The messengers went away, saying that they would talk it over and reply the next day. They consulted and discussed that night and then resolved to agree to it. The next day they went to the *doge* and

said: "Sire, we are ready to make this agreement." The *doge* said that he would speak to his people and tell them the result.

30. It was explained in council that they would go to Babylon, (Cairo), because at Babylon they could do more injury to the Turks than anywhere else. And in public it was announced that they would go across the sea. It was then Lent (March, 1201), and on St. John's Day the following year, the 1202nd year after the Incarnation of Jesus Christ, the barons and pilgrims were to be at Venice and the vessels were to be ready on their arrival.

2. Compact of the Venetians with the Sultan of Babylon.

L'Estoire de Eracles Empereur, xxviii, 2, in *Recueil des historiens des Croisades, hist, occ, II,*

(A. D. 1199?) After this he (the Sultan of Babylon) summoned messengers and servants and sent them to Venice, loaded with great wealth and great riches. He sent them to the doge and gave beautiful presents to the Venetians, and commanded the latter, if they could do so, not to go to the land of Egypt; he would give them great treasures and many privileges in the port of Alexandria. The messengers went to Venice, did as they were commanded, and returned as quickly as possible.

3. The Crusaders unable to pay the Venetians.

Robert de Clari: *La Prise de Constantinople,* xi and xii, in Hopf: *Chroniques Gréco-Romanes.*

XI. . . . . While the pilgrims were staying on the island of St. Nicholas, (the Lido), the Doge of Venice and the Venetians went to speak to them and demanded the pay for the navy which had been prepared. And the *doge* said to them that they had acted wrongly in commanding through their messengers that vessels should be prepared for 4,000 knights and their equipment, and for 100,000 foot-soldiers. Of these 4,000 knights, there were not more than 1,000 present, for the others had gone to other ports. And of these 100,000 foot-soldiers there were not more than 50,000 or 60,000.

"Nevertheless," said the *doge,* "we want you to pay us the sum which you promised." When the crusaders heard this, they debated and arranged that each knight should pay four *marks* and four *marks* for each horse, and each esquire two *marks*; and those who paid less, should pay one *mark.* When they collected this money, they paid it to the Venetians. But 50,000 *marks* still remained due.

When the *doge* and the Venetians saw that the pilgrims had not paid more, they were all so incensed that the *doge* said to the pilgrims:

"My Lords, you have imposed upon us, shamefully. For, as soon as your messengers had made the agreement with me and my people, I issued orders throughout my whole land that no merchant should undertake a voyage, but all were to aid in preparing this fleet. They have been waiting ever since and have gained nothing for the last year and a half; and, accordingly, they have lost much. Therefore my men and I want you to pay us the money which you owe us. If you do not pay us, you shall not leave this island before we get our money; and no one shall bring you anything to eat or drink"

The *doge*, however, was a very excellent man and did not prevent the people from bringing enough food and drink.

XII. When the count and the crusaders heard what the *doge* said they were much troubled and grieved. They made another collection and borrowed all the money they could from those who were thought to have any. They paid it all to the Venetians, but after this payment 36,000 *marks* still remained due. They said to the Venetians that they had been imposed upon; that the army was greatly impoverished by this last collection; that they could not pay any more money at all, for they had hardly enough to support the army.

When the *doge* perceived that they could not pay all the money and that they were in sore straits, he said to his people:

"Sirs, if we let these people go back to their own country, we shall always be considered base and tricky. Let us go to them and say that, if they are willing to pay us the 36,000 *marks* which they owe us out of their part of the first conquests which we make, we will carry them across the sea."

The Venetians were well pleased with the *doge*'s proposition. Accordingly, they went to the camp of the pilgrims. When they came thither, the *doge* said to the crusaders:

"Sires, we have agreed, I and my people, that if you are willing to guarantee faithfully to pay us the 36,000 *marks*, which you owe us, out of your share of the first conquests, we will carry you across the sea."

When the crusaders heard what the *doge* proposed they were very glad and fell at his feet for joy. They bound themselves very willingly to do faithfully what the *doge* had proposed. They were so joyous that night that there was no one so poor that he did not make a great illumination, and each one carried great torches made of candles on the end of his lance, both outside of the camp and inside, so that the whole army seemed intoxicated.

2. The Diversion to Zara.

According to Robert de Clari there were two separate propositions made by the doge; the one, given above, which was received so joyfully, and a second, given below, which was kept secret. Ville-Hardouin would have us understand that there was but one proposition, namely, to capture Zara. In fact, the official account given by Ville-Hardouin differs in many respects from the non-official versions of Robert, Gunther and others. Gunther describes how unwilling many were to go to Zara. The pope, who had learned something of the plan, protested vigorously against an attack on a Christian city. We see clearly from Ville-Hardouin's own account, given in the second extract, that there were many in the army opposed to the plan.

1. The new agreement with the Venetians.
Robert de Qari, in Hopf: *Chroniques.*

Afterwards the *doge* came to the army and said:

"Sirs, it is now winter, we cannot cross the sea, nor does this depend upon me. For I would have had you cross already, if it had not depended upon you. But let us do the best we can. There is a city near here, named Zara. The people of this city have done us much evil, and I and my men want to punish them, if we can. If you will take my advice, we will go there this winter and stay until Easter. Then we will make ready our navy and go to *Outre-mer* at Lady-day. The city of Zara is very rich and well supplied with all kinds of provisions." The barons and the nobles among the crusaders agreed to what the *doge* proposed. But no one in the army knew this plan, except the leaders.

2. The capture of Zara.
Ville-Hardouin

80. The day after the feast of St. Martin, (Nov. 12, 1202), some people from Zara came to speak to the *doge* of Venice, who was in his tent. They said to him that they would surrender the city and all their property to his mercy, if their lives were spared. The *doge* said that he would not accept these or any other conditions without the advice of the counts and barons, and that he would go and discuss the matter with them.

81. While he went to talk to the counts and barons, that party, of which I have already spoken, who wanted to break up the army, said to the messengers:

"Why do you want to surrender your city? The pilgrims will not attack you and you have nothing to fear from them. If you can defend yourselves against the Venetians, you need have no anxiety."

And they sent one of them, Robert de Boves, who went to the walls of the city and announced the same thing. So, the messengers returned to the city and the plan of surrender was given up.

82. The Doge of Venice, when he came to the counts and barons, said to them:

"Sirs, the people yonder want to surrender the city to my mercy, on condition that their lives be spared. But I will not make this agreement or any other without your advice."

The barons replied: "Sire, we advise you to make this agreement and we pray you to do so." He said he would, and they all went back together to the *doge's* tent to make this agreement. They found that the messengers had gone away, following the advice of those who wanted to break up the army.

83. Then the Abbot of Vaux of the order of Citeaux rose and said to them: "Sirs, I forbid you, in the name of the Pope at Rome, to attack this city; for the inhabitants are Christians and you are pilgrims."

When the *doge* heard this, he was much irritated and troubled. He said to the counts and barons: "Sirs, this city was practically in my power, and your people have taken it from me; you had promised that you would aid me in conquering it; now I require you to do so."

84. Then the counts and barons and those who belonged to their party held a conference and said: "Those who have prevented this agreement have committed a very great outrage, and it was not right for them to try to break up the army. Now we shall be disgraced, if we do not aid in capturing the city." They went to the *doge* and said to him: "Sire, we will aid you in capturing the city, in spite of those who wish to prevent it."

86. Accordingly the city was surrendered to the mercy of the *doge* of Venice, on condition that the lives of the inhabitants should be spared. Then the *doge* went to the counts and barons and said to them: "Sirs, we have conquered this city, by the grace of God and through your aid. It is now winter and we cannot leave here until Easter. For we should find no provisions elsewhere; and this city is very rich and very well supplied with everything needful. Let us divide it accordingly into two parts; we will take one-half of it and you the other half."

3. THE DIVERSION TO CONSTANTINOPLE.

Pears discusses the causes of the diversion and gives the most important references. But he has formed his own conclusions and argues for his own belief.

1. The summons to Alexis,
Robert de Clari, xvi-xvii, in Hopf: *Chroniques.*

XVI. In the meantime the crusaders and the Venetians remained at Zara during the winter. They considered how great the expense had been and said to one another that they could not go to Babylon or Alexandria or Syria; for they had neither provisions nor money for the journey. They had already used up everything they had, either during the sojourn that they had made or in the great price that they had paid for the vessels. They said that they could not go and, even if they should go, they would accomplish nothing; they had neither provisions nor money sufficient to support them.

XVII. The Doge of Venice saw clearly that the pilgrims were ill at ease. He addressed them, saying: "Sirs, Greece is a very rich land and bountifully supplied with everything. If we can find a sufficient excuse for going there and taking food and other things, so as to recuperate ourselves, it would seem to me advisable, and then we could easily go across the sea."

Then the marquis (Boniface, Marquis of Montferrat, the leader of the crusaders), rose and said: "Sir, I was in Germany at the emperor's (Philip of Suabia), court last Christmas. There I saw a young man who was the emperor's brother-in-law. (Alexis IV., brother of the Queen Irene.) This young man was the son of the Emperor Kyrsae (Isaac II. Angelos) of Constantinople from whom his brother had taken the empire of Constantinople by treason. Whoever could get this young man could certainly go to the land of Constantinople and take provisions and other things; for this young man is the rightful heir."

2, The proposition made by King Philip.
Ville-Hardouin

91. "My Lords, king Philip sends us to you and sends also the son of the emperor of Constantinople, who is his wife's brother.

92. "My Lords, says the king, I shall send you my wife's brother; I place him in the hands of God (may He preserve him from death!), and in your hands. Since you are fighting for God, for the right and for justice, you ought, if it lies in your power, to restore to their inheritance those who have been wrongfully dispossessed. He (Alexis) will make with you the best agreement which has ever been made by any one, and he will give you the most powerful aid in conquering the land of *Outre-mer.*

93. "In the first place, if God permits you to restore him to his in-

heritance, he will put all the empire of Romania under the obedience of Rome, from which it has been separated for a long time. In the second place, he knows that you have spent your property and that you are poor; he will give you 200,000 *marks* of silver and provisions for all the members of the army, humble and noble. He will himself go with you to the land of Babylon or will send thither with you (if you think it better) 10,000 men at his expense. This service he will perform for you during one year. And so long as he lives, he will maintain at his own expense 500 knights in the land of *Outre-mer*, to guard the land.

94. "My Lords, we have full power," said the messengers, "to make this agreement, if you wish to do so. And be sure that such a fine offer was never made to anyone, and he who refuses this can have no great desire to conquer." The leaders said that they would discuss the matter, and an assembly was appointed for the next day. When the host had assembled, this offer was presented to them.

95. There it was hotly discussed, "*pro* and *con.*" The Abbot of Vaux of the order of Citeaux and the party that wanted to break up the army said that they would not agree to it; it was fighting against Christians; they had not set out for this purpose, but they wanted to go to Syria.

96. The other party replied: "Good sirs, in Syria you can do nothing, you can see that clearly from those who have left us and gone to other ports. You know that it is through the land of Babylon or through Greece that the land of *Outre-mer* will be reconquered, if it is ever recovered. If we refuse this offer, we shall always be ashamed."

97. The army was in discord just as you have heard. And do not wonder that the laymen could not agree; for the white monks of the order of Citeaux in the army were also in discord. The Abbot of Loos, who was a very holy and excellent man, and the other abbots who agreed with him, preached to the people and cried out to them to have mercy, saying that, for God's sake, they ought to keep the army together and to make this agreement; "for it is the best means of recovering the land of *Outre-mer.*" And the Abbot of Vaux in his turn, and those who agreed with him, preached very frequently and said that that was all wrong; that they ought to go to the land of Syria and do what they could.

98. Then the Marquis Boniface of Montferrat, Baldwin, count of Flanders and Hainault, Count Louis and Count Hugh of St. Pol and those who belonged to their party went and said that they would make this agreement; for they would be ashamed to refuse it. So, they

went to the *doge's* lodging and the messengers were summoned. They concluded the agreement, just as you have heard it above, by their oaths and by sealed compacts.

99. And in regard to this matter, the book tells you that there were only twelve of the French who made their oaths; and they could not get any more. Of these, the first was the Marquis of Montferrat, Count Baldwin of Flanders, Count Louis of Blois and Chartres, the Count of St. Pol, and eight others who agreed with them. So, the compact was made, the securities given, and the time fixed when the heir of Constantinople should come; it was to be a fortnight after Easter.

3. The discussion after the arrival of Alexis.
Robert de Clari, xxxiii, in *Hopf: Chroniques.*

Then all the barons of the army and the Venetians were summoned. When they had all assembled, the *doge* of Venice rose and said to them: "My lords, we have now a sufficient excuse for going to Constantinople, if you think it wise, for we have the lawful heir." Now some who did not want to go to Constantinople, spoke thus: "Bah! what are we going to do at Constantinople? We have our pilgrimage to make and intend to go to Babylon or Alexandria. Our ships are rented for only one year and the year is already half over."

The others said in reply: "What are we going to do at Babylon or Alexandria, since we have neither provisions nor money enough to go? It is better to go where we have a sufficient excuse for obtaining money and provisions by conquest, than to go where we shall die of hunger. Then we can do it, and he offers to go with us and to pay for our ships and our navy another year at his own expense." And the Marquis of Montferrat did all in his power to urge our going to Constantinople, because he wished to take vengeance for a wrong which the emperor of Constantinople had done him.

4. The Difficulties with Alexis.

It had been very easy for Alexis in exile to make great promises. When his father was replaced on the throne and he himself was crowned co-emperor, they found it absolutely impossible to fulfil the conditions which Alexis had offered, and to which Isaac had been obliged to agree.

1. The first payment.
Robert de Gari, lvi, in *Hopf: Chroniques.*

Afterwards all the barons assembled one day at the palace of the emperor (Alexis, the crusaders rarely speak of Isaac as emperor), and demanded of him their pay. He replied that he would pay them, but he wished first to be crowned. Accordingly, they made preparations and set a day for the coronation. On that day he was crowned emperor with due ceremony, with the consent of his father, who willingly granted it. After he had been crowned the barons demanded their pay. He said he would very willingly pay what he could and at that time he paid 100,000 *marks*. Of this sum the Venetians received one-half; for they were to receive one-half of the conquests. Of the 50,000 which remained, 36,000, which the Franks still owed for the vessels, were paid to the Venetians. And all those who had advanced money to pay for the passage were paid out of the 14,000 *marks* which the pilgrims had left.

2. The public defiance.
Ville-Hardouin.

212. They dismounted from their horses at the gate, entered the palace and found the emperor Alexis and the Emperor Isaac, his father, seated upon two thrones, side by side. Near them was seated the empress, who was the father's wife, the son's stepmother, and the sister of the King of Hungary; a beautiful and good lady. A great number of nobles were with them; and it certainly seemed the court of a rich prince.

213. According to the agreement with the other messengers, (Ville-Hardouin was one of the messengers), Conon of Bethune, who was very rich and very eloquent, spoke: "Sire, we have been sent to you by the barons of the army and by the Doge of Venice. Know that they reproach you because of the great service which they have done you, which everybody knows and which is apparent to you. You have sworn to them, you and your father, to keep the agreement that you have made with them; and they have your written compact. You have not kept your agreement with them as you ought.

214. "They have summoned you many times, and we summon you in their name, before all your barons, to keep the agreement which you have made with them. If you do so, all will be well; if you do not keep it, know that in the future they will consider you neither as lord nor as friend; but they will try to get their rights in any way they can. They announce to you that they would injure neither you, nor anyone else, before the defiance; for they have never acted treasonably, and in their country, it is not the custom to do so. You have heard what we have said to you and you can do as you please."

215. The Greeks marvelled much at this defiance and great insult. They said that no one had ever been so bold before as to defy the Emperor of Constantinople in his own halls. The Emperor Alexis looked savagely at the messengers, and so did all the Greeks, though they had on many occasions in the past looked very friendly.

3. The doge's threat.
Robert de Clari, lix, in Hopf: *Chroniques.*

At these words the barons left the palace and returned to their camp. After returning they deliberated upon the course to follow. Meanwhile they sent two knights to the emperor and demanded again that he should pay them. He replied to the messengers that he would pay nothing, he had already paid too much, and that he was not afraid of anyone. He also commanded them to go away and leave his land; they were to understand that if they did not depart, he would injure them. Then the messengers went back and told the barons the emperor's reply. When the barons heard this, they deliberated as to what they should do. The *doge* said that he wanted to speak to the emperor.

He sent a messenger to demand that the emperor should come to the harbour to speak to him. The emperor went on horseback. The *doge* prepared four armed galleys; he went in one and took the other three for protection. When he was near the shore, he saw the emperor who had come on horseback. He addressed the latter as follows:

"Alexis, what do you think you are going to do? Remember we have raised you from a very humble estate. We have made you lord and crowned you emperor. Will you not keep your agreement with us and will you not do more?"

"No," replied the emperor, "I will not do anything more."

"No?" said the *doge*, "wretched boy, we have raised you from the mire, (a coarse expression in the original), and we will throw you into the mire again; and be sure that I will do you all the injury that I can, from this time on."

5. The Sack of Constantine

In spite of the previous dissensions the crusaders were practically compelled to act as a unit in the final attack on Constantinople. Some of those who had been most opposed to the diversion of the expedition had left the army. The argument employed by the bishops in the first extract seems to have removed doubts still lingering in the minds of many.

The compact of division was made before the capture of the city. Ville-Hardouin's account is followed because it is accurate and brief.

The account of the sack, given by Nicetas, is not exaggerated, as is proved by the letters of Innocent III. (especially Bk. viii, Ep.), and the statement of many other contemporaries; see Riant: Exuviae sacrae Constantinopolitanae, passim. We regret that we have not space for other extracts from Nicetas, such as his account of how he saved his future bride when she was being carried off by a crusader; his description of the statues that were destroyed (Pears, translates his account of Helen), and many other picturesque passages. Gibbon, Ch. LX, can still be read with profit. Wilken: Geschichte der Kreuzzüge, gives a long account of the destruction of the works of art in the "Beylagen." References might be indefinitely multiplied, but Riant: Exuviae contains the most important.

The last two extracts are added because they show so fully the feelings of the age and give some indication of the immense quantity of relics brought from Constantinople.

1. The sermons before the final attack on Constantinople.
Robert de Clari, ch. lxxii-lxxiii, in Hopf: *Chroniques*

LXXII. When the pilgrims saw this, (that the attack was repulsed), they were very angry and grieved much; they went back from the other side of the harbour. to their lodgings. When the barons had returned and had gotten ashore, they assembled and were much amazed, and said that it was on account of their sins that they did not succeed in anything and could not capture the city. Meanwhile the bishops and the clergy in the army debated and decided that the war was a righteous one, and that" they certainly ought to attack the Greeks. For formerly the inhabitants of the city had been obedient to the law of Rome and now they were disobedient, since they said that the law of Rome was of no account, and called all who believed in it "dogs." And the bishops said that for this reason one ought certainly to attack them, and that it was not a sin, but an act of great charity.

LXXIII. Then it was announced to all the host that all the Venetians and everyone else should go and hear the sermons on Sunday morning, (Apr. 11, 1204); and they did so. Then the bishops preached to the army, the Bishop of Soissons, the Bishop of Troyes, the Bishop of Havestaist (Halberstadt) Master Jean Faicette, (De Noyon, Chancellor of Baldwin of Flanders) and the Abbot of Loos, and they showed to the pilgrims that the war was a righteous one; for the Greeks were traitors and murderers, and also disloyal, since they had murdered their rightful lord, and were worse than Jews.

Moreover, the bishops said that, by the authority of God and in the name of the pope, they would absolve all who attacked the Greeks.

Then the bishops commanded the pilgrims to confess their sins and receive the communion devoutly; and said that they ought not to hesitate to attack the Greeks, for the latter were enemies of God. They also commanded that all the evil women should be sought out and sent away from the army to a distant place. This was done; the evil women were all put on a vessel and were sent very far away from the army.

2. The compact of division,
Ville-Hardouin, ch. li.

234. Then the members of the host debated and consulted upon the best course to pursue. The discussion was long and stormy, but the following was the result of the deliberation: If God granted that they should capture the city, all the booty that was taken should be brought together and divided fairly, as was fitting. And, if they captured the city, six men (Robert de Clari says ten), should be chosen from the Franks (collective name for all the crusaders), and six from the Venetians; these were to take oath upon relics that they would elect as emperor him whom they should judge to be the most useful for the good of the land.

And he whom they chose as emperor should have one-quarter of all the conquests both in the city and outside; and in addition he should have the palace of the Lion's mouth and of Blachern. The other three-quarters should be divided into two parts, one-half for the Venetians and one-half for the crusaders. Then twelve from the wisest of the army of the pilgrims and twelve of the Venetians should be chosen to divide the fiefs and the offices among the men and to define the feudal service which each one owed to the emperor.

235. This compact was guaranteed and sworn to both by the Franks and the Venetians, with the condition that anyone who wished could go away within one year from the end of March. Those who remained in the country must perform the feudal service to the emperor, as it might be arranged. Then the compact was made and sworn to and all who should not keep it were excommunicated by the clergy.

3. Account of the sack
Nicetas: *Alexii Ducae Impcrium*, ch. iii-iv, in *Recueil des historiens des Croisades, hist, grec.*

3. How shall I begin to tell of the deeds wrought by these nefarious men! Alas, the images, which ought to have been adored, were trodden underfoot! Alas, the relics of the holy martyrs were thrown

into unclean places! Then was seen what one shudders to hear, namely, the divine body and blood of Christ was spilled upon the ground or thrown about. They snatched the precious reliquaries, thrust into their bosoms the ornaments which these contained, and used the broken remnants for pans and drinking cups,—precursors of Anti-Christ, authors and heralds of his nefarious deeds which we momentarily expect. Manifestly, indeed, by that race then, just as formerly, Christ was robbed and insulted and His garments were divided by lot; only one thing was lacking, that His side, pierced by a spear, should pour rivers of divine blood on the ground.

Nor can the violation of the Great Church (St. Sophia), be listened to with equanimity. For the sacred altar, formed of all kinds of precious materials and admired by the whole world, was broken into bits and distributed among the soldiers, as was all the other sacred wealth of so great and infinite splendour.

When the sacred vases and utensils of unsurpassable art and grace and rare material, and the fine silver, wrought with gold, which encircled the screen of the tribunal and the ambo, of admirable workmanship, and the door and many other ornaments, were to be borne away as booty, mules and saddled horses were led to the very sanctuary of the temple. Some of these which were unable to keep their footing on the splendid and slippery pavement, were stabbed when they fell, so that the sacred pavement was polluted with blood and filth.

4. Nay more, a certain harlot, a sharer in their guilt, a minister of the furies, a servant of the demons, a worker of incantations and poisonings, insulting Christ, sat in the *patriarch's* seat, singing an obscene song and dancing frequently. Nor, indeed, were these crimes committed and others left undone, on the ground that these were of lesser guilt, the others of greater. But with one consent all the most heinous sins and crimes were committed by all with equal zeal. Could those, who showed so great madness against God Himself, have spared the honourable matrons and maidens or the virgins consecrated to God?

Nothing was more difficult and laborious than to soften by prayers, to render benevolent, these wrathful barbarians, vomiting forth bile at every unpleasing word, so that nothing failed to inflame their fury. Whoever attempted it was derided as insane and a man of intemperate language. Often, they drew their daggers against anyone who opposed them at all or hindered their demands.

No one was without a share in the grief. In the alleys, in the streets, in the temples, complaints, weeping, lamentations, grief, the groaning of men, the shrieks of women, wounds, rape, captivity, the separation of those most closely united. Nobles wandered about ignominiously, those of venerable age in tears, the rich in poverty. Thus, it was in the streets, on the corners, in the temple, in the dens, for no place remained unassailed or defended the suppliants. All places everywhere were filled full of all kinds of crime. Oh, immortal God, how great the afflictions of the men, how great the distress!

4. Abbot Martin's theft of relics

Gunther: *Historia Constantinopolitana*, ch. xix, in Riant: *Exuviae*, Vol. 1.

While the victors were rapidly plundering the conquered city, which was theirs by right of conquest, the Abbot Martin began to cogitate about his own share of the booty, and lest he alone should remain empty-handed, while all the others became rich, he resolved to seize upon plunder with his own sacred hands. But since he thought it not meet to handle any booty of worldly things with those sacred hands, he began to plan how he might secure some portion of the relics of the saints, of which he knew there was a great quantity in the city.

Accordingly, having a presentiment of some great result, he took with him one of his two chaplains and went to a church (Pantokrator), which was held in great reverence because in it the mother (Irene, died 1124), of the most famous Emperor Manuel (Manuel I. Komnenos), had a noble grave, which seemed of importance to the Greeks, but ours held for naught. There a very great amount of money brought in from all the surrounding country was stored; and also, precious relics which the vain hope of security had caused them to bring in from the neighbouring churches and monasteries. Those whom the Greeks had driven out, had told us of this before the capture of the city. When many pilgrims broke into this church and some were eagerly engaged in stealing gold and silver, others precious stones, Martin, thinking it unbecoming to commit sacrilege except in a holy cause, sought a more retired spot where the very sanctity of the place seemed to promise that what he desired might be found.

There he found an aged man of agreeable countenance, having a long and hoary beard, a priest, but very unlike our priests in his dress. Thinking him a layman, the abbot, though inwardly calm, threatened him with a very ferocious voice, saying: "Come, perfidious old man, show me the most powerful relics you have, or you shall die immediately." The latter, terrified by the sound rather than the words, since he heard but did not understand what was said, and knowing that Martin could not speak Greek, began in the *Romana lingua*, of which he knew a little, to entreat Martin and by soft words to turn away the latter's wrath, which in truth did not exist.

In reply, the abbot succeeded in getting out a few words of the same language, sufficient to make the old man understand what he wanted. The latter, observing Martin's face and dress, and thinking it more tolerable that a religious man should handle the sacred relics with fear and reverence, than that worldly men should, perchance, pollute them with their worldly hands, opened a chest bound with iron and showed the desired treasure, which was more grateful and pleasing to Martin than all the royal wealth of Greece. The abbot hastily and eagerly thrust in both hands and working quickly, filled with the fruits of the sacrilege both his own and his chaplain's bosom. He wisely concealed what seemed the most valuable and departed without opposition.

Moreover, what and how worthy of veneration those relics which the holy robber appropriated were, is told more fully at the end of this work. (See no. 5 below). When he was hastening to his vessel, so stuffed full, if I may use the expression, those who knew and loved him, saw him from their ships as they were themselves hastening to the booty, and inquired joyfully whether he had stolen anything, or with what he was so loaded down as he walked. With a joyful countenance, as always, and with pleasant words he said: "We have done well." To which they replied: "Thanks be to God."

5. List of relics stolen by Abbot Martin
Gunther, ch. xxiv, in *Riant: Exuviae*, Vol. 1.

Therefore "Blessed be the Lord God, who only doeth wondrous things," who in His unspeakable kindness and mercy has looked upon and made glorious His church at Paris (in upper Elsass), through certain gifts of His grace, which he deigned to transmit to us through the venerable man, already so frequently mentioned, Abbot Martin. In the presence of these the church exults and by their protection any soul faithful to God is aided and assisted. In order that the readers' trust in these may be strengthened, we have determined to give a partial list.

First, of the highest importance and worthy of all veneration: A trace of the blood of our Lord Jesus Christ, which was shed for the redemption of all mankind.

Second, a piece of the cross of our Lord on which the Son of the

Father, the new Adam, sacrificed for us, paid the debt of the old Adam.

Third, a not inconsiderable piece of St. John, the fore-runner of our Lord.

Fourth, the arm of St. James, the Apostle, whose memory is venerated by the whole church.

There were also relics of the other saints, whose names are as follows:

Christopher, the martyr.
George, the martyr.
Theodore, the martyr.
The foot of St. Cosmas, the martyr.
Part of the head of Cyprian, the martyr.
Pantaleon, the martyr.
A tooth of St. Lawrence.
Demetrius, the martyr.
Stephen, the proto-martyr.
Vincentius, Adjutus, Mauritius and his companions.
Crisantius and Darius, the martyrs.
Gervasius and Protasius, the martyrs.
Primus, the martyr.
Sergius and Bacchus, the martyrs.
Protus, the martyr.
John and Paul, the martyrs.

Also relics from the following: the place of the Nativity of our Lord; Calvary; our Lord's Sepulchre; the stone rolled away; the place of our Lord's Ascension; the stone on which John stood when he baptised the Lord; the spot where Christ raised Lazarus; the stone on which Christ was presented in the temple; the stone on which Jacob slept; the stone where Christ fasted; the stone where Christ prayed; the table on which Christ ate the supper; the place where He was captured; the place where the mother of our Lord died; His grave; the grave of St. Peter, the apostle; the relics of the holy apostles, Andrew and Philip; the place where the Lord gave the law to Moses; the holy *patriarchs*, Abraham, Isaac and Jacob; St. Nicholas, the bishop; Adelasius, the bishop; Agricius, the bishop; John Chrysostom; John, the almsgiver; the milk of the mother of our Lord; Margaret, the virgin; Perpetua, the virgin; Agatha, the virgin; Agnes, the virgin; Lucia, the virgin; Cecilia, the virgin; Adelgundis and Euphemia, the virgins.

Written and sealed—in this year of our Lord's Incarnation, 1205, in the reign of Philip, King of the Romans, Innocent the Supreme *Pontiff* presiding over the holy Roman church—under the direction of the Bishops Lutholdus of Basel and Henry of Strassburg.

6. Attitude of Innocent III.

This has given rise to much discussion. He was very anxious for a new crusade, and offered large privileges (see Ville-Hardouin, ch. 1, No. 2). He wrote:

"If men perish, if the churches are weakened, if the poor are oppressed, all this is of less consequence than the loss of Palestine." (See Pears.)

But he seems to have mistrusted the Venetians (see Gesta Inn., No. 84), and did not heartily approve of the arrangements made. He felt very indignant at the capture of Zara; "Satan has impelled you to turn your swords against a Christian people. You have offered to the devil the first fruits of your pilgrimage."

He excommunicated all who took part in the capture and released the crusaders from the ban only under necessity. The Venetians were still excommunicated. He commanded them not to go to Constantinople, and was extremely indignant at the first attack on that city. Even after the final capture of Constantinople and the restoration of the Greek church to obedience to Rome, he seems to have regretted the failure of the crusade. He continues his reproaches, although he seems to have believed that the divine Providence had miraculously used the deeds of sinful men for its own good purpose.

1. Crusaders to stay at Constantinople.

Epistolae, Bk. viii, No. 63, in Tessier: *Diversion*, etc.

To all the clergy and people in the Christian Army at Constantinople.

If the Lord had granted the desires of His humble servants sooner, and had transferred, as He has now done, the Empire of Constantinople from the Greeks to the Latins before the fall of the Holy Land, perhaps Christianity would not be weeping today over the desolation of the land of Jerusalem.

Since, therefore, through the wonderful transference of this empire God has deigned to open to you a way to recover that land, and the detention of this may lead to the restoration of that, we advise and exhort you all, and we enjoin upon you for the remission of your sins, to remain for a year in Romania, in order to strengthen the empire in its devotion to the Apostolic See and to us, and in order to retain it in the power of the Latins; and to give wise advice and efficient aid to Baldwin, our most beloved, son in Christ, the illustrious Emperor of Constantinople; unless, perchance, your presence in the Holy Land should be necessary before that time, in which case you ought to hasten to guard it before the year elapses.

Dated, ... (Potthast: *Regesta pont. Rom.*, No. 2507, gives date as possibly May 20, 1205.)

The Final Crusades
T. A. Archer

THE KINGDOM OF ACRE—THE STRUGGLE FOR RECOVERY, (1192-1244)

Saladin did not long survive the conclusion of the Third Crusade. Early in November, 1192, he left Palestine for Damascus, where, despite ill health, he spent the winter in hunting. When Baha-ed-din rejoined him in February, he remarked that his master had lost his old elasticity of spirit. On February 19th the illness took a serious form, and a fortnight later terminated fatally. Baha-ed-din writes:

Never since the death of the first four *caliphs*, had religion and the faithful received such a blow.

Saladin had won the respectful admiration of Christian and Moslem alike. Both in history and romance his name has always been coupled with that of his great rival Richard. Hubert Walter said:

Could each be endowed with the faculties of the other, the whole world could not furnish two such princes.

A Western legend, of somewhat later date, is so eminently characteristic of Saladin that it deserves repetition. When Saladin lay dying, he charged his standard-bearer, saying:

As thou didst bear my banner in war, bear also my banner of death. And let it be a vile rag, which thou must bear through all Damascus set upon a lance, crying, 'Lo! at his death the lord of the East could take nothing with him save this cloth only.'

Saladin's dominions were divided at his death. His sons, El-Afdal, El-Aziz, and Ez-Zahir, became Lords of Damascus, Egypt, and Aleppo. His brother, El-Adel, ruled at Kerak, and his great-nephews, Shirkuh and El-Mansur, at Emesa and Hamah. But this arrangement did not long subsist, for El-Adel first expelled El-Afdal from Damascus, and afterwards, in February, 1200, from Egypt, where the latter prince had become guardian for his infant nephew, El-Mansur. Two years later, by the subjection of Ez-Zahir, El-Adel became, like his brother before him, lord supreme of Syria, Mesopotamia, and Egypt. At his death, on August 31, 1218, the Moslem lands were once more divided, but his descendants reigned as *Sultans* of Egypt with more or less power for thirty years afterwards.

For the Franks the years that followed on the death of Saladin were disturbed only by disputes between the military orders and the warfare of Bohemond of Antioch with the Christian prince of Armenia. But if the Syrian Franks were content to enjoy what they still possessed, the opportunity afforded by the death of Saladin did not pass unheeded in Western Europe. Pope Celestine III. renewed his endeavours in the cause of the Holy War. In France and England, he met with little success; Philip was too intent on his ambitious projects, and Richard too busy counteracting them, whilst their subjects had too lively a recollection of their recent sufferings.

But in Germany the Pope's appeal accorded with the emperor's designs on Sicily and Constantinople. In 1196, Henry entered Italy at the head of forty thousand men, intending to proceed by sea to Palestine as soon as he had secured his authority in his wife's kingdom. He was destined to accomplish only the first part of his plan, but a large contingent of German Crusaders came to Acre late in 1197, under the leadership of Conrad of Wurzburg. Somewhat against the will of the native lords, the war was renewed; El-Adel at once retaliated by an attack on Jaffa; before the Franks could come to the rescue from Acre, Henry of Champagne was killed by a fall, and during the confusion consequent on his death, Jaffa was taken by the Saracen.

Isabella now bestowed her hand and kingdom on Amalric de Lusignan, who two years previously had succeeded his brother Guy as ruler of Cyprus. Encouraged by the arrival of a fresh force of Crusaders from Northern Germany, the new king resolved to attack Beyrout. The Saracens abandoned the city in panic, and about the same time a Crusading army won a great victory over El-Adel between Tyre and Sidon. These successes were followed by the recovery of all the coast towns, and the Crusaders had laid siege to Toron, when in December, 1197, the news of the emperor's death called the Germans home. The partial success of this Crusade was thus marred by its hasty termination, which left the recovered territory without defenders in the face of an embittered foe.

Next year (1198) the preaching of a French priest, Fulk of Neuilly, stirred up a new Crusade. Fulk was credited with strangely miraculous powers; he cured the blind and the lame, at his bidding the prostitute forsook her calling and the usurer his treasure. Even before kings he was not ashamed, and in God's name bade Richard of England provide for his three daughters.

"Liar!" said the angry king, "I have no daughter."

"Nay! thou hast three evil daughters—Pride, Lust, and Luxury."

With mocking words Richard turned to his courtiers:

He bids me marry my daughters. I give Pride to the Templars, Lust to the Cistercians, and Luxury to the prelates.

Fulk's efforts were aided by the new Pope, Innocent III., who mourned over the return of the Germans after such slight achievements, and endeavoured to make peace between the kings of France and England.

The kings turned a deaf ear to priest and Pope alike, but many of the great French nobles did under Fulk's influence, take the Cross. Foremost were Baldwin of Flanders and his brother Henry, Theobald of Champagne and his cousin Louis of Blois, the Count of St. Pol, Simon de Montfort, and John de Nesles. But the expedition was long delayed, and only started in 1202. Fulk meantime had died of grief, and though the treasure he had collected was sent over sea to Palestine, his projected Crusade proved, so far as the Holy Land was concerned, a miserable failure. The great part of the Crusaders allowed themselves to be diverted from their proper aim, and after conquering Zara for the Venetians, sailed against Constantinople. How they captured that city, chose Baldwin for emperor, and portioned out the European lands of the Eastern Empire amongst themselves, belongs to another story. (See Mr. C. W. C. Oman's *The Byzantine Empire*.)

A smaller force, however, passed through the Straits of Gibraltar, and under the leadership of Reginald de Dampierre reached Palestine in 1203. Some plundering raids were followed by concessions on the part of El-Adel, who surrendered Nazareth and concluded peace. Reginald, in wrath, went off to join Bohemond of Antioch; on his way he fell into an ambush, and of all his army only a single knight escaped. When, a little later, John de Nesles reached Acre with a further contingent, he also went north to aid the Prince of Antioch in his warfare with Armenia.

During the last years of the twelfth century the power of the Christian princes of Armenia had much increased. After long disputes between the kinsmen of Thoros, a prince called Rupin secured the throne about 1175. Rupin acquired Tarsus from Bohemond III., and ruled on the whole prosperously till 1188. His successor and brother, Leo, though married to a niece of Bohemond, sought to secure the independence of his country, which up to this time had been subject to the princes of Antioch. Bohemond treacherously endeavoured to capture Leo at a conference, but the Armenian, suspicious of his host, had taken such precautions that it was Bohemond, and not Leo, who became the prisoner. As the price of Bohemond's release, Leo was confirmed in his conquests and independence, and a few years later, in 1198, was anointed king by the German chancellor, Conrad of Wurzburg. (The date is not certain; it may be 1199. Another account makes Conrad of Mentz perform the coronation. Leo seems to have held his crown as vassal of the emperor and Pope.)

The death of Bohemond III. in 1201, was followed by further wars, for Leo supported the claims of his nephew Rupin, the child of the late princes elder son, Raymond, against the new prince, Bohemond IV. It was to aid in this warfare that John de Nesles went north in 1203. (Rupin contested Antioch till his death in 1222, when Bohemond IV. became undisputed prince.)

The close of the twelfth century had been grievous for the East. Egypt was vexed with a sore famine, and the consequent pestilence spread into Syria, so that all the lands from the Euphrates to the Nile were filled with mourning and desolation. Next year a terrible earthquake ruined almost all the cities of Palestine, with the exception of Jerusalem. The treasure collected by Fulk of Neuilly now proved of timely service for the rebuilding of the walls of Acre.

The pressure of these calamities did not avail to enforce observance of the truce. Amalric's Cypriote subjects were vexed by piratical Egyptian galleys, and when El-Adel would make no restitution, the king retaliated by a series of raids, which extended even to the east of Jordan. But eventually the truce was renewed for five years. A little later, in 1205, Amalric died, leaving an infant son, Amalric III.; but the youthful king and his mother both died within the year. The throne then passed to Mary, Isabella's eldest daughter by Conrad of Montferrat. John of Ibelin was made bailiff for the little queen, and Philip of France was asked to recommend a suitable husband. His choice fell on John de Brienne—an experienced warrior, but not a man of any great rank.

John accepted the proposal, and after some delay, with the aid of money lent him by the French king and the Pope, equipped three hundred knights, with which little force he reached Acre on September 14, 1210. (This date is almost certainly correct, though some authorities give 1209, or even 1208.) On the following day he was married to the young Queen Mary, and a week later was crowned with his wife at Tyre.

Before John's arrival in Palestine the Christians had refused to renew the truce. But though the new king took the field with courage, he presently found himself unable to cope with his powerful foe, the more so as most of his own knights had soon returned to Europe. Accordingly, in 1212, he appealed to the Pope to send him fresh succour from the West.

Innocent III. had long desired to make good the unhappy Crusade of 1203, but the intervening years had not been propitious. The death of Henry VI. had left Sicily with a child ruler, and Germany with a disputed succession. Both in France and England the Pope was involved in a serious quarrel with the royal power. But although these troubles hampered the execution of Innocent's projects, he did not abandon them.

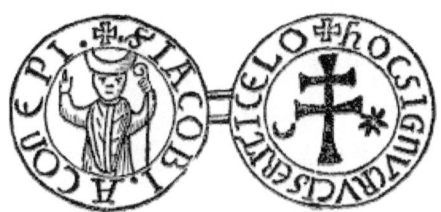

SEAL OF JAMES DE VITRY.

SEAL OF JAMES DE VITRY . . . . .
He was a Cardinal, and Bishop of Acre from about 1217 to 1229. James de Vitry was the historian of the Fifth Crusade, and indeed of the whole kingdom from 1099 to his own day.

At the Lateran Council, which met in November, 1215, and had been summoned over two years previously, four hundred and twelve bishops were present, including the Latin *patriarchs* of Jerusalem and Constantinople. Through Innocent's influence the project of a new Crusade was adopted, and preached with vigour; James de Vitry, the future Bishop of Acre and historian of the Holy Land, and the English Cardinal, Robert de Curzon, who died in 1218, at Damietta, being foremost in the work. Chief amongst those who took the Cross were Andrew, King of Hungary; Leopold, Duke of Austria; William, Count of Holland; and the English Earl Ranulf of Chester.

So, towards the autumn of 1217, there were gathered at Acre the four kings of Hungary, Armenia, Cyprus, and Jerusalem, besides many nobles and men of lesser degree A great foray was made to Bethshan and the Saracen castle on Mount Tabor besieged; but the *Sultan* would not permit his son Corradin to offer battle, and the Crusaders were at length forced to retire after effecting but little. The kings of Hungary and Armenia then returned to their own land, whilst Hugh of Cyprus went to Tripoli, where he soon fell ill and died.

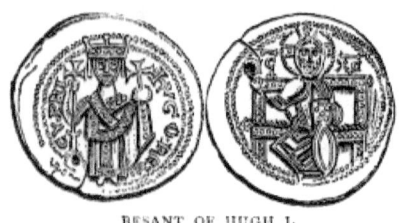

BESANT OF HUGH I.

BESANT OF HUGH I. OF CYPRUS . . . . .

This fine gold coin has the king in his royal robes on the obverse, and Christ seated on the reverse, with the legend, "HVGO REX CYPRI": I[ησου]Σ X[ιστο]Σ. The besants struck in Cyprus contained only one-sixth part of gold, the remainder being chiefly silver; hence from their colour they were called "white besants." The average weight of a white besant was 88 grains.

During the winter many Crusaders who had made the long sea voyage from Northern Europe arrived at Acre. John de Brienne now proposed an expedition to Damietta, and accordingly in May, 1218, the great host set sail with a fair wind for Egypt Damietta was well fortified with towers and walls, and protected by the river and a moat. In mid-stream rose an immense tower of great strength, which was the first point for attack. An assault was made on July 1st, but without success, and many of the Crusaders were drowned. On August 24th (St Bartholomew's Day), the attack was renewed; the Saracens poured down fire and sulphur on their assailants, so that the ladders were set ablaze, and the Crusaders reduced to despair.

Suddenly it seemed that the fire was extinguished, and the Christians saw the banner of the Holy Cross waving from the tower. With fresh vigour they returned to the attack, and now their efforts were crowned with success. Men soon fabled that this was due to no earthly prowess, but to a band of heavenly knights in white armour, the brilliancy whereof had dazzled the eyes of the Saracens, whilst their leader, clad in red, was hailed as none other than St Bartholomew himself.

In September the Papal *legate*, Cardinal Pelagius, reached the camp. A little later there came many French and English knights—the former under the Counts of Nevers, and Marche; the latter under the earls of Chester, Winchester, and Arundel. But winter was now coming on, the camp was flooded, provisions destroyed, and many ships lost. With the spring, however, the Crusaders renewed their efforts; by crossing the river on February 5th, they secured a better position for the attack, and then prepared their engines for an assault.

Meantime El-Adel had been succeeded by his son, El-Kamil. The new *Sultan* was in such despair that he meditated a retreat to Yemen; but on Palm Sunday, after reinforcements had come from Syria, he made a fierce though unsuccessful attack on the Christian camp. In May, Leopold of Austria went home, whilst on the other side, on Feb. 7, El-Kamil's brother, El-Muazzam, or, as the Crusaders called him, Corradin, Prince of Damascus, arrived with a great army of Saracens. But Pelagius and King John had made a Lombard "*caroccio*" to bear the Christian banner, and the sight of this novel engine with its mysterious emblem scared Corradin from a fresh attack. During the summer famine and disease raged within the city, and in the Saracen camp outside.

Nor were the Crusaders in much better plight; for if many Saracens sought relief and baptism in the Christian camp, certain evil Spaniards and English fled to the Moslem and denied Christ. At last the Saracens sent envoys offering to deliver up the land, "because the power of God was against them." But meantime El-Kamil succeeded in throwing reinforcements into the town, thanks to the departure of the Count of Nevers, whose name became a by-word among the Christians. The Crusaders then broke off the negotiations, and on November 5th, at midnight—the hour when, according to the mediaeval belief, Christ harrowed Hell, the Crusaders forced their way within the walls. The credit of this achievement belongs to certain "Latins and Romans," who, taking one of the towers by stealth, thundered out the "*Kyrie Eleeson*," as a sign of success to their comrades below. Then the Templars and Hospitallers forced their way into the city, and so Damietta was captured.

Scarcely was the city taken when a quarrel broke out between John and Pelagius. John was angry because the *legate* had lordship over him, and seeing that Leo of Armenia was now dead, departed to prosecute his wife's rights to that kingdom. John was absent for a whole year, during which time Pelagius vainly endeavoured to keep the Christian host from melting away. The Saracens in their despair offered extravagant terms for the recovery of Damietta—the whole land of Jerusalem excepting Kerak, and all their Christian prisoners. This the Crusaders refused because they hoped that if the Emperor Frederick came on his long-promised expedition, they might then conquer all Egypt. Thus, in their folly they threw away the best chance of recovering the Holy City. Philip of France said with reason that they must have been daft to prefer a town to a kingdom.

When, however, Frederick did not come, it was decided to advance against Cairo. Pelagius was reduced to appeal to John de Brienne for his assistance, but the king would not leave his own land till a liberal sum had been promised for his services. When John arrived, June 29, 1221, the Crusaders had already started. Two months later he found the host in a perilous position, for the Saracen galleys prevented provisions from being brought up from the sea, whilst the Nile was already rising. The *Sultan* ordered the dykes to be cut, and the waters rose so high that it was impossible to advance or to retreat.

The Crusaders were at the mercy of the Saracens, and John had to make the best terms he could. El-Kamil, in pity for the Christians, offered to let them go free if Damietta was restored. There was no alternative but to consent, and the *Sultan* further promised to release all his prisoners, restore the Holy Cross, and grant a truce for eight years. John de Brienne and James de Vitry became hostages for the fulfilment of the treaty. It is related that as John sat before the *Sultan*, he wept for thought of his starving companions. El-Kamil, on learning the cause of his tears, was moved to compassion, and sent enough store of food for all the people.

After his release John appointed Eudes de Montbeliard his bailiff at Acre, and went over sea to ask aid for his unhappy kingdom. He visited Rome, France, England, and Spain, where he married the King of Castile's sister. Later he joined the emperor in Apulia, and gave his daughter, Isabella or Yolande, in marriage to Frederick. After a time, John quarrelled with the emperor, and took service with the Pope; but he does not again appear in Crusading history.

The Emperor Frederick, who, by this marriage became Lord of Palestine, was certainly the greatest prince, and in some respects also the most remarkable man of his time; it was not without justice that an

English chronicler called him the "Wonder of the World." His natural gifts and acquired accomplishments were alike extraordinary; he was not only a great ruler, but a poet, and lover of art and all intellectual pursuits; the many tongues of his wide dominions—German, Italian, Greek, Latin, and Saracen—were alike familiar to him. But among men of the next generation he was remembered best as the foe of the papacy, and as the rumoured scoffer at all things holy. His relations with the Roman See can hardly have disposed him to reverence for the faith of which it was the centre, and his attitude to religion was no doubt one of indifference. It was even fabled that he had written a book of extreme blasphemy on the Three Impostors—Moses, Christ, and Mohammed.

False though this accusation was, there is something almost grotesque in the fate which made him the leader of Christendom in its Holy War.

After his coronation by Honorius III. in 1220, Frederick publicly renewed his vow of a Crusade. Year after year the Christians had hoped for his coming, and still he had never come—not even on the conquest of Damietta, when it would seem that the very rumour of his coming would suffice to lay the whole East at his mercy. Four months before his marriage to Yolande, in November, 1225, Frederick once more promised to cross the sea for two years; if he failed to fulfil his covenant he would fall under the interdict of the Church. Before the appointed time had elapsed, Honorius III. had been succeeded by Frederick's destined foe Gregory IX. But although one of Gregory's earliest acts was to urge Frederick in a somewhat imperative letter to fulfil his vow, the relations of the new Pope with the emperor were not at first unfriendly.

Frederick, indeed, had made his preparations in all sincerity, and in the appointed month of August, 1227, a large host had assembled at Brindisi. The emperor embarked, and the fleet set sail; but three days later the former entered the harbour of Otranto, whilst the latter dispersed. Frederick pleaded sickness as the excuse for his return, but Gregory nevertheless pronounced the excommunication which the emperor had incurred under his oath two years before. The sentence and its subsequent confirmations were treated with contempt by Frederick, who determined to prove his sincerity by starting on the Crusade in the spring.

The hostility of the Pope caused the desertion of many who had intended to join the Crusade. But Frederick probably counted more on the negotiations, which for some time past he had maintained with El-Kamil, than on the strength of his arms. So, it was with only six hundred knights—more like a pirate than a great king, as Gregory declared—that he landed at Acre on September 7, 1228. Frederick was received with hostility not only by the clergy, but also by the military orders, who presently refused to serve under his commands. El-Kamil, not unaware of the emperor's difficulties, endeavoured to renew their old amity, and made overtures for a compromise.

The negotiations proceeded slowly, but meanwhile there was much friendly intercourse between the two monarchs. Frederick's first demands were for the restoration of the kingdom in its fullest extent, together with liberal privileges for his merchants in the ports of Alexandria and Rosetta. But El-Kamil would not surrender Jerusalem entirely since the Saracens held the Temple in no less esteem than did the Christians the Holy Sepulchre. At first Frederick was disposed to war, but the news that Gregory and John de Brienne were capturing his Italian cities made him anxious to return at any cost. He therefore came to terms with El-Kamil, who agreed to surrender Jerusalem, Bethlehem, and Nazareth, if the site of the Temple, whereon stood the Mosque of Omar, was left to the Saracens.

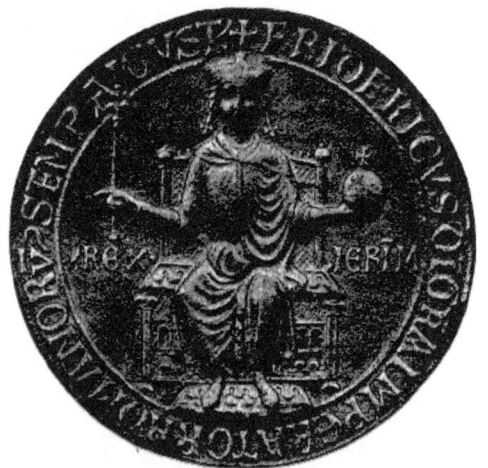

SEAL OF FREDERICK II. AS KING OF JERUSALEM.

As soon as the treaty was arranged Frederick and his Germans went up to Jerusalem on March 18, 1229. Next day—it was Sunday in Mid-Lent—he took the crown from the high altar, in the Church of the Holy Sepulchre, and with his own hands placed it on his head; "but there was no prelate, nor priest, nor clerk, to sing or speak." His pilgrimage to the Sepulchre over, and his coronation accomplished,

Frederick displayed his strange Catholicity by visiting the Mosque of Omar also. So, likewise, when the *cadi* out of regard to the emperor's feelings, forbade the *muezzin* to give the usual call for prayer, Frederick rebuked him:

> You were wrong to fail in duty to your religion for my sake. God knows, if you were to come to my country, you would find no such respectful deference.

After a pretence of refortifying Jerusalem, Frederick suddenly went back to Acre, and thence set sail for Europe. The peace which he had secured was extremely distasteful to his foes the Templars, whose great church at Jerusalem was left in the hands of the Moslem. Frederick announced his treaty in Western Europe as a great achievement Gerold the *patriarch*, on his part, wrote a, letter condemning it as a betrayal of religion and the Church. Gregory had already described it as a monstrous reconciliation of Christ and Belial. But with the effect of this treaty on its authors subsequent fortunes we have nothing to do. Frederick did not again visit his Oriental kingdom. He died in 1250, the victim of a strange and novel crusade. By his will he left a large sum of money for the succour of the Holy Land.

On his way to Palestine Frederick had stopped at Cyprus. The King of the island, Henry I, (son of Hugh I., by Alice, daughter of Henry of Champagne and Isabella), was then a child of eleven; the emperor claimed the right of wardship, and forced the bailiff, John of Ibelin, to do him homage. John accompanied Frederick to Palestine, but after his departure returned to Cyprus in June, 1229, and besieged the emperor's officers in the fortress of Dieudamour. His enterprise had just met with success when the arrival of a German fleet led to a new series of troubles.

The Saracens had not long kept the peace. Within little over a year they began to harass the pilgrims, and declaring that they would no longer suffer the Holy City to remain in Christian hands, broke into Jerusalem itself. Frederick's representatives were able to expel the intruders, and the emperor on hearing of the violation of the truce at once despatched a fleet to Palestine under Richard Filangier, whom he appointed bailiff of the kingdom. An order to Henry de Lusignan to dismiss John of Ibelin was met with a refusal, and an attempt to dispossess that noble of Beyrout was no more successful The native lords declared that Frederick was violating the ancestral customs of their land, and together with John of Ibelin appealed to the King of Cyprus for assistance. Henry and his lords responded readily; but even with their aid John could not venture to take the field against the bailiff Richard, who was besieging Beyrout

Sometime later, on May 3, 1232, Richard surprised the Cypriot lords near Casal Imbert, whilst John of Ibelin chanced to be absent at Acre. Though the young king managed to escape, his followers were utterly routed, and the disaster was fatal to John's ambitions. Richard was even able to carry the war into Cyprus, and for a time held possession of the greater part of that island, until John expelled him in 1233. The Imperial power on the mainland did not last much longer, and when John of Ibelin died in 1236, Queen Alice of Cyprus persuaded the barons to accept her third husband, Ralph of Soissons as bailiff, since Yolande had long been dead and Frederick would not send her young son Conrad to take her place.

Whilst these feuds weakened the Christian cause in the kingdom, similar troubles were working mischief in the principalities further north, where the Prince of Antioch endeavoured to reap advantage from the weakness of the infant daughter of Leo the Armenian. Such a state of affairs gradually wore away whatever powers of resistance the Syrian Franks might yet possess, and so when a new source of danger made its appearance, they proved quite incapable to cope with it.

Meantime there had been great changes in the lands of the Ayubites. At the death of El-Adel on August 31, 1218, his son El-Kamil had succeeded him at Cairo, with the title of *Sultan* and some kind of supremacy over his brothers who ruled in the various cities of Syria. El-Kamil reaped some advantage from the dissensions of his kinsfolk, but his rule in Syria was not altogether prosperous, and his last years were troubled by the dangers which threatened from the Turks of Iconium in the north, and the advancing Tartars to the east. His sudden death at the beginning of 1238, was the signal for general warfare amongst the Ayubite princes of Syria. Eventually Es-Saleh Ayub, El-Kamil's eldest son, became lord of Damascus; with the support of his cousin Dawud, the son of Corradin, he invaded Egypt and overthrew his brother El-Adel, in May, 1240. But the new *Sultan* soon quarrelled with his powerful kinsman Dawud, and the troubles of the Ayubites were still unsettled, when the landing of a new Crusade marked the termination of the ten years' truce concluded by the Emperor Frederick.

In the midst of his conflict with Frederick II., Gregory IX was not unmindful of his fellow Christians in the East. As the conclusion of the ten years' truce made by Frederick II. drew near he issued a summons to a new Crusade. The time was opportune for a fresh effort; the feuds of the Ayubites within, and the pressure of the Tartars from without, had much shaken the power of Islam. The chief response to Gregory's appeal came from France and Spain. King Louis being unable to go in person sent his constable Amalric, Count of Montfort; other French nobles were the Duke of Burgundy and the Counts of Bar and Nevers, whilst the leader of the expedition was Theobald, King of Navarre.

The host mustered at Marseilles, and refusing to wait a year for the emperor to join them, sailed for Palestine in August, 1239. After landing at Acre, they resolved on an expedition for the recovery of Ascalon, and with this purpose marched out towards Jaffa on the 2nd of November. Whilst halting in this town, the Count of Brittany made a successful raid on the Saracens. Emulous of this good fortune the Count of Bar and other nobles determined to make a raid towards Ascalon. Theobald expostulated, but to no purpose; the knights, bent on gain, declared that at least they would ride to Gaza and return on the morrow. So, they went along the coast, (Sunday, the 13th of November), till they reached the brook that divided the kingdom of Jerusalem from Egypt.

Here Count Walter of Jaffa advised that they should rest, but his comrades insisted on proceeding further. At length they halted in a place shut in by mountains, and prepared to feast on the delicate provisions they had brought with them. Whilst thus engaged the Saracens of Gaza came upon them. Count Walter, at their approach, rode off with the Duke of Burgundy, knowing that it was hopeless to fight in such a position. But the Counts of Bar and Montfort persisted in giving battle; they and all their followers were captured or slain before Theobald, who had now advanced to Ascalon, could come to their aid. On the news of this disaster Theobald withdrew in haste to Acre. Next year he sought for the release of the prisoners by making a truce with the *Sultan*, but before the treaty was completed went home by stealth and most of his host with him.

Shortly afterwards Earl Richard of Cornwall reached Acre, and the release of the prisoners was finally secured through the assistance of his wealth. With Richard came Simon de Montfort, Amalric's more famous brother, whom a year or two later the Syrian barons begged Frederick to appoint as bailiff of the kingdom during the minority of Conrad. The quarrels of the military orders rendered any active warfare impracticable, and the English earls shortly went home after accomplishing no more than the release of the prisoners.

The Christians soon found that the *Sultan* had only granted a truce to gain time for the conquest of his rivals. So in 1243, or 1244, they negotiated with the lords of Kerak (Dawud, son of El Muazzam, or Corradin), and Damascus, who promised the Franks all the land west of Jordan save Hebron, Nablûs, and Bethshan. By this means Jerusalem was restored to the Christians, and in the words of a letter of the time, "all the Saracens were expelled, and the sacred mysteries celebrated daily in all the holy places, wherein for fifty-six years the name of God had not been invoked." But hardly had the Christians in Europe time to rejoice over this news, when they heard that Jerusalem was lost again.

Es-Saleh Ayub, in need of aid to reassert his power, called in strangers from outside. His new allies were the Charismians, an eastern tribe, who, driven from their own land by Genghis Khan, had conquered themselves a new home on the Euphrates. They offered their services to the highest bidder, and so fought first for one and then for another of the Ayubite princes. As the Charismians marched south to join Es-Saleh they fell upon the city of Jerusalem, and slew its inhabitants, men, women, and children, to the number of thirty thousand. Mohammedans and Christians united in face of a common danger.

Ismail of Damascus sent an army under El-Mansur of Hamah to help the muster of the military orders, which had marched out from Acre. Count Walter de Brienne joined them at Jaffa, and by the time the army reached Ascalon it mustered six thousand knights without counting the men-at-arms, both horse and foot.

El-Mansur advised that they should abide safely in a place well stored with food till the inevitable time when a savage horde with no settled base must melt away. Some of the Christians approved, but others distrusted an *infidel's* advice. The latter prevailed, and the army marched out to encounter the Charismians near Gaza on October 14, 1244.

The battle was short but fierce; El-Mansur and his host fled from the field; the Christian Army was almost annihilated. Of the Templars, who numbered three hundred, only four knights survived, and of the Hospitallers only nineteen, and but three men-at-arms of the Teutonic order. The grand masters of the Temple and Hospital, and Count Walter were taken prisoners—the last two died in captivity. This disaster was fatal to the power of the Franks in Palestine, and from this moment even the semblance of the Christian kingdom began to fade away.

The Crusades of St. Louis and Edward I.

It might have been expected that the destruction of Jerusalem would send a shock of horror throughout Christendom, and rouse all Christians to the reconquest of the Holy Land. Just one hundred years previously the loss of Edessa, far removed as that city was from the interests of the European west, had been a trumpet call to king and noble and peasant. But things were not in the thirteenth century as they had been in the twelfth. The new era had different ideals, different hopes, and different aims; the political energy of the West was being transfused into new channels.

The great cities were winning privileges at the expense of lords and emperor; new kingdoms were rising into prominence or developing into strength. Here the king was gathering all power more and more into his own hands; there the nobles were asserting their rights to his detriment. But in the fervour and industry of a new age, that was building the noblest churches ever seen, inventing fresh heresies, opening out new studies, there was little place for true religious enthusiasm. The age of Roger Bacon and Albertus Magnus was beginning, that of Anselm and Peter the Hermit dying out. Religion was no longer a matter for the emotions only; but was more and more a thing for philosophers to wrangle over, not one that a practical man need trouble himself about.

But above all else the thirteenth century had no St. Bernard to rouse it to the service of God. Such religious zeal as remained was frittered away in internecine crusades against the Albigeois and a heretic emperor, or diverted its energies from warfare with the *infidel* abroad, to the rescue of afflicted Christians at home. The Templar and Hospitaller had warred in Palestine for the Holy Sepulchre, the followers of St. Francis and St. Dominic toiled in the crowded cities for the poor, the friendless, and the sick.

Europe was, moreover, confronted by a danger unknown for many centuries past The Tartars threatened to sweep away all civilisation from the Volga to the Atlantic. Frederick, even had he not been excommunicate, was too busy with this grave trouble to undertake a new Crusade. In the west the kings of Spain were still waging their perpetual crusade with the Saracens of their own peninsula, and the King of England in the pressure of incident at home could spare no time for Jerusalem and the East Italy was distracted by the feuds of emperor and Pope. To France alone could the Latin Christians of the East look for help.

Louis IX. of France was now about twenty-seven years old. The great-grandson of our English Henry II. and the grandson of Philip Augustus, he had been left an orphan at the age of ten, but through the prudence of his mother Blanche the troubles of his minority had been averted. About the end of 1244, Louis fell so ill that his life was despaired of; as he lay unconscious, his nurse thinking all was over, was about to draw the sheet across his face, when a companion stayed her hand. At the sound of their voices the king roused from his trance, and calling for a cross vowed himself to God's service for the recovery of Jerusalem. It was not, however, for more than three years that Louis sailed from Marseilles on the 25th of August, 1248.

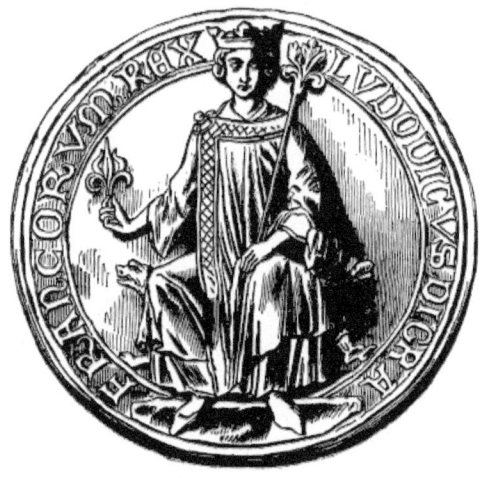

SEAL OF LOUIS IX.

Louis was perhaps the most truly religious king that ever lived. His whole life was a prayer; his whole aim to do God's will. His horror of sin was deep and unaffected. "Would you rather be a leper, or commit a deadly sin?" he once asked Joinville. The *seneschal* bluntly blurted out that he would rather commit thirty deadly sins than have his body covered with leprosy. Louis reproved his choice: for the leprosy of the body would disappear at death, but the leprosy of sin last hereafter. Everything about the king is charming from the *As-you-Like-it* scene where he administered justice beneath the great oak at Vincennes, to his washing of the feet of the poor in imitation of Christ.

Nor was he regardless of learning, even though he commended the knight who closed an unsuccessful disputation with a Jew by a blow from his stick. He had a great library of books at Royaumont, was the patron of Robert of Sorbonne, and chose Vincent of Beauvais, the greatest scholar of his day, to be his reader and the teacher of his sons. But with all this he was no weakling or do-nothing. All men trusted him, and the English barons accepted him as arbiter in their disputes with Henry, knowing that he would never seek his own advantage from quarrels among his neighbours. But that which most struck his contemporaries was his extreme sobriety of language; Joinville, who was with him constantly for two and twenty years, declares that he never heard him utter a word of blasphemy though this was the commonest fault of that age.

Such was the king who now started on the last Crusade but one. With him though not in his immediate following, went Jean de Joinville his biographer. All history might be racked in vain for a passage of more simple pathos than that in which the great French noble tells how on his way to Marseilles he passed beneath the walls of his own castle, and dared not cast a look upon them lest his heart should melt at the thought of his little children, who there lay all unconscious of the perils on which their father was embarking. Louis reached Cyprus towards the end of 1248, and remained there till the following May. Great preparations had been made in the island long beforehand, and Joinville remarks on the great heaps of corn that were turning green upon the top where the grain was sprouting into active life, with the wine casks piled up into "houses" as it seemed—all in readiness for the start to Syria or Egypt.

Joinville, whose own money was now spent, took service with the king, and on the 21st of May the French host set forth in eighteen hundred vessels, whose white sails made a very fair sight. A sudden storm, however, dispersed the fleet; but on Whit-Monday the wind fell, and Louis reached Damietta three days later on the 27th of May (so Joinville; William of Nangis puts the capture of Damietta a week or two later), with seven hundred ships. He had scarcely landed when the Saracens fled in terror from the city, and the French became masters of this great port without striking a serious blow.

For six months the army lay in or near Damietta, until the remainder of the fleet under the king's brother, the Count of Poitiers, could arrive from Syria. This was not till October, and then a council determined to waste no time in attacking Alexandria, but to push on boldly for Cairo itself; for said the Count of Artois it were better if they wished to kill the serpent to crush him on the head. Accordingly, at the end of November, the army marched south; but at the Delta, or to use the mediaeval expression " The Island," formed by the Damietta branch of the Nile and one of the other numerous river channels, (Joinville says the "Rexi" or Rosetta branch, which is clearly impossible; other writers come nearer the truth in saying the Tanis branch; no doubt it was the canal of Ashmun), their further advance was stayed; for they could not cross the river in the face of the great army that opposed them on the southern side.

The French determined to construct a causeway to enable them to pass over, but whenever the work seemed to be making progress the enemy managed to destroy it. The Saracen stone-casters, and other military engines troubled the labourers incessantly, whilst the wooden towers or belfries which the Crusaders had erected for their protection were twice destroyed by Greek fire. Louis was now in a most perilous position, for a hostile force which had crossed Damietta branch into "the island" threatened his rear. In this emergency he accepted the offer of a Bedouin who agreed for five hundred *besants* to guide the French to a secret ford. On Shrove Tuesday, February 8, 1250, Louis marched out for the ford, leaving the Duke of Burgundy to guard the camp. In the van went the Templars, with the Count of Artois in the centre, and the king in the rear.

Amongst the few English who took part in this Crusade, the most distinguished was William Longsword, second earl of Salisbury, the grandson of Henry II., and in all probability of Rosamond Clifford. Though the king's cousin and titular earl of Salisbury he was a poor man, and had been obliged to collect money for his expedition to the East, by what practically amounted to the sale of dispensations to the timid or the old, who at the last moment lacked courage for the journey. In the earlier days of the expedition he had succeeded in capturing an Egyptian caravan on its way with spices to Alexandria.

Of this spoil, however, so says a contemporary English writer, the French had robbed him; William appealed to Louis for justice, but the king though admitting his wrong declared himself powerless to grant redress. The angry earl forswore the authority of so weak a prince and withdrew to Acre. There he awaited the coming of the main body of the English, but in vain, for the Pope at King Henry's request forbade their passage. Eventually at Louis' wish, probably when the army was marching on Cairo, Earl William returned to Egypt, and was thus present on this fatal day.

The Templars and the Count of Artois crossed the river with such ease that the count was for moving on Mansurah in the first flush of their success. To this rash project the Master of the Templars objected,

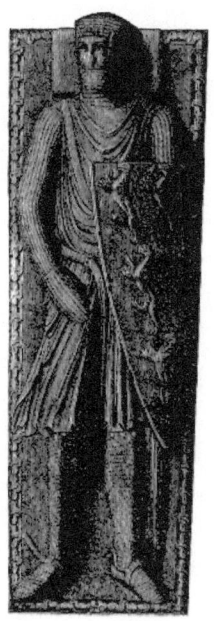 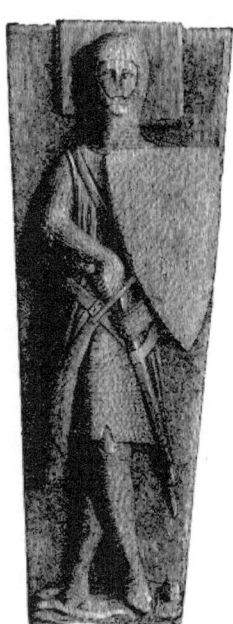

THE TWO WILLIAM LONGSWORDS.

THE TWO WILLIAM LONGSWORDS FROM THEIR TOMBS IN
SALISBURY CATHEDRAL . . . . . .
William Longsword I., Earl of Salisbury (*d.* 1226), was son
of Henry II., and perhaps of Fair Rosamond, and was
possibly present at the siege of Damietta; his tomb affords a
beautiful example of early thirteenth-century armour. The
other effigy is traditionally that of his son, the William
Longsword mentioned in the text. The two effigies are
much alike, except that the latter has the legs crossed, has
no blazonry on the shield, and has small *plates* of armour to
protect the elbows and knees. If this is really the tomb of
William Longsword II., it perhaps affords the earliest known
instance of such plates—the beginnings of plate armour.

advising that they should wait for the king. But the fiery temper of the French prince would brook no delay. He accused the Grand Master roundly of treachery, and of a desire to avoid any decisive victory since the power of the military orders depended on the preservation of something like equality between the Eastern Christians and the Saracens. The intervention of the Earl of Salisbury only aggravated the dispute.

"See how timid are these tailed English!" cried the angry count; "it would be well if the army were purged of such folk."

This taunt stung the English earl to the quick. "At least," he retorted, "we English today will be where you will not dare to touch our horses' tails."

All prudent thoughts were now cast aside, and the whole van charged into Mansurah. The wisdom of the Templar and the boast of Longsword were alike justified. The earl was slain refusing to fly, while the Count of Artois, in his endeavour to escape, was either killed or drowned in the river. The French were only saved from annihilation by the arrival of the king, and by the valour of Joinville, who held, at all hazards, a small bridge that led from Mansurah.

After this battle Louis remained on the south bank of the stream for several weeks, till the news came that the Saracens had blocked the Damietta stream. As he was now on the verge of starvation, he reluctantly ordered a retreat into "the island," and commenced negotiations with the *Sultan* for the exchange of Damietta against the kingdom of Jerusalem. But on the 29th of March matters had become so intolerable that the order was given for a further retreat towards Damietta. Then the Saracens seeing what plight the French were in, refused to abide by the terms they had been discussing. They threw themselves on the sick, and began to murder them as they were warming themselves by the fires.

Louis himself, despite the desperate valour of his attendant, Sir Geoffrey de Sergines, was taken prisoner as he was attempting to guard the river. Joinville had already gone on board his ship, and reached the place where the *Sultan's* galleys blocked the river. Four of these Saracen vessels bore down on him, and his life vas only saved by the generous deceit of a Saracen, who swore that he was the king's cousin. The good knight, though he would not tell a lie himself, did not scruple to take advantage of his protector's falsehood. Nor is it unpleasing to find that afterwards the same Saracen, as he led Joinville away, slipt into his hand that of a little lad, Bartholomew de Montfaucon, bidding him never let himself be parted from him, or the child's life would be sacrificed.

Such was the end of the French Army. After protracted negotiations Louis was set free. In spite of many tortures with which he was threatened the king refused to surrender the Christian fortresses in Palestine, or to forswear his faith, but agreed to purchase his freedom and that of his army by the payment of one hundred thousand *livres* and the surrender of Damietta. In the midst of the negotiations the Sultan Turan Shah was murdered by his Mamluks on the 4th of May, and Louis had once more to display his constancy in the presence of danger. (Turan Shah succeeded his father, Es-Saleh Ayub, on November 23, 1249; but he only reached Egypt on February 24, 1250, for he was at Hisn Keifa when his father died.) But after the payment of an increased ransom, Louis and the remains of his host were able to sail for Acre in the middle of the month.

After the murder of Turan Shah the power in Egypt fell into the hands of the widow of Es-Saleh, who ruled in the name of her son Khalil; but after a little the *emirs* displaced her in favour of Musa, a great-grandson of El-Kamil. (Musa was deposed in 1254, and with him the line of the Ayubite *Sultans* in Egypt came to an end.) The Mohammedan princes of Aleppo and Damascus were offended at the ransom of Louis; such a prince, they said, should have been kept in perpetual captivity and not set free for money. They placed themselves at the head of a great league, and marched against Musa, to be utterly routed on February 3, 1251. Musa, in the stress of his contest with his kinsmen entered into communications with the French king, and concluded a truce for fifteen years.

In the West men spoke of Musa as a possible convert and whispered that Louis had sworn to spend the remainder of his life in the Holy Land. The king had sent home his brothers to collect the remainder of his ransom; they had urged the Pope to compose his quarrel with the emperor in the interests of Christendom, and lend them his aid; but Innocent remained immovable in the pursuit of his feud with Frederick and his sons. So, the time wore on with nothing done, for though Henry of England took the cross his motives were seemingly sinister. A little later the regent of France, Louis' mother Blanche, died, and this event appears to have called the king home. Louis had spent nearly four years in the Holy Land, busy with the fortification of the great seaports. Caesarea, Jaffa, Sidon, were all rebuilt during these years, and it was not till the spring of 1254, that the king departed reaching his own country about July 11th.

Sixteen years later King Louis embarked upon a second Crusade. In the interval he had always remained a Crusader at heart, and amidst all the troubles of his home life his real ambition was set upon the Holy Land, though the duties of his position forced him to remain in France. It was not till July, 1270, that the king started on his second expedition from Aigues Mortes. Despite Louis's earnest request Joinville would not accompany him, pleading that his first duty was to his own vassals, who suffered so many wrongs during his absence on the previous Crusade.

Louis, who was accompanied by his eldest son Philip, and the kings

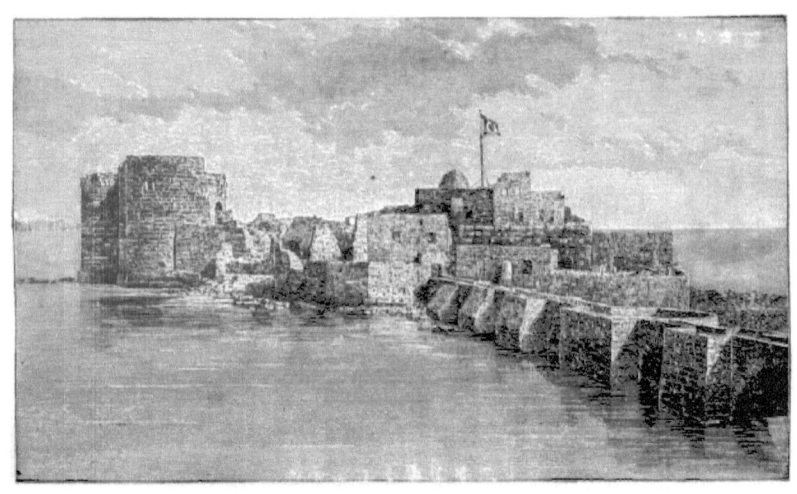

FORTIFICATIONS OF SIDON.

FORTIFICATIONS OF SIDON
This represents the work of Louis IX. in 1250, which was almost perfect till the English bombardment in 1840.

of Navarre and Aragon, was induced to turn aside to Tunis in the hope of converting its ruler to Christianity. Whilst encamped near this city he was seized with dysentery. On Sunday, the 24th of August, he crept from bed to confess his sins and receive the last sacrament from the hands of Geoffrey de Beaulieu, to whom we owe most of our knowledge of this expedition. In the night as he lay on his ash-sprinkled couch the words "Jerusalem! Jerusalem!" showed in what direction his thoughts were turning. As morning drew on the watchers caught fragments of the good king's prayer for his people, and a little later heard his last cry, "*Domine in manus tuas animam meam commendavi*;" shortly afterwards, about the hour of *nones*, St. Louis expired.

With him may be said to have perished the last hope of the Latin kingdom in the East For over a century the French kings had been the recognised defenders of this outpost of the Christian religion and French culture. But the old spirit of piety was dying out; the new king, an illiterate warrior, had little care for a distant land, and after a few years the complex problems of a new age forced the grandson of St. Louis into a very different line of policy. In his life St. Louis afforded the most perfect illustration of the aspiration of two centuries towards an impossible ideal, and his death tolled the knell of hopes, which if essentially futile were no less essentially sublime. The good king did not leave his peer behind, and the dream of a united Christendom mustering its

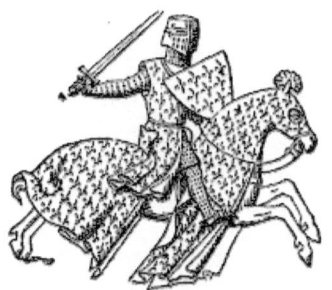

SEAL OF PHILIP III. OF FRANCE.

SEAL OF PHILIP III. OF FRANCE . . . . .
He accompanied his father to Tunis in 1270, but left Sicily for France the same year, and never fulfilled his promise to return to the East. This is a splendid example of the luxurious blazonry now so fully in vogue, with coat-of-arms, horse barding and vizored helmet all complete.

forces for the subjugation of a common foe was destined to fade away among the ruder visions of national integrity and feudal dissolution.

Amongst those who had taken the cross at the same time as St. Louis was Edward, the eldest son of Henry of England. In his company went many of the great English nobles—especially those of the younger generation, whom he is said to have taken with him to divert them from the wars at home. Edward reached Tunis about the 9th of October with his cousin Henry of Almaine. He found the French barons, who had been victorious in more than one engagement, bent on enforcing the tribute which they said was due from Tunis to the King of Sicily.

After exacting a great treasure, the Crusading host set sail for Sicily, meaning to winter there; but a storm fell upon them outside the harbour of Trapani, and the tribute of the Mohammedan prince was lost in the sea. Next spring Edward, finding the French princes unwilling to accompany him, set sail with his English followers and reached Acre fifteen days after Easter, (May 9th, according to the Templar of Tyre), just in time to save the city from the Saracens. After a month's rest he made a raid to the *casal* of S. George between Acre and Safed, and at the end of November led another expedition as far as Chaco (Kakoun), and Castle Pilgrim or Athlit on the south.

These trifling successes were probably intended to pave the way to greater achievements. At his request the barons of Cyprus, who had refused the summons of their own lord, the King of Jerusalem, came over with a great following and declared themselves the faithful

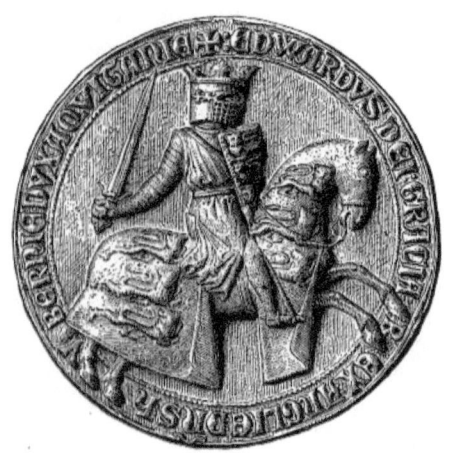

SEAL OF EDWARD I. OF ENGLAND.

SEAL OF EDWARD I.
This shows well chain armour and grand hauberk at their fullest development. Notice the vizored helmet completely hiding the face, the coat-of-arms worn over the hauberk and the horse barding. Compare the seal of Richard I.

servants of the English king, whose predecessor had won their island for the Latin Church; it was only on their coming that Edward had ventured so far afield. (This is the statement of an English writer and as such must be discounted. Edward seems to have been called on to decide as to the rival claims of Hugh III. of Cyprus, and Mary of Antioch, see next chapter.)

After his return to Acre Edward commenced negotiations with a Saracen *emir* who professed himself ready to become a Christian. His messenger was admitted time after time to Edward's presence and all suspicion was lulled asleep. At last, on his fifth visit, on June 18, 1272, the assassin found his opportunity. After a cursory examination for arms he was permitted to pass into the prince's presence. The day was hot and Edward, clad in a tunic only, was resting on a couch; he took the *emir's* letter from the messenger who, as he bent in Eastern fashion to answer the prince's questions, drew a knife from his belt and struck a blow at his intended victim.

Edward caught the blow on his arm, and tripping the villain to the ground with his foot wrenched the dagger from his grasp and stabbed him as he lay. The English servants coming in found the would-be murderer dead, but to make assurance doubly sure, battered out his brains with a footstool. Edward's life was in much danger, for the weapon was poisoned, and though the Master of the Temple gave him what was declared to be a certain antidote, the wound grew daily worse. At last, an English doctor pledged himself to effect a perfect cure. He bade the nobles lead the weeping Eleanor from her husband's presence; then he cut away the poisoned flesh, and thus, under his care, Edward was within fifteen days able to appear on his horse in public. (The romantic story of her devotion is first related by Ptolemy of Lucca fifty years later.)

Very shortly afterwards Edward concluded a ten years' truce with the *Sultan*. His departure was accelerated by a letter from King Henry urging his son to return immediately since his health was failing, Edward left Palestine on the 14th of September, but did not reach England till two years later, long after his father's death. Throughout his life he cherished the hope of completing the exploits of his earlier manhood, and at the very close of his career vowed himself once more to the service of God, if He would but grant him vengeance on his enemy Bruce.

THE KINGDOM OF ACRE—ITS DECAY AND DESTRUCTION, (1244–1291)

We must now turn back thirty years to trace the last fortunes of the Latin colonies in Syria. After the departure of Frederick II. Jerusalem was to all intents and purposes a kingless realm, and during the greater part of this period even the bare tenure of the title of king was not allowed to go undisputed. It may seem strange that under such circumstances the Frankish rule should have dragged out even a moribund existence for so many years. But a variety of circumstances contributed to delay its dissolution. Chief among these we must place the extreme weakness of the Ayubite *Sultans* during the sixteen years that elapsed between the death of El-Kamil and the final destruction of their power by the Mamluks in 1254; and, in the second place, we have the fact that the very existence of a Mussulman Empire was threatened by the rise of a new power in the person of the Tartar *khans*. No credit can be placed to the continuance of any vitality in the Franks themselves; for saddest of all features in these fifty years of Crusading history is the presence of perpetual feuds among the Christians in the East.

After Frederick's death in 1250, his rights should have passed to Yolande's son Conrad, but the emperor, in bequeathing his own dominions to his eldest son, expressly stipulated that Jerusalem should go to Henry, the offspring of his marriage with Isabella of England. But both Conrad and Henry died within a few years, and the title passed to Conradin, the youthful son of the former, on whose tragic death in 1267, the line of Yolande came to an end. Meantime in Palestine the office of bailiff was held for the most part by one member or another of the house of Ibelin. Henry of Cyprus died in 1253, leaving an infant son Hugh by his wife Plaisance of Antioch.

The claims of this child were asserted by his uncle Bohemond VI. of Antioch in 1258, but resisted by the Hospitallers and Genoese, who supported Conradin. Hugh died in 1267, and his cousin and namesake, who had been warden of Cyprus in the boy-king's name, then asserted his right to succeed him both in Cyprus and Jerusalem. Hugh III. of Cyprus was actually crowned King of Jerusalem at Tyre on September 24, 1269; but though he maintained a more or less shadowy authority on part of the mainland during seven years, his claims were disputed by his aunt Mary of Antioch. At last, in 1276, the opposition of the Templars drove Hugh to leave Acre; the knights of the other orders and the Genoese would have supported him, and were anxious for his return.

But the Templars declared: "If he wants to "come he can come, and if he does not, let him stay away." Hugh contented himself with a declaration to the Western Powers that he could not maintain justice or order in the strife of contending parties at Acre; whilst Mary, his opponent, went to Europe in person, and there sold her rights to Charles of Anjou, whom the Pope had made King of Sicily. Charles sent Roger of St. Severin as his bailiff to Acre next year, but though Roger had the support of the Templars there was no longer any pretence of a supreme authority in the Frankish possessions.

The divisions among the Latins in the East had a twofold origin; on the one side, there was the commercial rivalry of the Venetians, the Pisans, and the Genoese; on the other, the military jealousy of the two great orders. In 1249, the Pisans and Genoese had fought against one another at Acre for eight and twenty days with two and twenty kinds of engines, stone casters, *tribuchets*, and *mangonels*. Louis IX., during the four years of his residence in Palestine, was able through the preponderance of his authority to maintain some sort of peace.

At his departure he left Geoffrey de Sergines as his lieutenant with a force of one hundred knights. Geoffrey fought with some success before Jaffa, which was excepted from the truce, but it was not long before these old jealousies broke out with new force, and "the Chris-

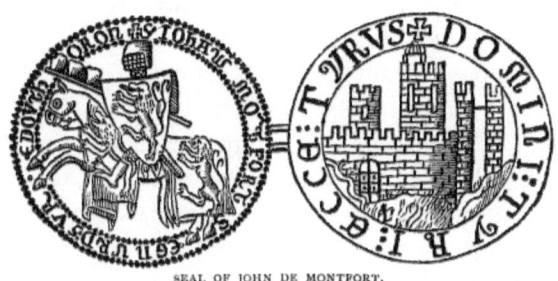

SEAL OF JOHN DE MONTFORT.

SEAL OF JOHN DE MONTFORT, LORD OF TYRE AND TORON.
He was son of Philip de Montfort, a cousin of the famous
Earl Simon of Leicester, who married the heiress of Toron,
and acquired Tyre after the expulsion of Richard Filangier,
in which he took a prominent part; he died November 27th,
1283.

tians waged war with each other villainously." On the one side, were the Venetians, the Pisans, and *Pullani*, or Syrian Franks, supported as it would seem by the Templars; on the other side, the Genoese, the Spaniards, and the Hospitallers. It was in the midst of this war in 1258, that Bohemond VI. paid his visit to Acre, and endeavoured without success to make peace. The struggle continued during two years till at last, in a great sea fight off Acre, a fleet of fifty Genoese galleys was defeated by forty Venetians with a loss of seventeen hundred men.

A little later the Templars were disastrously defeated in a pitched battle with their rivals. Much of this warfare had been conducted in the streets of Acre, where the contending parties battered each other's quarters and towers till a great portion of the city was utterly destroyed. In the end the Genoese had to abandon their quarter and withdraw to Tyre. There was no such open and prolonged war after this, but the continued dissensions of the Christians lasted till the very day when Acre was taken.

It was at the time of this warfare among the Christians that the Tartars began to threaten Syria. In the early years of the thirteenth century Genghis Khan had established his authority over the Mongols and laid the foundations of an empire, which within a few years extended from the most eastern confines of Asia to the borders of Germany. The sons of Genghis held rule in China, Persia, and Russia; Europe was with difficulty preserved by the valour of Conrad; and when at length in 1258, Bagdad was taken and the orthodox *Caliphate* extinguished by Hulagu Khan, the son of Genghis, it seemed as though the very existence of Islam was at stake.

Despite the terror which the first invasions of the Tartars had inspired, the eyes of the Christians had already been turned towards the new power as a possible ally for the destruction of the Moslem. From the council of Lyons, in 1245, Innocent IV. despatched Dominicans on a mission to the great *khan*; and four years later Louis IX. received at Cyprus an embassy from Ilchikadai, a Tartar *khan*, with promises of assistance. In response the king sent certain friars, who, returning after an absence of two years, found Louis at Caesarea; afterwards Louis despatched the Franciscan Rubruquis, who has left us a graphic account of his long journey, and of the court of the great *khan*.

It was no doubt, therefore, with mingled feelings of hope and dread that the Franks beheld the Tartars enter Syria in the year after the fall of Bagdad. Aleppo, Hamah, and Damascus fell before them. The *Sultan* appealed to the Franks for assistance, but through the counsel of the Hospitallers and Teutonic knights the proffered alliance was refused. On September 3, 1260, the Sultan Kutuz met and defeated the Tartar host at Ain Talut; it was one of the decisive battles in the world's history, for not only was the tide of Tartar conquest stemmed, but the fate of Palestine was settled. The fruits of the victory did not, however, fall to Kutuz, for as he was returning to Cairo, he was murdered on October 24th by his Mamluks, and the throne of Egypt passed to Bibars Bendocdar.

Bibars was the true founder of the Mamluk rule in Egypt, and was the most formidable and relentless foe that the Christians had had to encounter since the death of Saladin. The first year of his reign was signalised by the discomfiture of the Tartars in a second battle near Emesa; from this moment Bibars was able to turn his arms against the Franks, and win for himself the titles of the Pillar of Religion and Father of Victories.

The lax authority among the Franks gave Bibars an easy opportunity to disregard the truce, which nominally subsisted between the Christians and Mohammedans in Syria. In 1263, he appeared for the first time before the walls of Acre, and two years later commenced his career of conquest by the capture of Arsûf. The next year was marked by the fall of Safed and massacre of all its defenders, and in 1267, whilst the Venetians and Genoese were contending for the mastery outside the harbour of Acre, Bibars was plundering the gardens beneath its very walls. In 1268, the victorious *Sultan* appeared once more in Palestine, Jaffa was taken on March 2nd, and then passing northwards the Mohammedans laid siege to Antioch in May.

The prince was absent at Tripoli, and this great city, which 170 years previously had resisted the Crusaders for over six months, fell once more beneath the sway of the Mohammedans after a siege that had not lasted so many days. The fall of Antioch led to the Crusade of Edward, but that enterprise as we have seen, did little to check the progress of Bibars. It were tedious to trace in detail the steps by which the last poor remnants of the Latin colonies perished. One by one the strong castles of the military orders were captured, until the Franks were confined to a few isolated cities on the coast, which were separated yet more by mutual jealousy or discord.

Bibars died, perhaps of wounds received in battle with the Tartars, in 1277, but his death brought no relief to the Franks. His successor, Malek El-Mansur or Kalaun, took Markab in 1285, and the great and rich city of Tripoli in 1289. As one by one the different towns were taken, their inhabitants were either put to the sword, or suffered to escape with their lives to Acre. Thus, the population of that city was much increased, and within its walls there were gathered representatives from every nation in Christendom.

For every one there was a separate commune, and the various lords of the land, the masters of the great orders, the representatives of the kings of France, England, and Jerusalem, each exercised separate authority, so that there were in one city seventeen independent powers, "whence there sprang much confusion." It is not strange that under such circumstances the city became, as it were, the sink into which all the vileness of Christendom found its way. Over its mixed population many ruled but none had authority; within its walls the precepts of religion, law, and morality were alike void, so that in its last days Acre became a byword in all Christian lands for the luxury, turbulence, and vice of its inhabitants. Popes did not cease to preach with more or less sincerity the duty of a new Crusade, but the spirit of self-denial and heroism which inspired the warriors of the Cross in an earlier age was now extinct. Such assistance as the West afforded came in the shape of mercenary troops, and it was the dissolute violence of some of these mis-called Crusaders that precipitated the end of the Christian rule in Syria.

Pope Nicholas IV., in his zeal for the Eastern Christians, had sent, as it is said, no less than seventeen hundred mercenaries at his own cost to Acre. These men, being left without pay and in lack of means of subsistence, fell to plundering the Saracen merchants, who, under cover of a truce, had come to Acre for the purpose of peaceful trade. The *Sultan* appealed to the rulers of Acre for redress, but it was in vain that the Templars urged the justice and prudence of concession. Malek Eh-Ashraf or Khalil, who just at this time succeeded Kalaun as *Sultan*, then had resort to arms, and on the 25th of March, 1291, his troops appeared before the walls of Acre.

There were not wanting enough soldiers to have successfully defended the city; but even in this the last hour of their extremity, its inhabitants were more intent upon feasting than upon fighting, and when the trumpet called them to battle, could not tear themselves from the pleasures of love. Cowardice and discord also played their part in ruining the hopes of a successful defence. Many at the first threat of danger made haste to flee oversea; whilst others who stayed

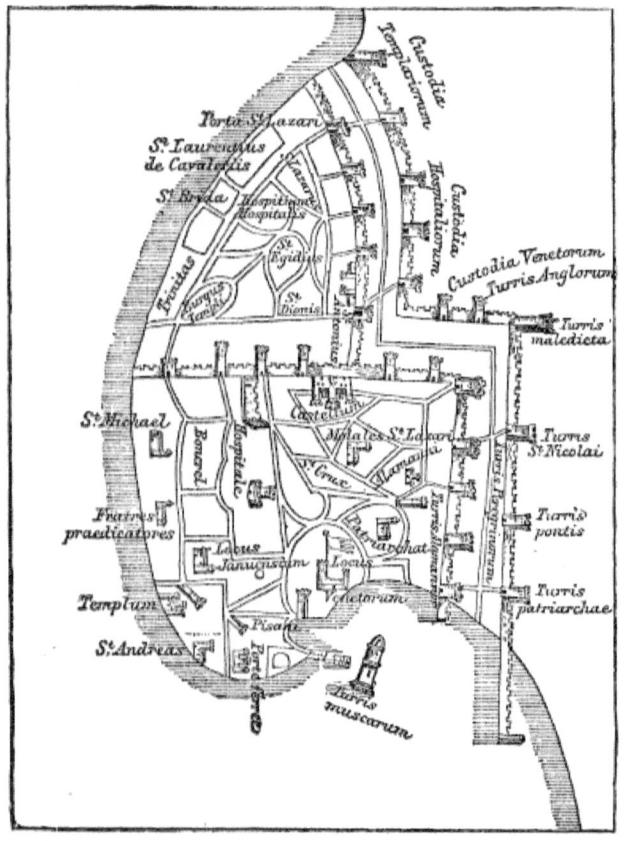

ACRE AS IT WAS ABOUT 1291 A.D.

From the manuscript of Marino Sanuto's treatise, "Secreta Fidelium Crucis," written in 1307 and presented to Pope John XXII. in September, 1321. The work was intended to urge upon the Church and princes of Western Europe the duty of a new Crusade. It was by the Turris Maledicta— name of ill-omen—that Khalil forced his entry.

for a time departed when the prospects of success grew desperate. Among these latter, to his shame, went the Burgundian knight, Otho de Grandison, whom Edward of England had sent with treasure and men to the assistance of the Christians in the East. Not even when the whole purpose of their existence was in peril could the Templars and Hospitallers lay aside their mutual jealousy; and so, the defence, if conducted with valour in parts, lacked that general unity of purpose which could alone have made it successful.

At length on Friday, the 18th of May, Khalil's engines had wrought such a breach in the walls, that the moat being filled with the stones and the bodies of the dead, his army forced its way into the city. The people fled before him to the towers, the palaces of the nobles, or the great house of the Templars. Others, making their way to the harbour, crowded on board the ships in such numbers, that some vessels were swamped as they lay at anchor. Henry II. of Cyprus, who had played a not unworthy part in the early days of the siege, had already escaped to his island kingdom, whither the Grand Master of the Hospital and a number of other fugitives now followed him.

But there yet remained sixty thousand Christians whose fate was slavery, or the sword, or worse. The Templars and those who had taken refuge with them met the noblest end; for, resisting to the last, they succumbed only when their fortress was undermined, and together with numbers of their assailants perished in its ruins. Thus almost exactly a century after its recovery by the soldiers of the Third Crusade was Acre finally lost to the Christians; and since Tyre and the few other places that still remained to the Franks could offer no effectual resistance, the last vestiges of the Latin kingdom of Jerusalem were swept away.

The Close of the Crusades

It would be wrong to suppose that the feelings of Western Europe were not deeply excited by the fall of Acre. Pope Nicholas in particular was eager that this loss should be made the occasion of a new Crusade. But neither his influence, nor the feelings of princes and people themselves, were strong enough to bring about the serious undertaking of such an enterprise. The century that had elapsed between the capture of Jerusalem by Saladin, and that of Acre by Khalil had witnessed great and marvellous changes in Europe. In a mis-called Crusade the papacy had crushed the power of the Empire, and destroyed the semblance of unity in the Western world.

The triumph of the papacy had fostered the growing seed of the principle of separate and independent nationalities. It had been fatal also to its own authority. When the Popes debased their spiritual office for the furtherance of their political aims, they lost the substance which they possessed, and obtained but the shadow of what they clutched at. The coming century was filled with the national warfare of the French and English, and with a divided papacy and a nerveless empire there was no central authority that might have rallied the nations of the West to a new Crusade.

Yet in a half-hearted way Popes preached and princes talked of renewed warfare for the Church against the *infidel*. Nicholas IV. spent his last days in calling on the rulers of Germany, France, and England to take the Cross; but he did not survive the fall of Acre by a twelve-month, and after his death the papacy was vacant over two years. Of his successors, Boniface VIII. was too full of his schemes for papal aggrandisement; Clement V. too much the tool of the French king to seriously resume the initiative. John XXII. took up once more the cause of Christendom, and obtained from Philip of Valois and Edward III. a promise to go on the Crusade. But in the midst of his labours John was cut off by death, and within a few years his two allies had involved their countries in a war that was to last with but little intermission for over a hundred years.

Meantime the power of the Ottoman Turks was growing yearly, at the expense of the Greek Empire in the East. At the end of the fourteenth century the victorious Bayazid had overwhelmed Bulgaria and Servia, and threatened to destroy Hungary also. The imminence of the danger stirred the chivalry of the West to take up arms against the common foe of Christendom. In 1396, a goodly band of French knights, under the Comte de Nevers, went to aid Sigismund in his warfare with the Turks, but only to share in his defeat at Nicopolis. If Bayazid failed to accomplish the conquest of Constantinople, it was due, not to the valour of Christendom, but to the might of Timur the Tartar.

The Greek Empire was further preserved by the quarrel of Bayazid's sons, and it was only in 1453, that the capture of Constantinople by Mohammed II. stirred a Pope to proclaim once more to the princes of the West the duty of a Crusade. For another two centuries the Turks hung as a storm-cloud over Eastern Europe, and in one sense the victories of Don John at Lepanto in 1571, and of Sobieski at Vienna in 1683, may be counted amongst the Triumphs of the Cross. Yet these exploits cannot, any more than the frequent wars with the Algerine

Corsairs from the fourteenth to the nineteenth centuries, properly be counted as Crusades; for though politically speaking they aimed at averting what was substantially the same danger, they did not possess that religious characteristic which is essential to the idea of a Holy War.

It is indeed to the decay of that spirit of enthusiasm which had imparted to the Crusades their religious characteristic, that we must attribute the discontinuance of the attempt to preserve the Holy Places under Christian rule. Some instances we do, however, find of men who were to all appearance fired with the true Crusading fervour. Such was our own king, Henry V., who died with these words on his lips:

> Good Lord, Thou knowest that mine intent hath been, and yet is, if I may live, to rebuild the walls of Jerusalem.

Henry's intention seems to have been sincere, and only a short time previously he had despatched the Burgundian knight Gilbert de Lannoy to Egypt and Syria to report on the practicability of a fresh Crusade. So too Columbus dreamt of a new war for the faith in the East, before he took up that marvellous enterprise in the West, which, by diverting the course of commerce, made a new Crusade more than ever unlikely. But these men stand out as solitary exceptions, and with the changing spirit of the times it was impossible that the world should witness again such strange scenes of enthusiasm as had marked the early days of the First Crusade, or as that perhaps still stranger delusion which in the years 1212, and 1213, sent numbers of children wandering off, in the belief that by their means should be accomplished that which had been beyond the power of kings.

But if the Crusading spirit had run its course in Europe the Latin kings of Cyprus and the knights of St. John at Rhodes maintained during two centuries a gallant struggle in defence of the Cross. The latter were avowedly dependent on recruits from Europe; the former no doubt also benefited by the aid of soldiers, who had left their homes for this purpose, or who, during a pilgrimage to the Holy Sepulchre, landed at Cyprus, and for a time gave their services to the king. Amongst these warrior pilgrims who came from our own land were Henry of Lancaster, father in-law of John of Gaunt; William, Lord Roos of Hamlake, who died in the East in 1352; and John, Lord Grey of Codnor, who, after serving his own sovereign with distinction in France, fought for Peter de Lusignan, King of Cyprus, with other English knights, at Alexandria in 1365.

Peter may in some sense not unfairly be called the last of the Crusaders, and had made an endeavour to rouse the flagging interest of the West, in the course of which he paid a visit to England and was handsomely entertained by Edward III. But his fight at Alexandria had no practical result, and the city was abandoned almost as soon as it was taken. Still it was the last notable achievement of Western chivalry in the East, and it is perhaps in this spirit that Chaucer says of his perfect knight—

At Alisaundre he was whan it was wonne.

If, however, military enthusiasm had declined, there was no falling off in pilgrim zeal. From John of Wurzburg and Theoderic, in the days of the kingdom, to Burcard and Felix Fabri, in the latter years of the fifteenth century, the pilgrim record runs on in an unbroken line. So numerous were the pilgrims that a regular system was organised for their conveyance under the superintendence of the Venetian senate. An *Information for Pilgryms*, by William Wey, Fellow of Eton, was of sufficient interest to be printed by Caxton. Wey gives the would-be pilgrim careful directions for his journey to Venice, and details of various excursions to be made in Palestine, together with such useful advice as where to buy a bed for the voyage in Venice; how it was well to avoid the lowest stage in the vessel, "for it is ryght evyll and smouldryng hote and stynkynge"; how Famagosta was unhealthy for Englishmen; how there was "good wine and dear" to be had in Jerusalem, and what payments it would be right to make in the Holy Land.

But the zeal which has maintained the stream of pilgrims to the present day was a thing apart from that enthusiasm for the Holy War which made the Crusades possible. Though in a sense the age of the Crusades was not closed till the dawn of the Renaissance, their interest as a living force came to an end when the last visible sign of the kingdom of Jerusalem perished with the fall of Acre.

Letters of the Crusaders
Dana Carleton Munro

THE CRUSADE OF FREDERIC I.

To protect his own interest from the crusaders, the Grecian emperor made an alliance with Saladin. This made the former a greater object of hatred than ever before. In the First Crusade, Alexius had been suspected and detested; Manuel had been openly blamed for the failure of the second crusade. Now in the third, no means are too odious to be attributed to the emperor of the East. In a few years, the hatred accumulated for more than a century will vent itself in the sack of Constantinople.

1. Frederic I. to Leopold of Austria. Adrianople, end of November

Frederic, by the grace of God, Emperor and always August, to his beloved kinsman Leopold, Duke of Austria—greeting and all good wishes.

We thought we ought to tell you, because of your love for us, that our brother, the emperor of Constantinople, although he ought to have been bound by brotherly love, has from the very first violated all the oaths which are known to have been sworn by his chancellor at Nuremberg, in the presence of the princes of the empire, in regard to our security on the march, and markets and exchanges. Moreover, he has seized and ignominiously thrown into prison our ambassadors, the Bishop of Münster, Count Rupert (of Nassau), and Markward, our chamberlain, together with all their attendants, whom we had sent to confirm the peace and to arrange for our peaceful march on this expedition of the quickening cross.

At length, however, after long negotiations, grievously delaying our march until the dangerous winter season, he has sent back to our excellency the aforesaid ambassadors on the feast of St. Simon and St. Jude, as if matters had been satisfactorily arranged, and he has again promised us good markets, the usual exchanges and an abundance of vessels.

Truly, because the burnt child dreads the fire, we can in the future have no confidence in the words and oaths of the Greeks. In order to avoid the stormy winter season, we propose to stay until spring at Philippopolis and Adrianople, and to cross over to Constantinople in the favourable season. Therefore, although we rejoice in a well-equipped army, yet we must seek divine succour in our prayers. For these reasons we ask and desire of your love, that in your prayers and pious devotions you commend us and the whole army of the crusaders to God. In addition, we ask of your prudence to see that the letters which we send to the Pope reach him through your aid and exertions, because you can arrange this more successfully than anyone else.

2. Sibylla, Ex Queen of Jerusalem to Frederic I. 1189.

To her venerable and most illustrious Lord Frederic, by the grace of God, most victorious Emperor of Rome and most friendly champion of the Holy Cross, Sibylla, formerly queen of Jerusalem, his most humble servant, greatly humiliated in the name of the Lord.

Spare the humble and conquer the proud. I, your most humble maid-servant—as I said above—am compelled to tell Your Highness and supreme excellency of the grief of the whole city and of the disgrace of the sacred Christians. For the Emperor of Constantinople, the persecutor of the church of God, has entered into a conspiracy with Saladin, the seducer and destroyer of the Holy Name, against the name of our Lord Jesus Christ.

I tell this, which I am indeed not able to say without tears. Saladin, the aforesaid enemy of Christ, has sent to the Grecian emperor and the persecutor of the Holy Name many presents very pleasing to mortals, in order to make a compact and agreement. And for the slaughter and destruction of the Christians wishing to exalt the name of God, he sent 600 measures of poisoned grain and added a very large vase of wine, filled with such a malignant poison that when he wanted to try its efficacy he called a man, who was killed by the odour alone when the vase was opened.

Along with the rest I am compelled to tell my lord another thing: the aforesaid emperor, in order to increase our misfortunes and magnify the destruction of the Christians, does not permit wheat or other necessary victuals to be carried from his country to Jerusalem. Wherefore, the wheat which might be sent by himself and others, is also shut up in the city of Constantinople.

However, at the end of this tearful epistle, I tell you truthfully that you ought to believe the most faithful bearer of this letter. For he himself witnesses what he has seen with his own eyes and heard with his own ears. This is the reason that with my head bowed to the ground and with bent knees, I ask Your Magnificence that inasmuch as you are the head of the world and the wall of the house of Israel, you should never believe the Grecian emperor.

THE GERMAN CRUSADE.

This letter shows the German Crusaders in the full course of victory, which was so soon to be checked by the death of Henry VI

1. The Duke of Lorraine to the Archbishop of Cologne, 1197.

Since we know that you rejoice greatly in the increase of our honour and in the prosperity of all Christianity, we announce to your discretion and prudence that after I had been chosen as the chief of the whole army by the princes of the Roman empire and the barons of the kingdom of Jerusalem and the common people, we directed our march toward Beyroot, by the advice of the princes and of the whole army.

When we were marching in most excellent order between Tyre and Sidon, on the night of the festival of St. Severinus, Saphadin and all the armies of Babylon and Damascus with a great multitude of the Saracens appeared on the side of the mountain; they surrounded our army from the rear as far as the sea-coast, and made severe and continuous attacks on our lines, and having drawn up their forces, the wicked people exercised against us all their strength. Their purpose indeed was to pour forth all their strength against us and make trial of all our strength.

But God, the Protector of those who trust in Him, and who frees the poor from the power of the mighty, snatched His poor from the hands of the impious, and not without great injury to the impious. For, forsooth, they left there the Lord of Sidon and very many other Saracens dead, and since then they have never dared to attack us. Accordingly, on the same day we fixed our tents with delight above the river of Sidon. Since, moreover, our ships were going in advance of the army, and the Saracens who dwelt in the fortress of Beyroot saw our ships coming, terrified by fear, they left the very strongly fortified fortress of Beyroot. And on the next day following with the army, we took the same fortress, which was very strongly fortified, without any difficulty.

And we found in the fortress so many weapons of *arbalisters* and bowmen that twenty wagons could scarcely carry them, and so many victuals that they were sufficient for 500 men for seven years. Moreover, after we had made a stay of twenty days in that place, other Saracens fearing our approach deserted the fortress which is called Gibel (Gibelin) and another very strong fortress which is called Lyeche (Laodicea). Having heard of this, and having ascertained that all the fortresses on the coast as far as Antioch were in the hands of the Christians, we turned towards Sidon and devastated in every direction all the land which the Saracens held. Thus, having routed the Saracens, by the aid of the Heavenly King, so that they never dare to appear, we hope very soon to capture the sacred city of Jerusalem. For the Saracens, having heard that our army is unanimous and strong, never dare to show themselves.

This is the reason that we strenuously exhort your reverence, as much as lies in your power, to keep the memory of us alive throughout your whole archbishopric, in behalf of our prosperity and that of all Christianity, and to compel all in your archbishopric who have taken the cross to fulfil their vows and to aid the cause of Christianity. Moreover, if any wish to remain in the land of promise, we will cause sufficient incomes to be assigned to them in the same land. Farewell.

THE FIFTH CRUSADE.

These are the most valuable sources for the crusade of Frederic II. Each of the contestants tells the story from his own standpoint. We have comparatively little data for controlling their statements and determining their motives.

1. Frederic II. to Henry III. of England. 1229.
Translation taken from Roger of Wendover.

Frederic, by the grace of God, the August Emperor of the Romans, King of Jerusalem and Sicily, to his well-beloved friend Henry, King of the English, health and sincere affection.

Let all rejoice and exult in the Lord, and let those who are correct in heart glorify Him, who, to make known His power, does not make boast of horses and chariots, but has now gained glory for Himself, in the scarcity of His soldiers, that all may know and understand that He is glorious in His majesty, terrible in His magnificence, and wonderful in His plans on the sons of men, changing seasons at will, and bringing the hearts of different nations together; for in these few days, by a miracle rather than by strength, that business has been brought to a conclusion, which for a length of time past many chiefs and rulers of the world amongst the multitude of nations, have never been able till now to accomplish by force, however great, nor by fear.

Not, therefore, to keep you in suspense by a long account, we wish to inform your holiness, that we, firmly putting our trust in God, and believing that Jesus Christ, His Son, in whose service we have so devotedly exposed our bodies and lives, would not abandon us in these unknown and distant countries, but would at least give us wholesome advice and assistance for His honour, praise, and glory, boldly in the name set forth from Acre on the fifteenth day of the month of November last past and arrived safely at Joppa, intending to rebuild the castle at that place with proper strength, that afterwards the approach to the holy city of Jerusalem might be not only easier, but also shorter and more safe for us as well as for all Christians.

When, therefore, we were, in the confidence of our trust in God, engaged at Joppa, and superintending the building of the castle and the cause of Christ, as necessity required and as was our duty, and whilst all our pilgrims were busily engaged in these matters, several messengers often passed to and fro between us and the Sultan of Babylon; for he and another *Sultan*, called Xaphat, his brother, were with a large army at the city of Gaza, distant about one day's journey from us; in another direction, in the city of Sichen, which is commonly called Neapolis, and situated in the plains, the Sultan of Damascus, his nephew, was staying with an immense number of knights and soldiers also about a day's journey from us and the Christians.

And whilst the treaty was in progress between the parties on either side of the restoration of the Holy Land, at length Jesus Christ, the Son of God, beholding from on high our devoted endurance and patient devotion to His cause, in His merciful compassion of us, at length brought it about that the Sultan of Babylon restored to us the holy city, the place where the feet of Christ trod, (see note) and where the true worshippers adore the Father in spirit and in truth.

But that we may inform you of the particulars of this surrender each as they happened, be it known to you that not only is the body of the aforesaid city restored to us, but also the whole of the country extending from thence to the sea-coast near the castle of Joppa, so that for the future pilgrims will have free passage and a safe return to and from the Sepulchre; provided, however, that the Saracens of that part of the country, since they hold the temple in great veneration, may come there as often as they choose in the character of pilgrims, to worship according to their custom, and that we shall henceforth permit them to come, however, only as many as we may choose to allow, and without arms, nor are they to dwell in the city, but outside, and as soon as they have paid their devotions they are to depart.

****

Note:—This is in Psalm 132. The English version is "Before thy footstool." The translation in the letter is from the Vulgate and is due to a mistake made by St. Jerome.

****

Moreover, the city of Bethlehem is restored to us, and all the country between Jerusalem and that city; as also the city of Nazareth, and all the country between Acre and that city; the whole of the district of Turon, which is very extensive, and very advantageous to the Christians; the city of Sidon, too, is given up to us with the whole plain and its appurtenances, which will be the more acceptable to the Christians the more advantageous it has till now appeared to be to the Saracens, especially as there is a good harbour there, and from there great quantities of arms and necessaries might be carried to the city of Damascus, and often from Damascus to Babylon.

And although according to our treaty we are allowed to rebuild the city of Jerusalem in as good a state as it has ever been, and also the castles of Joppa, Cesarea, Sidon, and that of St. Mary of the Teutonic order, which the Brothers of that order have begun to build in the mountainous district of Acre, and which it has never been allowed the Christians to do during any former truce; nevertheless the *Sultan* is not allowed, till the end of the truce between him and us, which is agreed on for ten years, to repair or rebuild any fortresses or castles.

And so, on Sunday, the eighteenth day of February last past, which is the day on which Christ, the Son of God, rose from the dead, and which, in memory of His resurrection, is solemnly cherished and kept holy by all Christians in general throughout the world, this treaty of peace was confirmed by oath between us. Truly then on us and on all does that day seem to have shone favourably, in which the angels sing in praise of God, "Glory to God on high, and on earth peace, and good-will toward men."

And in acknowledgment of such great kindness and of such an honour, which, beyond our deserts and contrary to the opinion of many, God has mercifully conferred on us, to the lasting renown of His compassion, and that in His holy place we might personally offer to Him the burnt offering of our lips, be it known to you that on the seventeenth day of the month of March of this second indiction, we, in company with all the pilgrims who had with us faithfully followed Christ, the Son of God, entered the holy city of Jerusalem, and after worshipping at the Holy Sepulchre, we, as being a Catholic emperor, on the following day, wore the crown, which Almighty God provided for us from the throne of His Majesty, when of His especial grace,

He exalted us on high amongst the princes of the world; so that whilst we have supported the honour of this high dignity, which belongs to us by right of sovereignty, it is more and more evident to all that the hand of the Lord hath done all this; and since His mercies are over all His works, let the worshippers of the orthodox faith henceforth know and relate it far and wide throughout the world, that He, who is blessed for ever, has visited and redeemed His people, and has raised up the horn of salvation for us in the house of His servant David.

And before we leave the city of Jerusalem, we have determined magnificently to rebuild it, and its towers and walls, and we intend so to arrange matters that, during our absence, there shall be no less care and diligence used in the business, than if we were present in person. In order that this our present letter may be full of exultation throughout, and so a happy end correspond with its happy beginning, and rejoice your royal mind, we wish it to be known to you our ally, that the said *Sultan* is bound to restore to us all those captives whom he did not in accordance with the treaty made between him and the Christians deliver up at the time when he lost Damietta some time since, and also the others who have been since taken.

Given at the holy city of Jerusalem, on the seventeenth day of the month of March, in the year of our Lord one thousand two hundred and twenty-nine.

2. Gerold to all the Faithful 1229.

Gerold, *Patriarch* of Jerusalem, to all the faithful—greeting.

If it should be fully known how astonishing, nay rather, deplorable, the conduct of the emperor has been in the eastern lands from beginning to end, to the great detriment of the cause of Jesus Christ and to the great injury of the Christian faith, from the sole of his foot to the top of his head no common sense would be found in him. For he came, excommunicated, without money and followed by scarcely forty knights, and hoped to maintain himself by spoiling the inhabitants of Syria. He first came to Cyprus and there most discourteously seized that nobleman J. (John) of Ibelin and his sons, whom he had invited to his table under pretext of speaking of the affairs of the Holy Land. Next the king, whom he had invited to meet him, he retained almost as a captive. He thus by violence and fraud got possession of the kingdom.

After these achievements he passed over into Syria. Although in the beginning he promised to do marvels, and although in the presence of the foolish he boasted loudly, he immediately sent to the Sultan of Babylon to demand peace. This conduct rendered him despicable in the eyes of the *Sultan* and his subjects, especially after they had discovered that he was not at the head of a numerous army, which might have to some extent added weight to his words. Under the pretext of defending Joppa, he marched with the Christian Army towards that city, in order to be nearer the *Sultan* and in order to be able more easily to treat of peace or obtain a truce. What more shall I say?

After long and mysterious conferences, and without having consulted anyone who lived in the country, he suddenly announced one day that he had made peace with the *Sultan*. No one saw the text of the peace or truce when the emperor took the oath to observe the articles which were agreed upon. Moreover, you will be able to see clearly how great the malice was and how fraudulent the tenor of certain articles of the truce which we have decided to send to you. The emperor, for giving credit to his word, wished as a guarantee only the word of the *Sultan*, which he obtained. For he said, among other things, that the holy city was surrendered to him.

He went thither with the Christian Army on the eve of the Sunday when "*Oculi mei*" is sung (third Sunday in Lent). The Sunday following, without any fitting ceremony and although excommunicated, in the chapel of the Sepulchre of our Lord, to the manifest prejudice of his honour and of the imperial dignity, he put the diadem upon his forehead, although the Saracens still held the temple of the Lord and Solomon's temple, and although they proclaimed publicly as before the law of Mohammed—to the great confusion and chagrin of the pilgrims.

This same prince, who had previously very often promised to fortify Jerusalem, departed in secrecy from the city at dawn on the following Monday. The Hospitalers and the Templars promised solemnly and earnestly to aid him with all their forces and their advice, if he wanted to fortify the city, as he had promised. But the emperor, who did not care to set affairs right, and who saw that there was no certainty in what had been done, and that the city in the state in which it had been surrendered to him could be neither defended nor fortified, was content with the name of surrender, and on the same day hastened with his family to Joppa. The pilgrims who had entered Jerusalem with the emperor, witnessing his departure, were unwilling to remain behind.

The following Sunday when *"Laetare Jerusalem"* is sung (fourth Sunday in Lent), he arrived at Acre. There in order to seduce the people and to obtain their favour, he granted them a certain privilege. God knows the motive which made him act thus, and his subsequent conduct will make it known. As, moreover, the passage was near, and as all pilgrims, humble and great, after having visited the Holy Sepulchre, were preparing to withdraw, as if they had accomplished their pilgrimage, because no truce had been concluded with the Sultan of Damascus, we, seeing that the holy land was already deserted and abandoned by the pilgrims, in our council formed the plan of retaining soldiers, for the common good, by means of the alms given by the King of France of holy memory.

When the emperor heard of this, he said to us that he was astonished at this, since he had concluded a truce with the Sultan of Babylon. We replied to him that the knife was still in the wound, since there was not a truce or peace with the Sultan of Damascus, nephew of the aforesaid *Sultan* and opposed co him, adding that even if the Sultan of Babylon was unwilling, the former could still do us much harm. The emperor replied, saying that no soldiers ought to be retained in his kingdom without his advice and consent, as he was now King of Jerusalem.

We answered to that, that in the matter in question, as well as in all of a similar nature, we were very sorry not to be able, without endangering the salvation of our souls, to obey his wishes, because he was excommunicated. The emperor made no response to us, but on the following day he caused the pilgrims who inhabited the city to be assembled outside by the public crier, and by special messengers he also convoked the prelates and the monks.

Addressing them in person, he began to complain bitterly of us, by heaping up false accusations. Then turning his remarks to the venerable master of the Templars he publicly attempted to severely tarnish the reputation of the latter, by various vain speeches, seeking thus to throw upon others the responsibility for his own faults which were now manifest, and adding at last, that we were maintaining troops with the purpose of injuring him.

After that he ordered all foreign soldiers, of all nations, if they valued their lives and property, not to remain in the land from that day on, and ordered Count Thomas, whom he intended to leave as bailiff of the country, to punish with stripes anyone who was found lingering, in order that the punishment of one might serve as an example to many. After doing all this he withdrew, and would listen to no excuse or answers to the charges which he had so shamefully made. He determined immediately to post some cross-bowmen at the gates of the city, ordering them to allow the Templars to go out but not to return.

Next, he fortified with cross-bows the churches and other elevated positions, and especially those which commanded the communications between the Templars and ourselves. And you may be sure that he never showed as much animosity and hatred against Saracens.

For our part, seeing his manifest wickedness, we assembled all the prelates and all the pilgrims, and menaced with excommunication all those who should aid the emperor with their advice or their services against the Church, the Templars, the other monks of the holy land, or the pilgrims.

The emperor was more and more irritated, and immediately caused all the passages to be guarded more strictly, refused to allow any kind of provisions to be brought to us or to the members of our party, and placed everywhere cross-bowmen and archers, who attacked severely us, the Templars and the pilgrims. Finally, to fill the measure of his malice, he caused some Dominicans and Minorites who had come on Palm Sunday to the proper places to announce the Word of God, to be torn from the pulpit, to be thrown down and dragged along the ground and whipped throughout the city, as if they had been robbers.

Then seeing that he did not obtain what he had hoped from the above-mentioned siege, he treated of peace. We replied to him that we would not hear of peace until he sent away the cross-bowmen and other troops, until he had returned our property to us, until finally he had restored all things to the condition and freedom in which they were on that day when he entered Jerusalem. He finally ordered what we wanted to be done, but it was not executed. Therefore, we placed the city under interdict.

The emperor, realising that his wickedness could have no success, was unwilling to remain any longer in the country. And, as if he would have liked to ruin everything, he ordered the crossbows and engines of war, which for a long time had been kept at Acre for the defence of the Holy Land, to be secretly carried onto his vessels. He also sent away several of them to the Sultan of Babylon, as his dear friend. He sent a troop of soldiers to Cyprus to levy heavy contributions of money there, and, what appeared to us more astonishing, he destroyed the galleys which he was not able to take with him. Having learned this, we resolved to reproach him with it, but shunning the remonstrance and the correction, he entered a galley secretly, by an obscure way, on the day of the Apostles St. Philip and St. James, and hastened to reach the island of Cyprus, without saying *adieu* to anyone, leaving Joppa destitute; and may he never return!

Very soon the bailiffs of the above-mentioned *Sultan* shut off all departure from Jerusalem for the Christian poor and the Syrians, and many pilgrims died thus on the road.

This is what the emperor did, to the detriment of the Holy Land and of his own soul, as well as many other things which are known and which we leave to others to relate. May the merciful God deign to soften the results! Farewell.

The Final Capture of Jerusalem.

The Christians had again prepared their own ruin by a mistaken policy toward Egypt. The grand master of the Hospitalers gives the most graphic picture of the final capture of Jerusalem.

1. *The Master of the Hospitalers at Jerusalem to Lord de Melaye. 1244.*

To the most potent lord, M. de Melaye, brother G. of Newcastle, by the grace of God, humble master of the holy house at Jerusalem, and guardian of the poor followers of Christ—greeting.

From the information contained in our letters, which we have sent to you on each passage, you can plainly enough see how ill the business of the Holy Land has proceeded, on account of the opposition which for a long time existed, at the time of making the truce, respecting the espousing the cause of the Damascenes against the Sultan of Babylon; and now wishing Your Excellency to be informed of other events since transpired, we have thought it worth our while to inform you that, about the beginning of the summer last past, the Sultan of Damascus, and Seisser, Sultan of Cracy, who were formerly enemies, made peace and entered into a treaty with the Christians, on the following conditions; namely, that they should restore to the Christians the whole of the kingdom of Jerusalem, and the territory which had been in the possession of the Christians, near the River Jordan, besides some villages which they retained possession of in the mountains, and that the Christians were faithfully to give them all the assistance in their power in attacking the Sultan of Babylon.

The terms of this treaty having been agreed to by both parties, the Christians began to take up their abode in the Holy City, whilst their army remained at Gazara, in company with that of the aforesaid *Sultans*, to harass the Sultan of Babylon. After they had been some time engaged in that undertaking, the *Patriarch* of Jerusalem landed from the transmarine provinces; and, after taking some slight bodily rest, he was inspired with a longing to visit the Sepulchre of our Lord, and set out on that pilgrimage, on which we also accompanied him. After our vow of pilgrimage was fulfilled, we heard in the Holy City that a countless multitude of that barbarous and perverse race, called Choermians, had, at the summons and order of the Sultan of Babylon, occupied the whole surface of the country in the furthest part of our territories adjoining Jerusalem, and had put every living soul to death by fire and sword.

A council was on this held by the Christians living at Jerusalem, and, as they had not the power to resist these people, it was prudently arranged that all the inhabitants of the Holy City, of both sexes and of every age, should proceed, under escort of a battalion of our knights, to Joppa, as a place of safety and refuge.

On that same night, after finishing our deliberations, we led the people cautiously out of the city, and had proceeded confidently half the distance, when, owing to the intervention of our old and wily enemy, the devil, a most destructive obstacle presented itself to us; for the aforesaid people raised on the walls of the city some standards, which they found left behind by the fugitives, in order by these means to recall the unwary, by giving them to believe that the Christians who had remained had defeated their adversaries. Some of our fellow-Christians hurried after us to recall us, comforting us with pleased countenance, and declaring that the standards of the Christians, which they well knew, were raised on the wall of Jerusalem, in token that they had defeated the enemy; and they, having been thus deceived, deceived us also.

We, therefore, in our exultation, returned confidently into the Holy City, thinking to dwell there safely, and many from feelings of devotion, and others in hope of obtaining and retaining possession of their inheritances, rashly and incautiously returned, either into the city itself or into the suburbs; we, however, endeavoured to dissuade them from this altogether, fearing treachery from these perfidious people, and so went away from them.

Not long after our departure, these perfidious Choermians came in great force and surrounded the Christians in the Holy City, making violent assaults on them daily, cutting off all means of ingress and egress to and from the city, and harassing them in various ways, so that, owing to these attacks, hunger and grief, they fell into despair, and all by common consent exposed themselves to the chances and risk of death by the hands of the enemy.

They therefore left the city by night, and wandered about in the trackless and desert parts of the mountains till they at length came to a narrow pass, and there they fell into an ambuscade of the enemy, who, surrounding them on all sides, attacked them with swords, arrows, stones and other weapons, slew and cut to pieces, according to a correct computation, about seven thousand men and women, and caused such a massacre that the blood of those of the faith, with sorrow I say it, ran down the sides of the mountain like water.

Young men and virgins they hurried off with them into captivity, and retired into the Holy City, where they cut the throats, as of sheep doomed to the slaughter, of the nuns, and aged and infirm men, who, unable to endure the toils of the journey and fight, had fled to the church of the Holy Sepulchre and to Calvary, a place consecrated by the blood of our Lord, thus perpetrating in His holy sanctuary such a crime as the eyes of men had never seen since the commencement of the world.

At length, as the intolerable atrocity of this great crime aroused the devotion of all the Christians to avenge the insult offered to their Creator, it was, by the common consent of all, agreed that we should all, after asking assistance from heaven, arrange ourselves in order, and give battle to these treacherous people.

We accordingly attacked them, and fought without resting from early in the morning till the close of the day, when darkness prevented us from distinguishing our own people from our enemies; immense numbers fell on our side; but four times as many of our adversaries were slain, as was found out after the battle.

On the following (St. Luke the Evangelist's) day, the Knights Templars and Hospitalers, having recovered breath, and invoked assistance from above, together with all the other religious men devoted to this war, and their forces, and the whole army of the Christians, in the Holy Land, assembled by proclamation under the *patriarch*, and engaged in a most bloody conflict with the aforesaid Choermians and five thousand Saracen knights, who had recently fought under the Sultan of Babylon, and who now joined these Choermians; a fierce attack was made on both sides, as we could not avoid them; for there was a powerful and numerous army on both sides of us.

At length, however, we were unable to stand against such a multitude, for fresh and uninjured troops of the enemy continued to come upon us, as they were ten times as numerous as we, and we wearied and wounded, and still feeling the effects of the recent battle; so, we were compelled to give way, abandoning to them the field, with a bloody and dearly-bought victory; for great numbers more fell on their side than on ours.

And we were so assisted by Him who is the Saviour of souls, that not a hundred escaped by flight, but, as long as we were able to stand, we mutually exhorted and comforted one another in Christ, and fought so unweariedly and bravely, to the astonishment of our enemies, till we were at length taken prisoners (which, however, we much tried to avoid) or fell slain. Hence, the enemy afterwards said in admiration to their prisoners: "You voluntarily threw yourselves in the way of death; why was this?"

To which the prisoners replied: "We would rather die in battle, and with the death of our bodies obtain glorification for our souls, than basely give way and take to flight: such people, indeed, are greatly to be feared."

In the said battle, then, the power of the Christians was crushed, and the number of slain in both armies was incomputable. The masters of the Templars and Hospitalers were slain, as also the masters of other orders, with their brethren and followers. Walter, count of Brienne, and the Lord Philip de Montfort, and those who fought under the *patriarch*, were cut to pieces; of the Templars only eighteen escaped, and sixteen of the Hospitalers, who were afterwards sorry that they had saved themselves. Farewell.

THE SIXTH CRUSADE.

This letter, although not "written from the Holy Land," and the composition of a humble pilgrim, gives such valuable—and in some cases otherwise unknown—details, concerning the capture of Damietta in St. Louis' first crusade, that it has seemed wise to insert it. The king's speech is very characteristic.

1. Guy, a Knight, to B. of Chartres.
From Damietta, 1249.

To his dear half-brother and well-beloved friend, master B. of Chartres, student at Paris, Guy, a knight of the household of the viscount of Melun, greeting and a ready will to do his pleasure.

Because we know that you are uneasy about the state of the Holy Land and our lord, the King of France, and that you are interested in the general welfare of the church as well as the fate of many relatives and friends who are fighting for Christ under the king's orders, therefore, we think we ought to give you exact information as to the events of which a report has doubtless already reached you.

After a council held for that purpose, we departed from Cyprus for the East. The plan was to attack Alexandria, but after a few days a sudden tempest drove us over a wide expanse of the sea. Many of our vessels were driven apart and scattered. The Sultan of Cairo and other Saracen princes, informed by spies that we intended to attack Alexandria, had assembled an infinite multitude of armed men from Cairo, Babylon, Damietta and Alexandria, and awaited us in order to put us, while exhausted, to the sword. One night we were borne over the waves by a violent tempest.

Toward morning the sky cleared, the storm abated, and our scattered vessels came together safely. An experienced pilot who knew all the coast in this part of the sea and many idioms, and who was a faithful guide, was sent to the masthead, in order that he might tell us if he saw land and knew where we were. After he had carefully and sorrowfully examined all the surrounding country, he cried out terrified, "God help us, God help us, who alone is able; we are before Damietta."

Indeed, all of us could see the land. Other pilots on other vessels had already made the same observation, and they began to approach each other. Our lord, the king, assured of our position, with undaunted spirit, endeavoured to reanimate and console his men. "My friends and faithful soldiers," said he to them, "we shall be invincible if we are inseparable in our love of one another. It is not without the divine permission that we have been brought here so quickly. I am neither the King of France nor the holy church, you are both. I am only a man whose life will end like other men's when it shall please God. Everything is in our favour, whatever may happen to us. If we are conquered, we shall be martyrs; if we triumph, the glory of God will be exalted thereby—that of all France, yea, even of Christianity, will be exalted thereby. Certainly, it would be foolish to believe that God, who foresees all, has incited me in vain. This is His cause, we shall conquer for Christ, He will triumph in us, He will give the glory, the honour and the blessing not unto us, but unto His name."

In the meantime, our assembled vessels approached the land. The inhabitants of Damietta and of the neighbouring shores could view our fleet of 1,500 vessels, without counting those still at a distance and which numbered 150. In our times no one, we believe, had ever seen such a numerous fleet of vessels. The inhabitants of Damietta, astonished and frightened beyond expression, sent four good galleys, with well-skilled sailors, to examine and ascertain who we were and what we wanted. The latter having approached near enough to distinguish our vessels, hesitated, stopped, and, as if certain of what they had to report, made ready to return to their own party; but our galleys with the fast boats got behind them and hemmed them in, so that they were compelled, in spite of their unwillingness, to approach our ships.

Our men, seeing the firmness of the king and his immovable resolution, prepared, according to his orders, for a naval combat. The king commanded to seize these mariners and all whom they met, and ordered us afterward to land and take possession of the country. We then, by means of our *mangonels* which hurled from a distance five or six stones at once, began to discharge at them fire-darts, stones, and bottles filled with lime, made to be shot from a bow, or small sticks like arrows.

The darts pierced the mariners and their vessels, the stones crushed them, the lime flying out of the broken bottles blinded them. Accordingly, three hostile galleys were soon sunk. We saved, however, a few enemies. The fourth galley got away very much damaged. By exquisite tortures we extracted the truth from the sailors who fell alive into our hands, and learned that the citizens of Damietta had left the city and awaited us at Alexandria. The enemies who succeeded in escaping and whose galley was put to flight, some mortally wounded, uttering frightful cries, went to tell the multitude of Saracens who were waiting on the shore, that the sea was covered with a fleet which was drawing near, that the King of France was coming in hostile guise with an infinite number of barons, that the Christians were 10,000 to one, and that they caused fire, stones, and clouds of dust to rain down.

"However," they added "while they are still fatigued from the labour of the sea, if your lives and your homes are dear to you, hasten to kill them, or at least to repulse them vigorously until our soldiers return. We alone have escaped with difficulty to warn you. We have recognized the ensigns of the enemy. See how furiously they rush upon us, equally ready to fight on land or sea."

In consequence of this speech, fear and distrust seized the enemy.

All of our men, assured of the truth, conceived the greatest hopes. In emulation of one another they leaped from their vessels into the barks; the water was too shallow along the shore, the barks and the small vessels could not reach the land. Several warriors, by the express order of the king, cast themselves into the sea. The water was up to their waists. Immediately began a very cruel combat. The first crusaders were promptly followed by others and the whole force of *infidels* was scattered. We lost only a single man by the enemy's fire. Two or three others, too eager for the combat, threw themselves into the water too quickly and owed their deaths to themselves rather than to others. The Saracens giving way, retired into their city, fleeing shamefully and with great loss. Great numbers of them were mutilated or mortally wounded.

We would have followed them closely, but our chiefs, fearing an ambuscade, held us back. While we were fighting some slaves and captives broke their chains, for the gaolers had also gone out to fight us. Only the women, children and the sick had remained in the city. These slaves and captives, full of joy, rushed to meet us, applauding our king and his army, and crying "Blessed is he who cometh in the name of the Lord." These events happened on Friday the day of our Lord's Passion; we drew from it a favourable augury.

The king disembarked joyfully and safely, as well as the rest of the Christian Army. We rested until the next day, when, with the aid and under the guidance of slaves who knew the country and the roads, we got possession of what remained to be captured of the land and shore. But during the night the Saracens, who had discovered that the captives had escaped, had killed those who remained. They thus made of them glorious martyrs of Christ, to their own damnation.

In the darkness of the following night and on Sunday morning, as they lacked weapons and troops, the Saracens seeing the multitude of the Christians who were landing, their courage and firmness, and the sudden desolation of their own city, lacking leaders, superiors and persons to incite them, as well as destitute of strength and weapons for fighting, departed, taking their women and children and carrying off everything movable. They fled from the other side of the city by little gates which they had made long before. Some escaped by land, others by sea, abandoning their city filled with supplies of all kinds. That same day at nine o'clock, two captives who escaped by chance from the hands of the Saracens, came to tell us what had happened.

The king, no longer fearing an ambuscade, entered the city before three o'clock without hindrance and without shedding blood. Of all who entered only Hugo Brun, Earl of March, was severely wounded. He lost too much blood from his wounds to survive, for he was careless of his life, because of the reproaches which had been inflicted upon him, and rashly rushed into the midst of the enemy. He had been stationed in the front rank, at his own request, because he knew that he was an object of suspicion.

I must not forget to say that the Saracens, after having determined to flee, hurled at us a great quantity of Greek fire, which was very injurious to us, because it was carried by a wind which blew from the city. But this wind, suddenly changing, carried the fire back upon Damietta, where it burned several persons and fortresses. It would have consumed more property, if the slaves who had been left had not extinguished it by a process which they knew, and by the will of God, who did not wish that we should take possession of a city which had been burnt to the ground.

The king, having then entered the city in the midst of cries of joy, went immediately into the temple of the Saracens to pray and thank God, whom he regarded as the author of what had taken place. Before eating, all the Christians, weeping sweet and sacred tears of joy, and led by the *legate*, solemnly sang that hymn of the angels, the *Te Deum Laudamus*. Then the mass of the blessed Virgin was celebrated in the place where the Christians in ancient times had been wont to celebrate mass and to ring the bells, and which they had now cleansed and sprinkled with holy water. In this place, four days before, as the captives told us, the foul Mohammed had been worshiped with abominable sacrifices, loud shouts and the noise of trumpets.

We found in the city an infinite quantity of food, arms, engines, precious clothing, vases, golden and silver utensils and other things. In addition, we had our provisions, of which we had plenty, and other dear and necessary objects brought from our vessels.

By the divine goodness, the Christian Army, like a pond which is greatly swollen by the torrents pouring in, was added to each day by some soldiers from the lands of Lord Ville-Hardouin and some Templars and Hospitalers, besides pilgrims newly arrived, so that we were, by God's grace, largely reinforced. The Templars and Hospitalers did not want to believe in such a triumph. In fact, nothing that had happened was credible. All seemed miraculous, especially the Greek fire which the wind carried back onto the heads of those who hurled it against us. A similar miracle formerly took place at Antioch. A few *infidels* were converted to Jesus Christ and up to the present time have remained with us.

We, instructed by the past, will in the future exercise much prudence and circumspection in our actions. We have with us faithful Orientals upon whom we can count. They know all the country and the dangers which it offers; they have been baptized with true devotion. While we write, our chiefs are considering what it is necessary to do. The question is whether to proceed to Alexandria or Babylon and Cairo. We do not know what will be decided. We shall inform you of the result, if our lives are spared. The Sultan of Babylon, having learned what has taken place, has proposed to us a general engagement for the morrow of St. John the Baptist's day, and in a place which the two armies shall choose, in order, as he says, that fortune may decide for the men of the East or the men of the West, that is between the Christians and themselves, and that the party to whom fate shall give the victory, may glory in it, and the conquered may humbly yield.

The king replied that he did not fear the enemy of Christ one day more than another and that he offered no time for rest, but that he defied him tomorrow and every day of his life, until he should take pity on his own soul and should turn to the Lord who wishes the whole world to be saved, and who opens the bosom of His mercy to all those who turn to Him.

We tell you these things in this letter through our kinsman Guiscard. He seeks nothing else than that he may, at our expense, prepare himself for a professorship and have a fit lodging for at least two years.

We have learned nothing certain worth reporting about the Tartars. We can expect neither good faith from the perfidious, nor humanity from the inhuman, nor charity from dogs, unless God, to whom nothing is impossible, works this miracle. It is He who has purged the Holy Land from the wicked Charismians. He has destroyed them and caused them to disappear entirely from under heaven. When we learn anything certain or remarkable of the Tartars, or others, we will send you word either by letter or by Roger de Montefagi, who is to return to France in the spring, to the lands of our lord the viscount, to collect money for us.

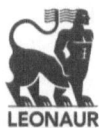

ALSO FROM LEONAUR
AVAILABLE IN SOFTCOVER OR HARDCOVER WITH DUST JACKET

THE FALL OF THE MOGHUL EMPIRE OF HINDUSTAN *by H. G. Keene*—By the beginning of the nineteenth century, as British and Indian armies under Lake and Wellesley dominated the scene, a little over half a century of conflict brought the Moghul Empire to its knees.

LADY SALE'S AFGHANISTAN *by Florentia Sale*—An Indomitable Victorian Lady's Account of the Retreat from Kabul During the First Afghan War.

THE CAMPAIGN OF MAGENTA AND SOLFERINO 1859 *by Harold Carmichael Wylly*—The Decisive Conflict for the Unification of Italy.

FRENCH'S CAVALRY CAMPAIGN *by J. G. Maydon*—A Special Correspondent's View of British Army Mounted Troops During the Boer War.

CAVALRY AT WATERLOO *by Sir Evelyn Wood*—British Mounted Troops During the Campaign of 1815.

THE SUBALTERN *by George Robert Gleig*—The Experiences of an Officer of the 85th Light Infantry During the Peninsular War.

NAPOLEON AT BAY, 1814 *by F. Loraine Petre*—The Campaigns to the Fall of the First Empire.

NAPOLEON AND THE CAMPAIGN OF 1806 *by Colonel Vachée*—The Napoleonic Method of Organisation and Command to the Battles of Jena & Auerstädt.

THE COMPLETE ADVENTURES IN THE CONNAUGHT RANGERS *by William Grattan*—The 88th Regiment during the Napoleonic Wars by a Serving Officer.

BUGLER AND OFFICER OF THE RIFLES *by William Green & Harry Smith*—With the 95th (Rifles) during the Peninsular & Waterloo Campaigns of the Napoleonic Wars.

NAPOLEONIC WAR STORIES *by Sir Arthur Quiller-Couch*—Tales of soldiers, spies, battles & sieges from the Peninsular & Waterloo campaingns.

CAPTAIN OF THE 95TH (RIFLES) *by Jonathan Leach*—An officer of Wellington's sharpshooters during the Peninsular, South of France and Waterloo campaigns of the Napoleonic wars.

RIFLEMAN COSTELLO *by Edward Costello*—The adventures of a soldier of the 95th (Rifles) in the Peninsular & Waterloo Campaigns of the Napoleonic wars.

AVAILABLE ONLINE AT **www.leonaur.com**
AND FROM ALL GOOD BOOK STORES

www.ingramcontent.com/pod-product-compliance
Lightning Source LLC
Chambersburg PA
CBHW020649220526
45464CB00001B/352